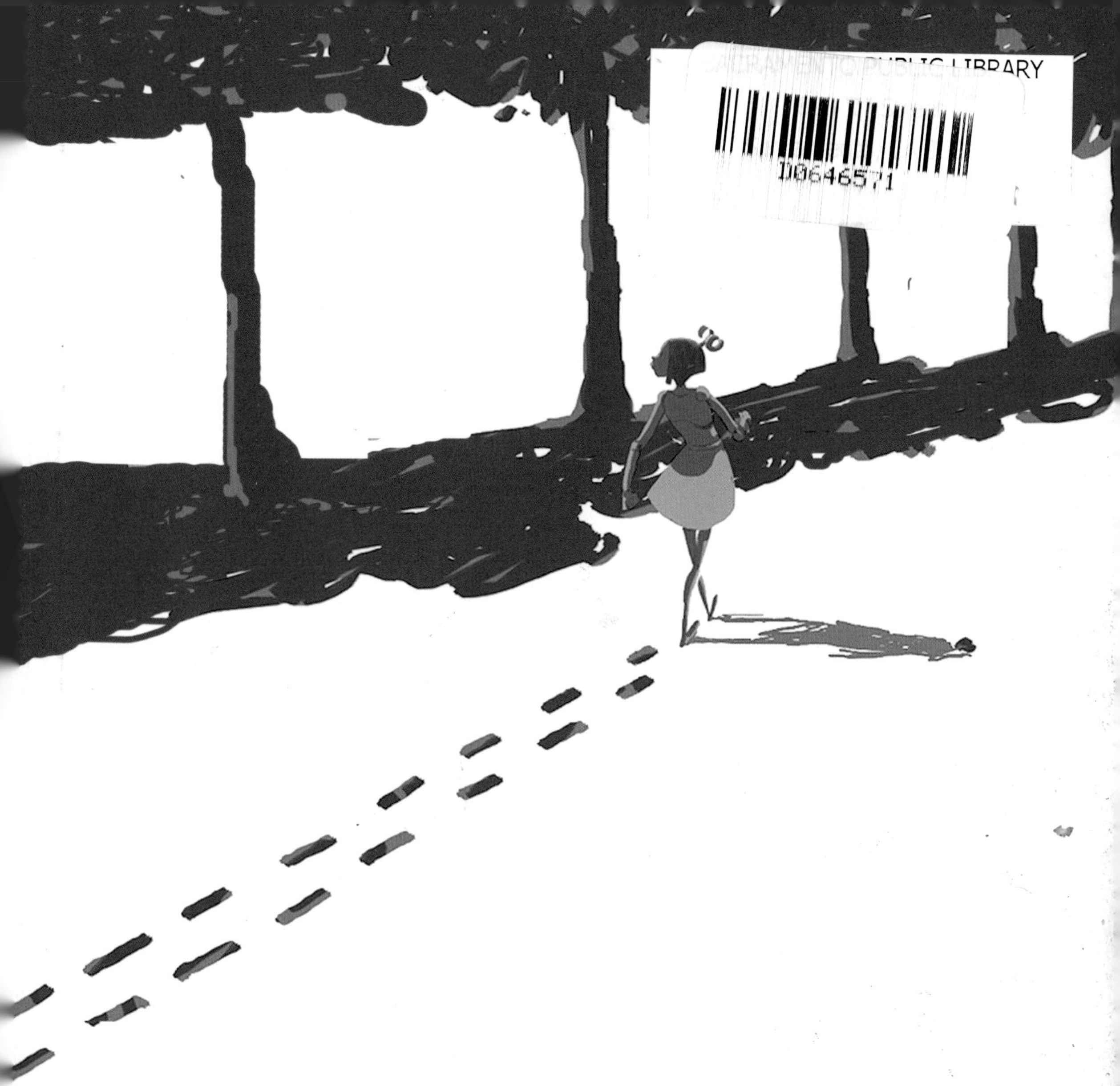

The
CLOCKWORK GIRL

The CLOCKWORK GIRL

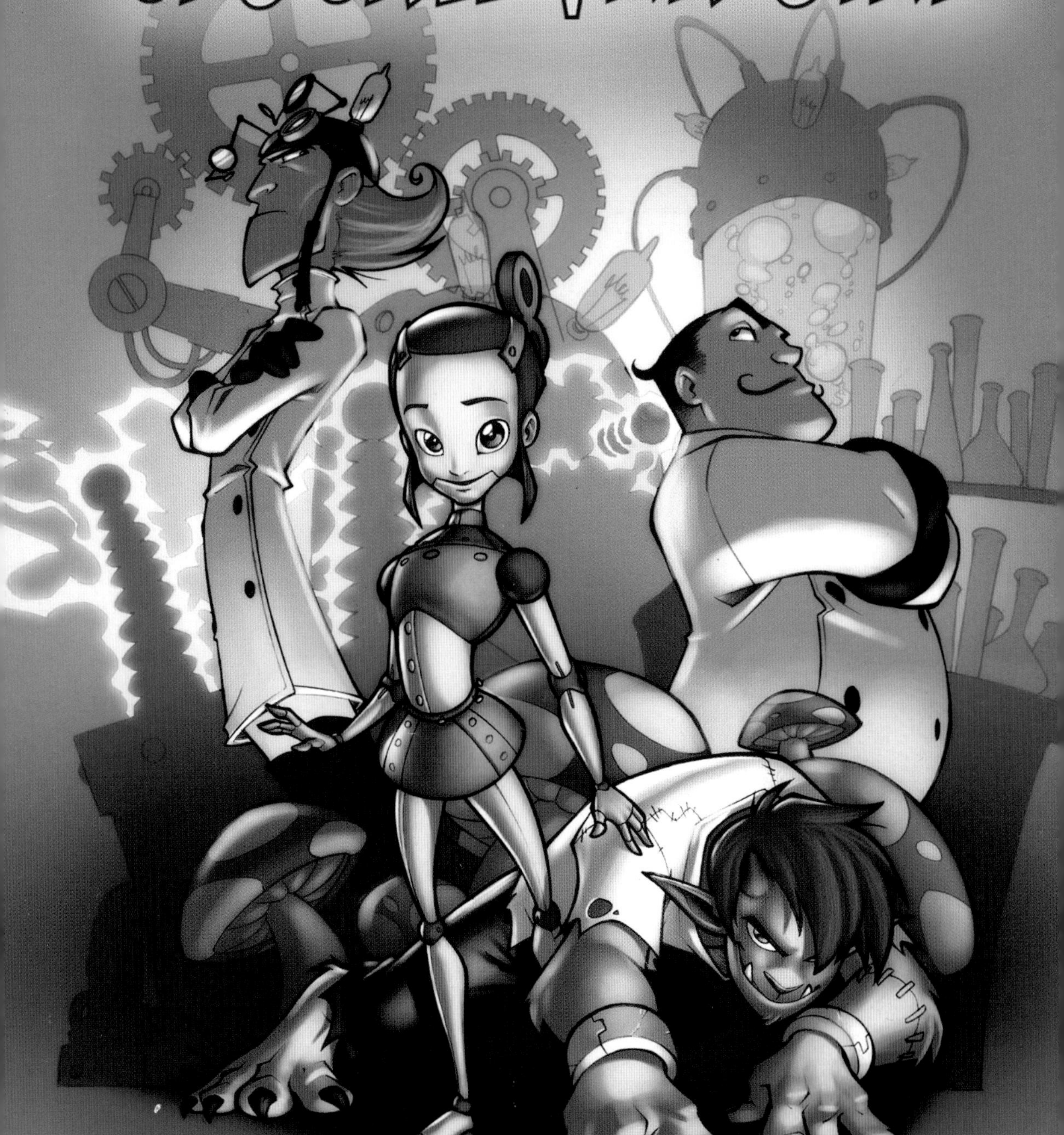

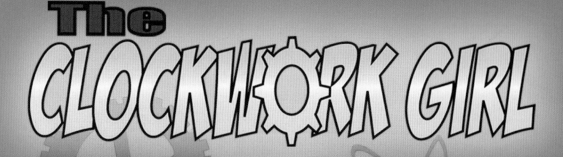

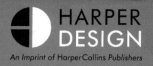

HARPER DESIGN

An Imprint of HarperCollins Publishers

Written and Created by
Sean O'Reilly and Kevin Hanna

Art by
Mike Thomas, Grant Bond, Karen Krinbrink, Mirana Reveier and Kevin Hanna

Collected Edition Cover Artist
Brandon Graham

Series Cover Artist
Pedro Delgado, Grant Bond, Kevin Hanna

Letters by
Shawn DePasquale

Graphic Design by
Emma Waddell

Special thanks to Eric and Natalie Johnson, Jessyca Dewey, Larry Ahern, Vincent Perea, Royden Lepp, Barnaby Ward, Mike Christian, Egg Embry, Deboragh Gabler, John Han, Sean Lee, and Julia Abramoff

www.arcana.com

CEO & Founder
Sean O'Reilly

VP of Operations
Mark Poulton

VP of Sales & Distribution
Michelle Meyers

General Manager
Emma Waddell

VP of Marketing
Erik Hendrix

Executive Assistant
Jaime Sambell

HarperCollins books may be purchased for educational, business, or sales promotional use. For information please write: Special Markets Department, HarperCollinsPublishers, 10 East 53rd Street, New York, NY 10022.
Published in 2011 by: Harper Design, An Imprint of HarperCollinsPublishers. 10 East 53rd Street New York, NY 10022.
Tel (212) 207-7000, harperdesign@harpercollins.com, www.harpercollins.com
Distributed throughout the world by: HarperCollinsPublishers, 10 East 53rd Street, New York, NY 10022
Library of Congress Control Number: 2011921581

ISBN 978-0-06-208039-4 (hardcover)   978-0-06-209129-1 (paperback)   Printed in the United States, 2011

To love and those who pursue it relentlessly.

Introduction

I grew up with the story of *The Clockwork Girl*—we all did. It's a story of the future. A world where wild mutants exist and machines look like people. Where families wage wars against one another—where nothing is safe and nothing is sacred. And yet in this land that is far, far away, a love story blooms.

I've told the story of *The Clockwork Girl* in over two hundred meetings. Each time the response is the same. The listeners' eyes light up. Grown men and women, often ones in business suits, act like curious children. A clockwork girl? What is that? A mutant circus boy? What does he look like? Is it *Romeo and Juliet* but with monsters? I look them squarely in the eyes, sometimes I pause for a minute or two to increase the suspense, and then I tell them the honest truth that *The Clockwork Girl* is much, much more than that.

The Clockwork Girl is a story we all know in our hearts, but it takes pictures and words to give life to it. Enter Kevin Hanna. I met Kevin at a comic book convention in Seattle in February 2005. We'd both grown up with comic books stashed in our knapsacks to be read under our desk when the teacher was speaking, read at night instead of doing our homework, and collected with all the pennies we could convince adults to give us. Kevin and I had both grown up with Superman and Lois Lane, but we'd also fallen in love with more futuristic comics, the ones exploring worlds we could only dream about.

Soon after our introduction, Kevin and I got to talking over burgers and soda. Kevin revealed his character the Tinkerer to me. Kevin had been dreaming up the Tinkerer, a technology-loving madman, since high school. A character so devoted to his robots, gizmos, and gadgets that he builds a castle to house them and then uses these mechanical toys to run errands for him, to cater to his every whim and desire. Fleshing out the Tinkerer, Kevin and I were whispering at first and slowly our voices rose with excitement. What if one of these robots was more than just a metal contraption? What if this robot machine was capable of feeling the grass beneath its feet? What if it could see the beauty of a butterfly or smell the sweet scent of roses? What then? Would this machine made up of gizmos and gadgets have a heart? Could it care for another being? Could it love?

From February 2005 to May 2007, we went back and forth on this world, tweaking and fine-tuning it. The Clockwork Girl was the first addition to the Tinkerer's story. And if a tinkerer and a clockwork girl, why not a grafter and a mutant boy? There were changes along the way, of course. Dendrus the Grafter's original name was Aristotle, and the opening started with Aristotle working on Huxley. But we soon had a full story fleshed out, and with a talented art team from my studio, Arcana Comics, in tow, we set about realizing it on the page. Our amazing art team sketched the characters until they perfectly resembled the ones we'd imagined and then colored them until they took on a life of their own.

We split the story into four comics and distributed them to comics stores. But we couldn't stock enough to fulfill demands. So we put our heads together, we took long walks, we sat at computers and twiddled our thumbs until we dreamed up *The Clockwork Girl* book. It would be one gorgeous keepsake graphic novel with pages that would do justice to the characters—and hey, we could even give them their own gallery in the back.

In the weeks and months that followed this idea, we began to dream a little bigger. If we're doing a book, let's give our readers—those loyal devotees to *The Clockwork Girl*—an additional way to experience it: a stereoscopic three-dimensional feature film! We originally titled this *The Astonishing Clockwork Girl and the Amazing Mutant Boy*, but heck—*The Clockwork Girl* was what this had always been and what it always should be!

The screenplay was written, and Kevin put together a talented team who created a two-minute sampler of the film we envisioned. It debuted at San Diego Comic Con in July 2009. Then the meetings began. I pitched the project at numerous meetings. We received countless offers of co-productions, options, letters of intent with 50% of the financing and everything in between. For one reason or another, the deals didn't transpire or the deals didn't work for us. We were at a standstill; we had a dream and we knew what we wanted, but it didn't seem to be working out.

Finally, in December 2009, we got a huge break. Deboragh Gabler, a producer who owns Legacy Filmworks, took me under her wing and into a trailer on the set of *Dancing Ninja* to meet John Han from Grape Vine Entertainment. I gave my pitch, showed them the graphic novel and the short film, and watched their eyes light up. John then brought the project to Sean Lee at CJ Entertainment and, inspired by our dream, they gave us the opportunity to make the film.

On March 22, 2010, we began preproduction on *The Clockwork Girl* with Kevin directing and myself producing, along with Deboragh Gabler and John Han as our partners. We created a three-dimensional fantasy world based on the amazing graphic novel you have in your hands—complete with lush organic landscapes, cold mechanical inventions, and a monster boy falling head over heels for a robot girl.

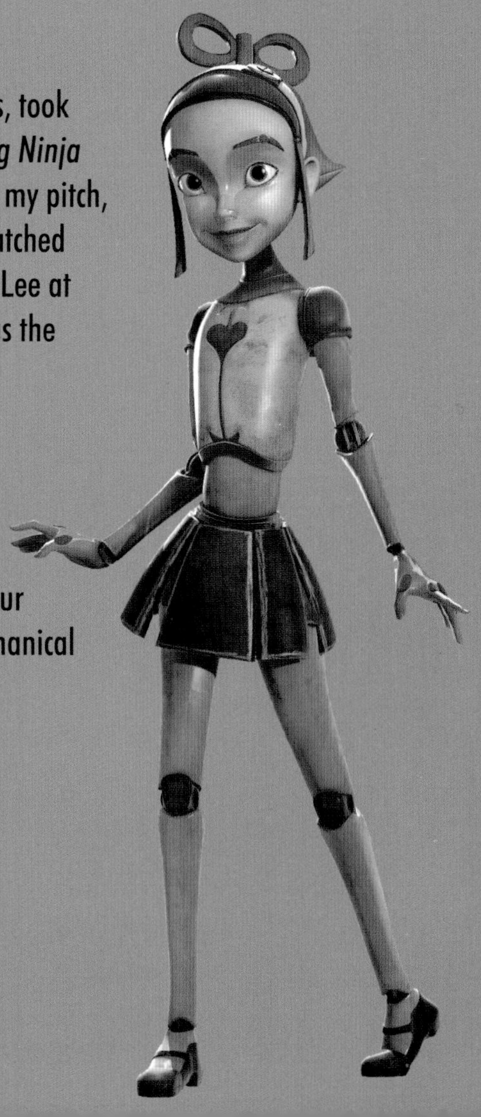

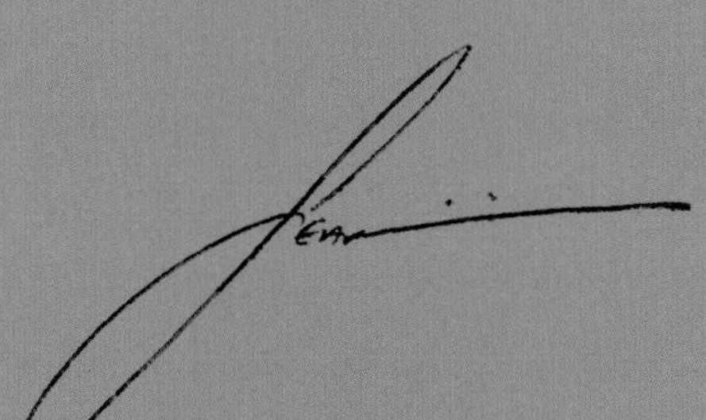

Chapter 1

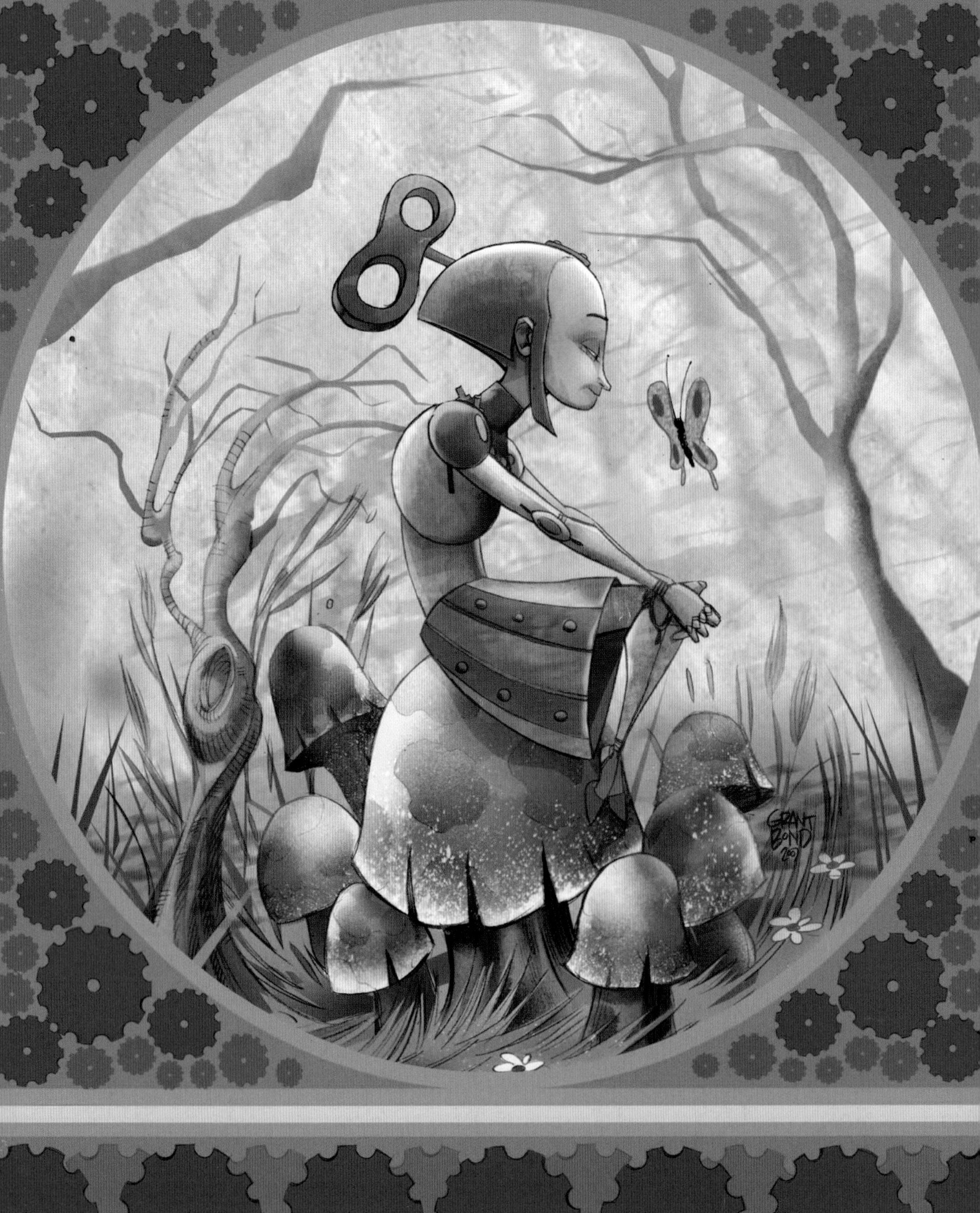
GRANT BOND

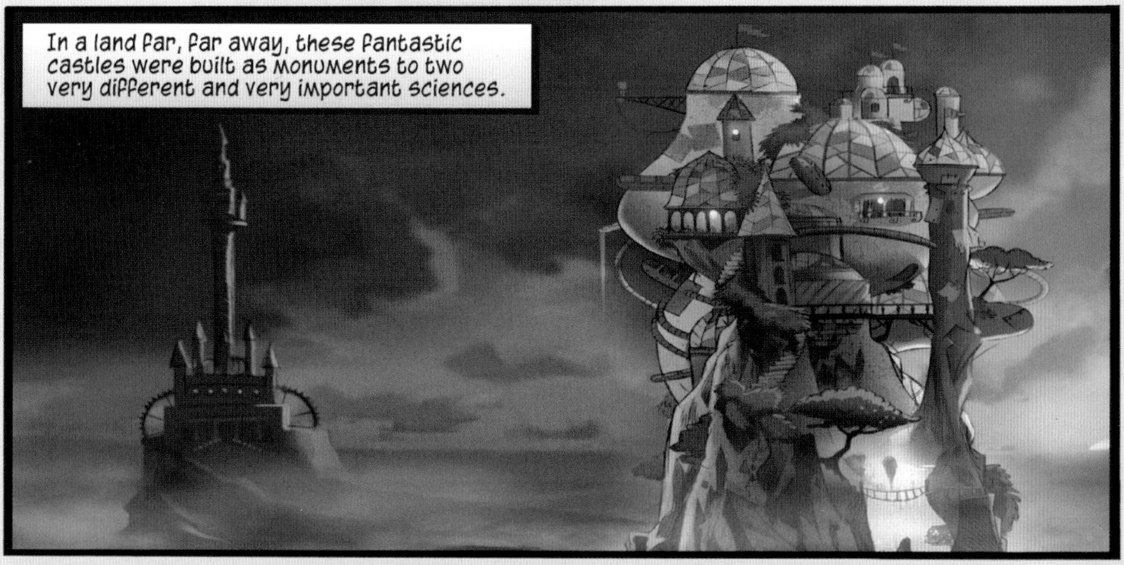
In a land far, far away, these fantastic castles were built as monuments to two very different and very important sciences.

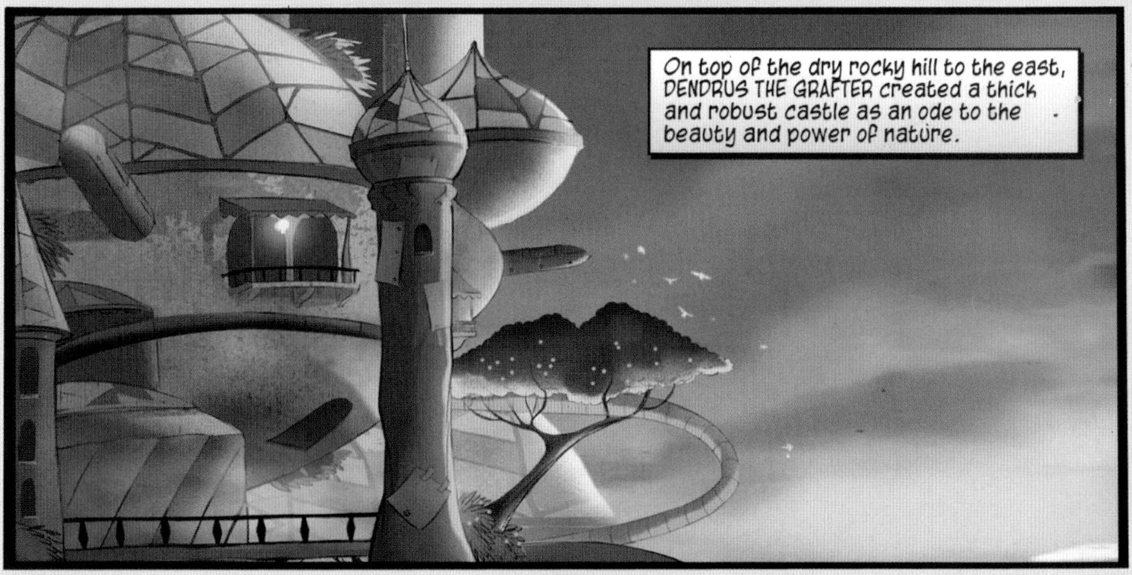
On top of the dry rocky hill to the east, DENDRUS THE GRAFTER created a thick and robust castle as an ode to the beauty and power of nature.

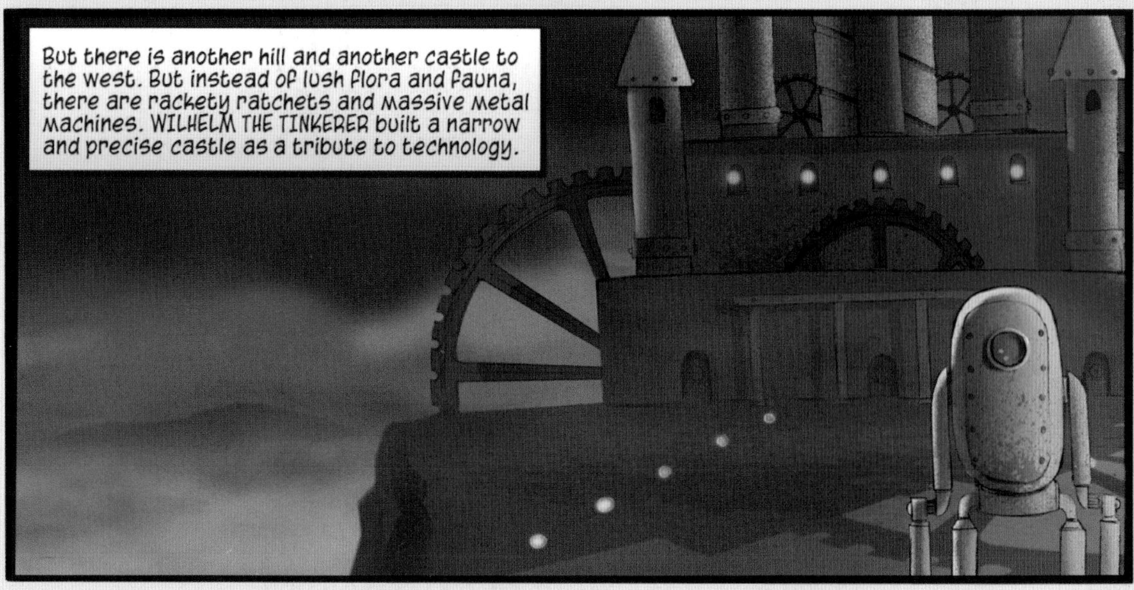
But there is another hill and another castle to the west. But instead of lush flora and fauna, there are rackety ratchets and massive metal machines. WILHELM THE TINKERER built a narrow and precise castle as a tribute to technology.

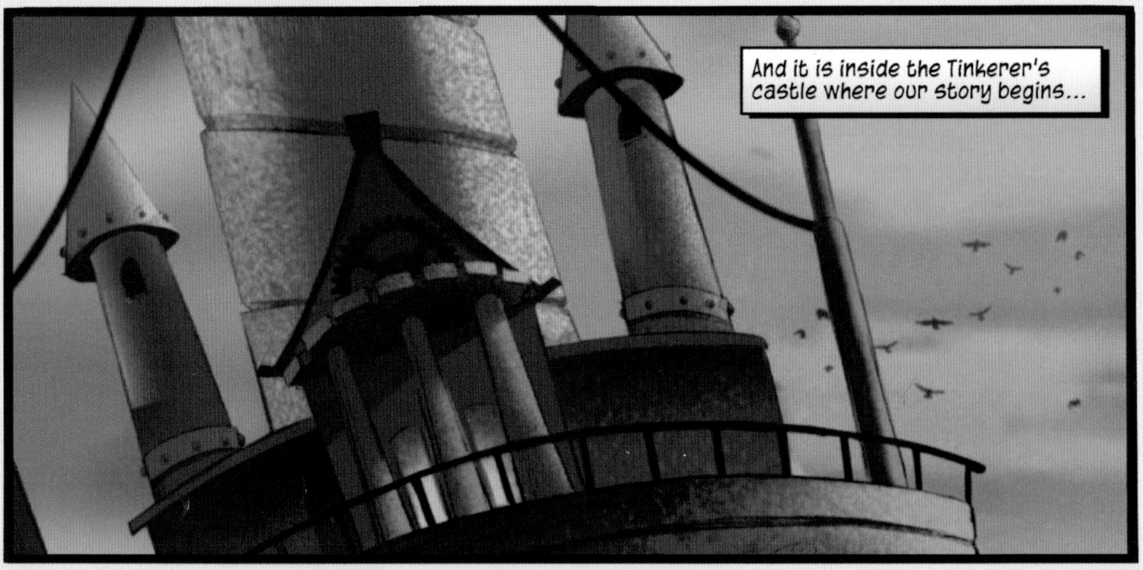
And it is inside the Tinkerer's castle where our story begins...

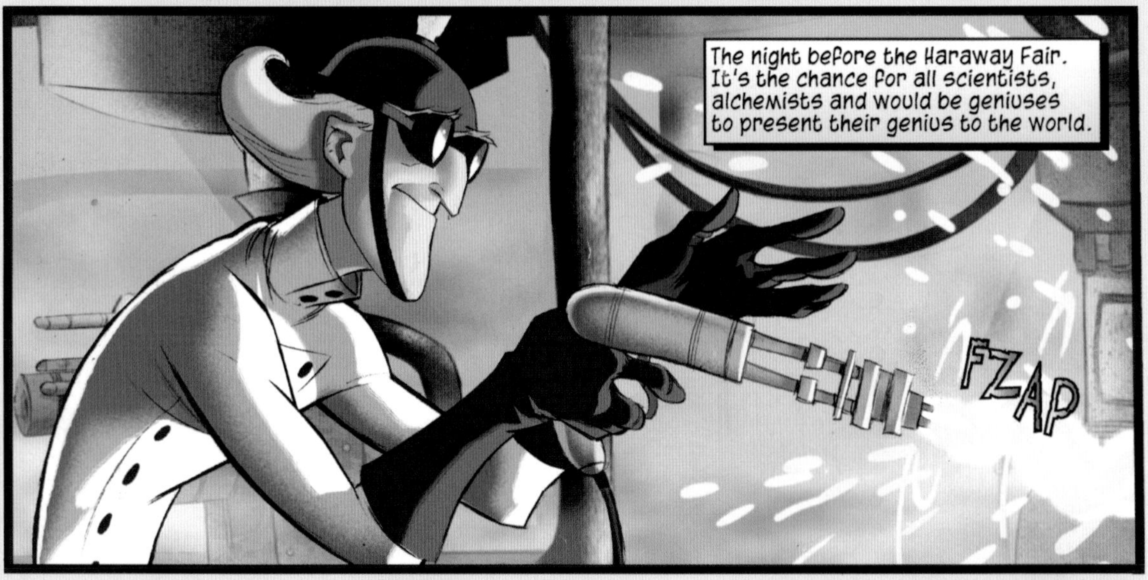
The night before the Haraway Fair. It's the chance for all scientists, alchemists and would be geniuses to present their genius to the world.
FZAP

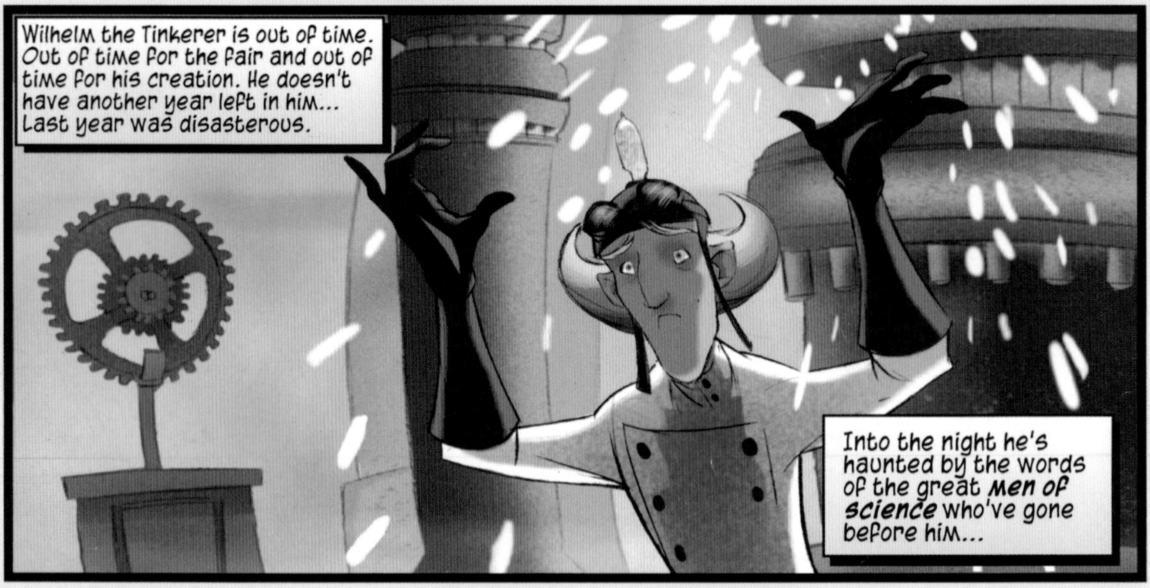
Wilhelm the Tinkerer is out of time. Out of time for the fair and out of time for his creation. He doesn't have another year left in him... Last year was disasterous.
Into the night he's haunted by the words of the great *Men of science* who've gone before him...

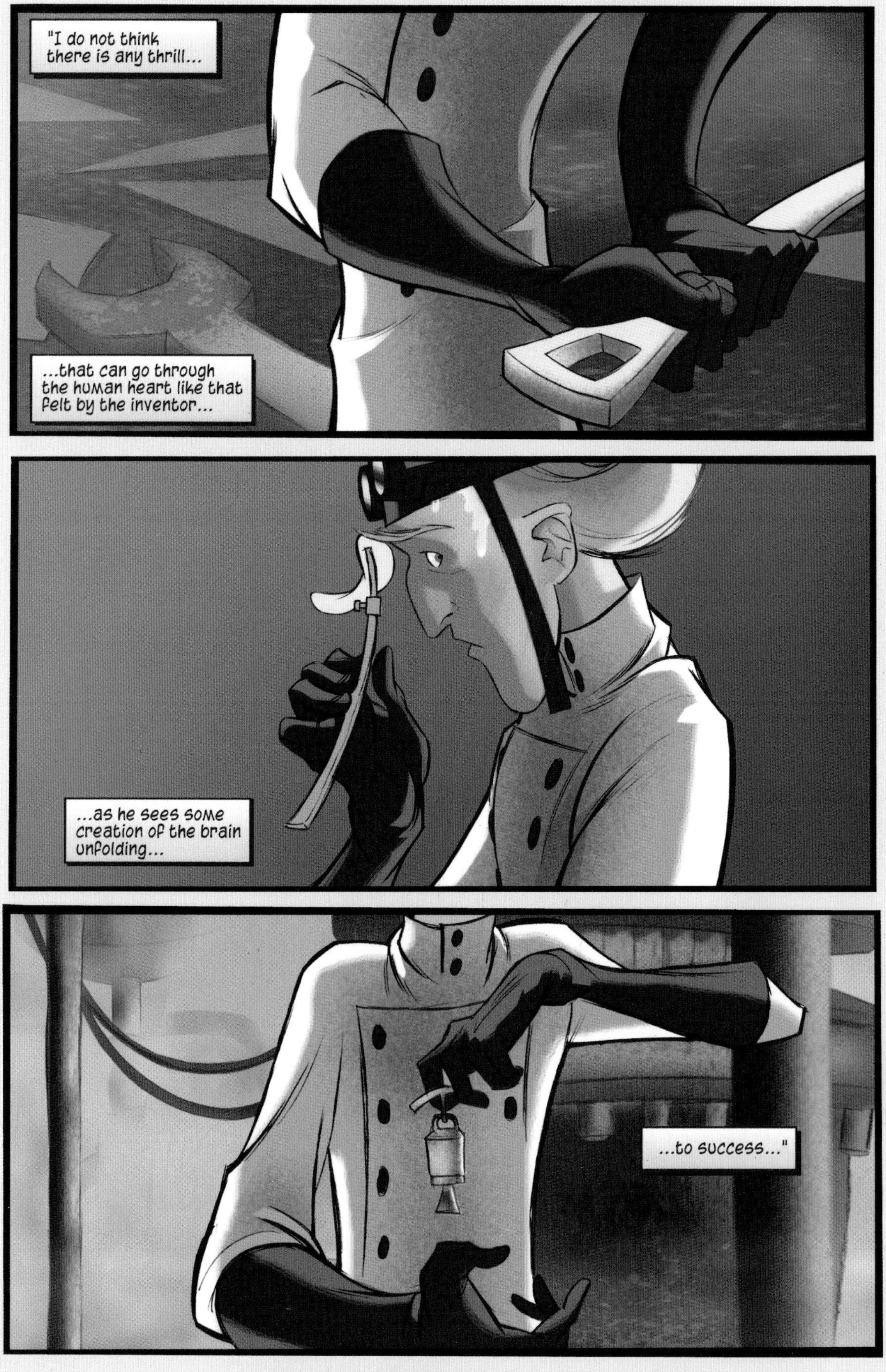
"I do not think there is any thrill...
...that can go through the human heart like that felt by the inventor...
...as he sees some creation of the brain unfolding...
...to success..."

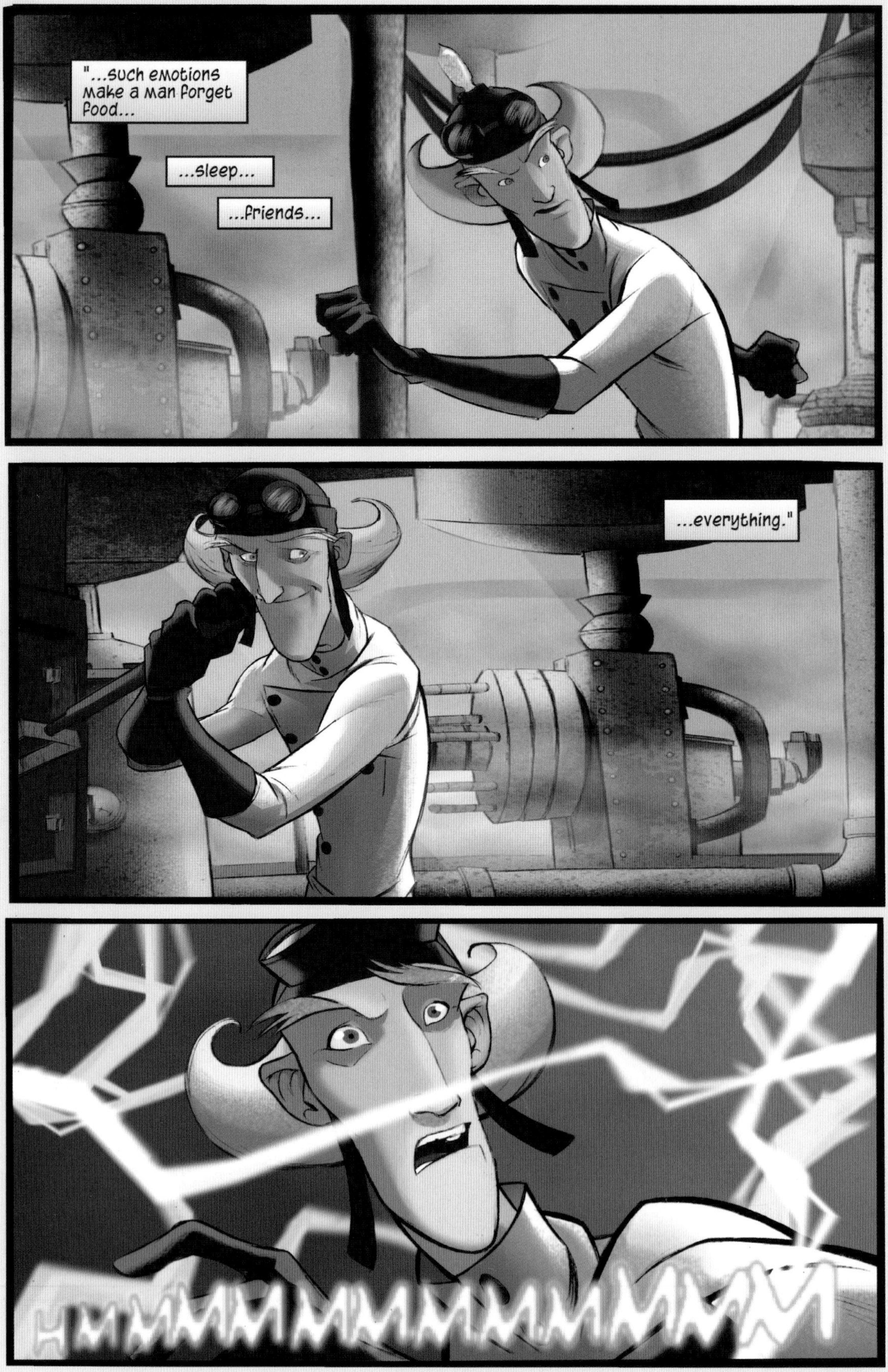
"...such emotions make a man forget food...
...sleep...
...friends...
...everything."
HMMMMMMMMMMMMMMM

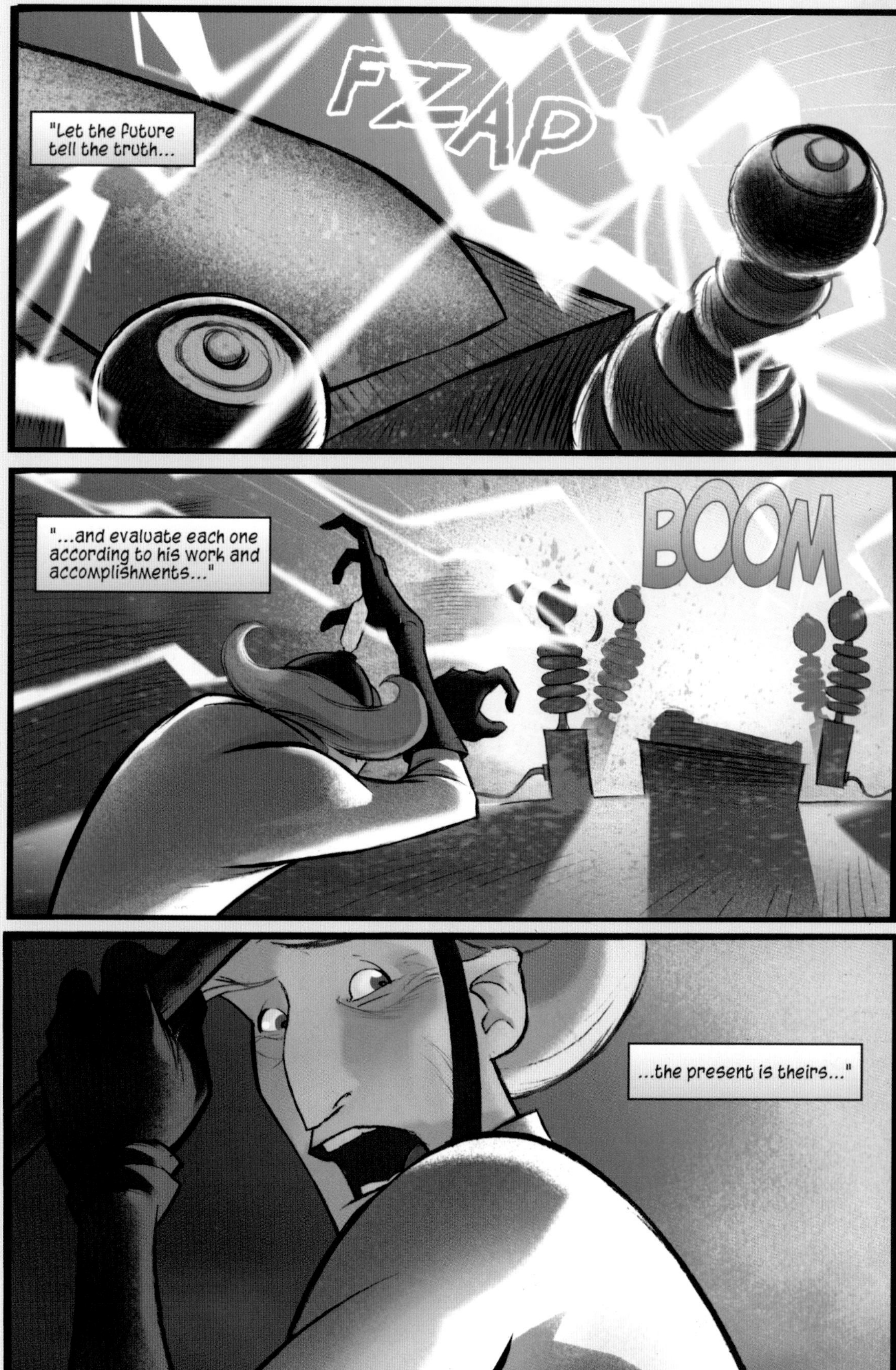
"Let the future tell the truth...
FZAP
"...and evaluate each one according to his work and accomplishments..."
BOOM
...the present is theirs..."

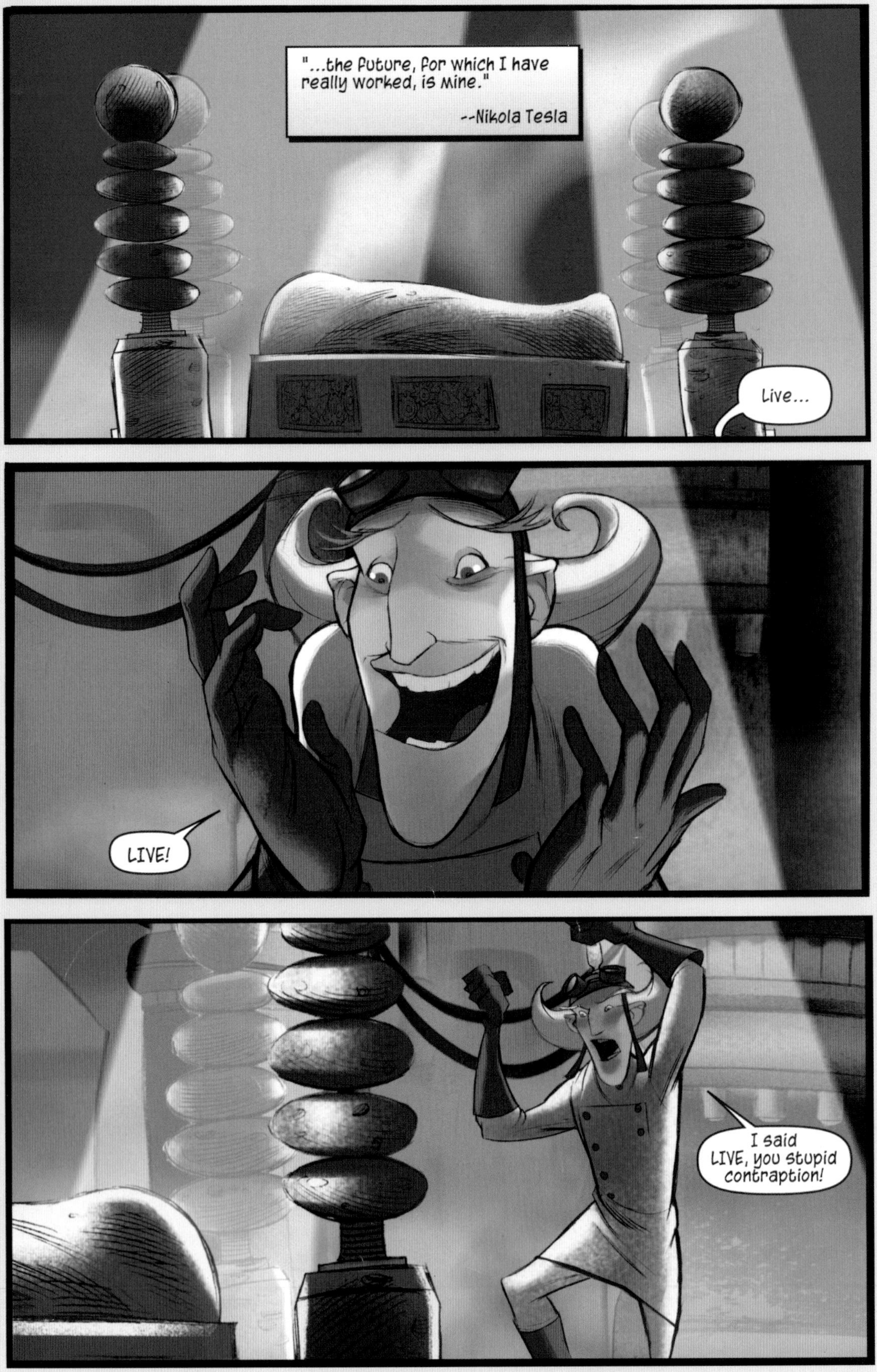
"...the future, for which I have really worked, is mine."
--Nikola Tesla
Live...
LIVE!
I said LIVE, you stupid contraption!

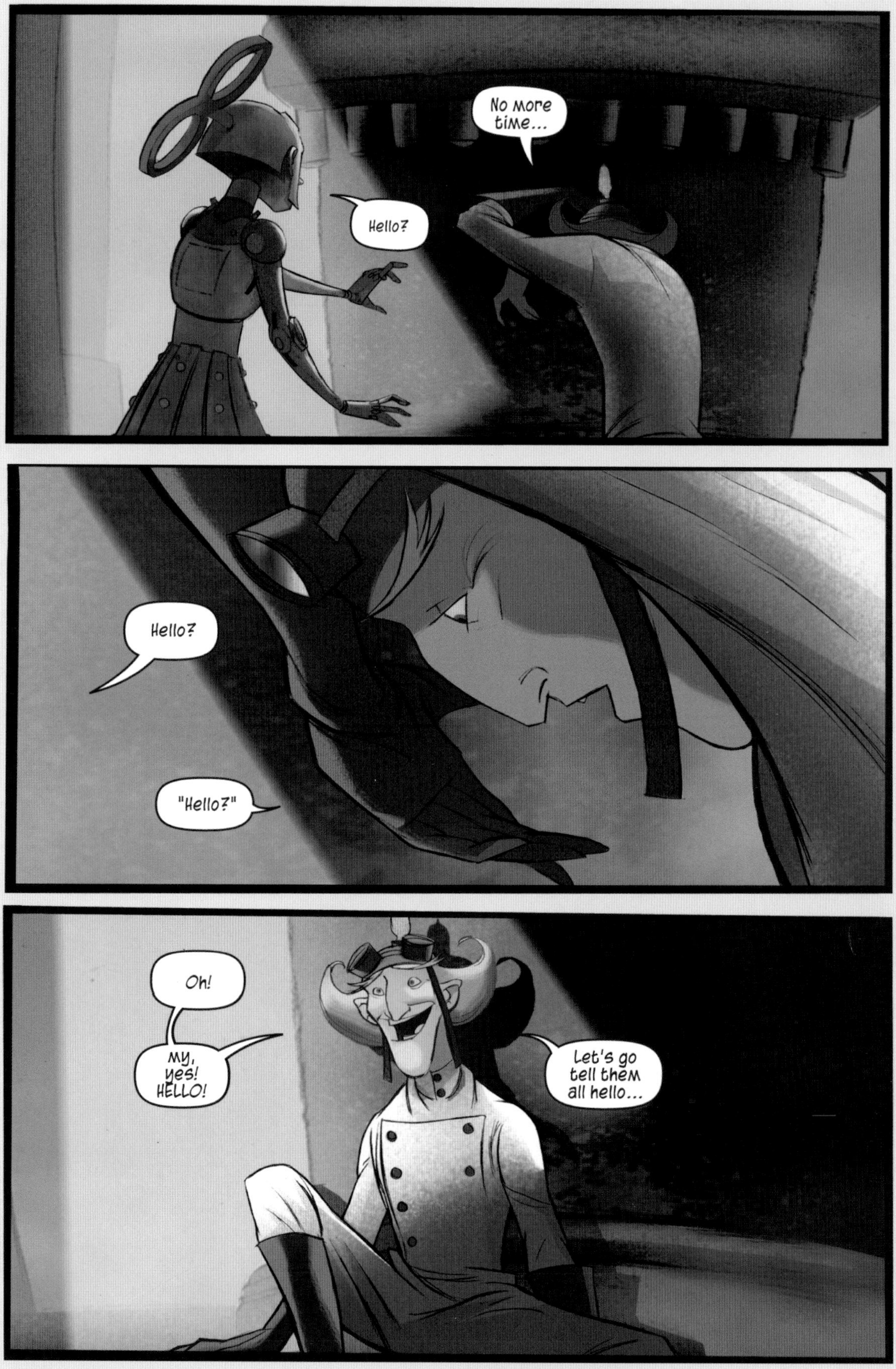
No more time...
Hello?
Hello?
"Hello?"
Oh!
My, yes! HELLO!
Let's go tell them all hello...

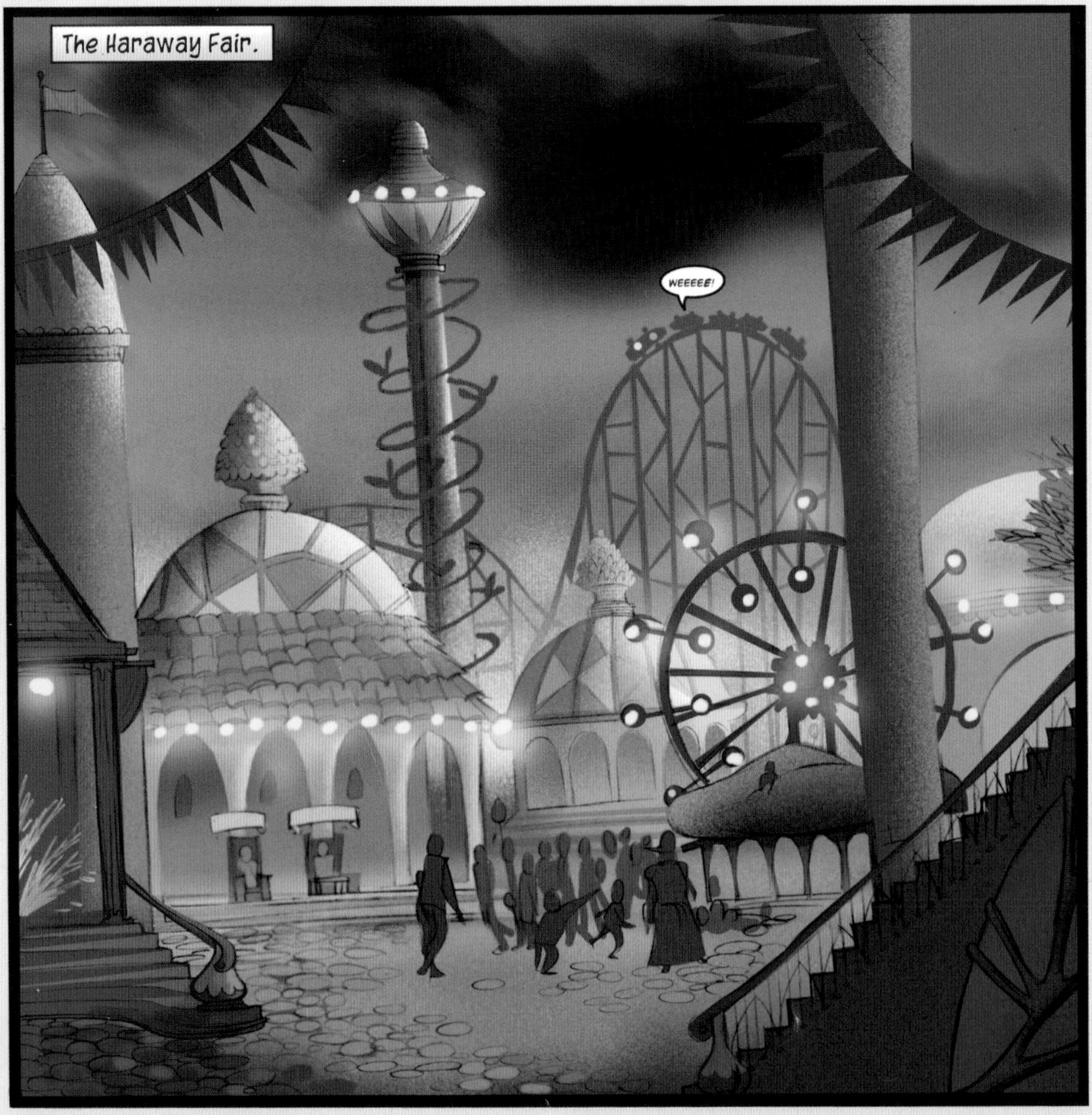
The Haraway Fair.
WEEEEE!

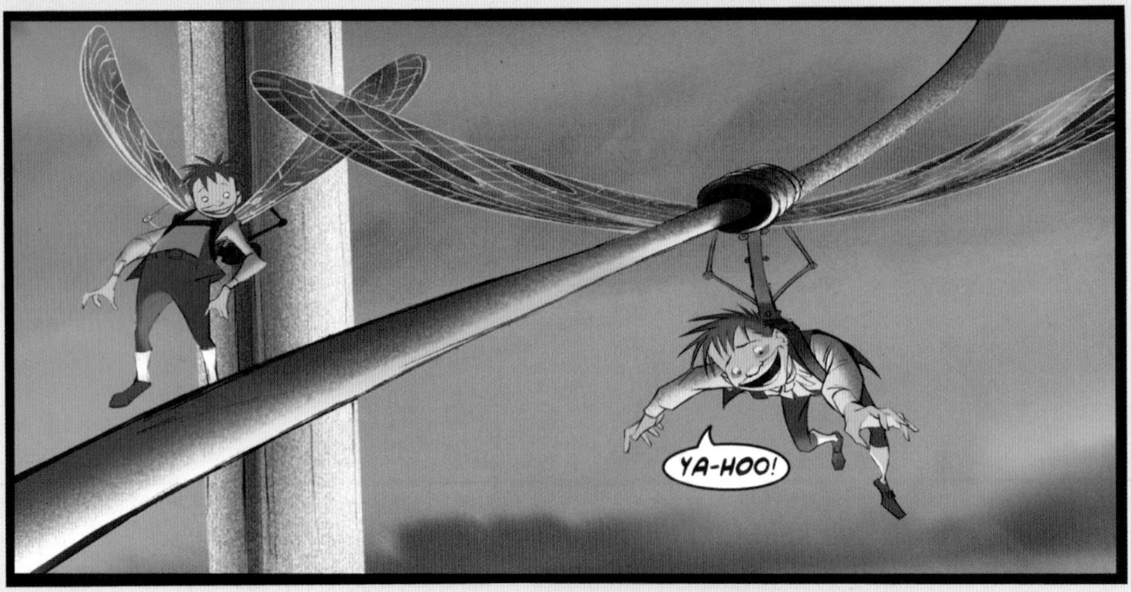
YA-HOO!

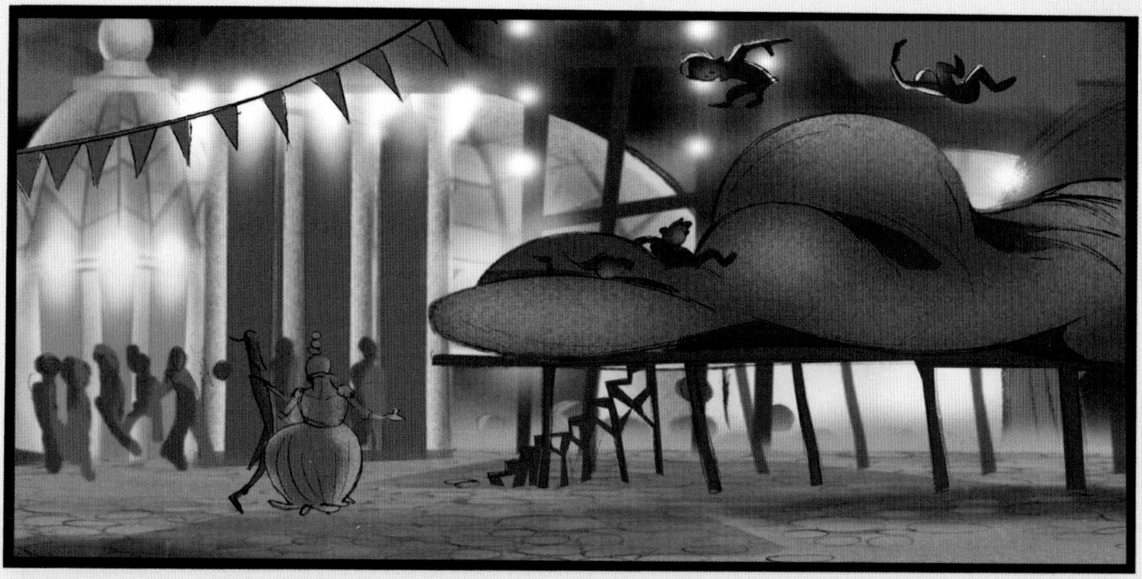

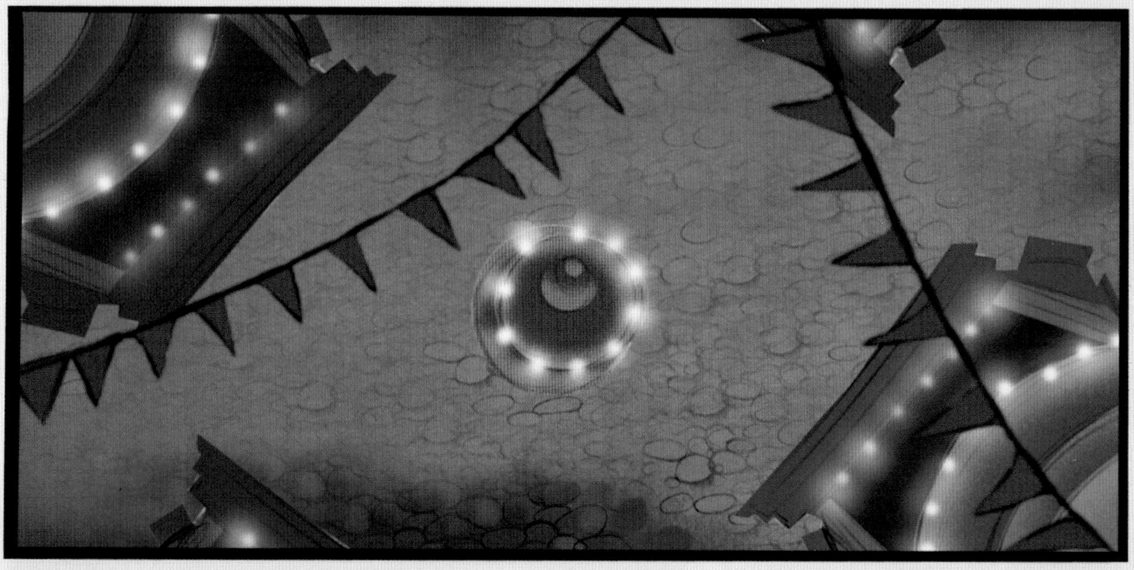

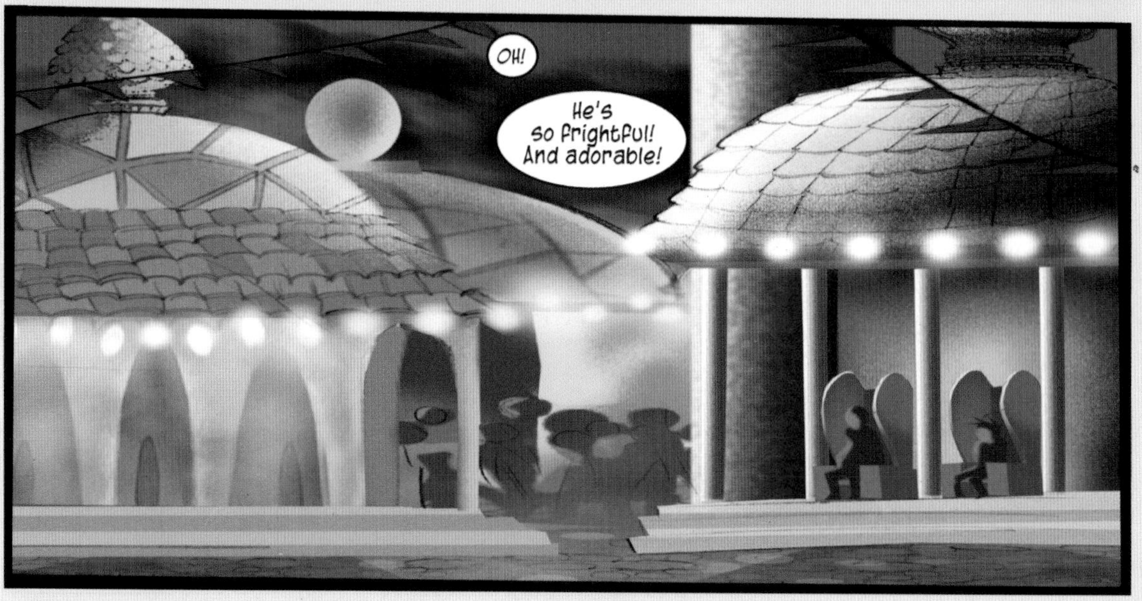
OH!
He's so frightful! And adorable!

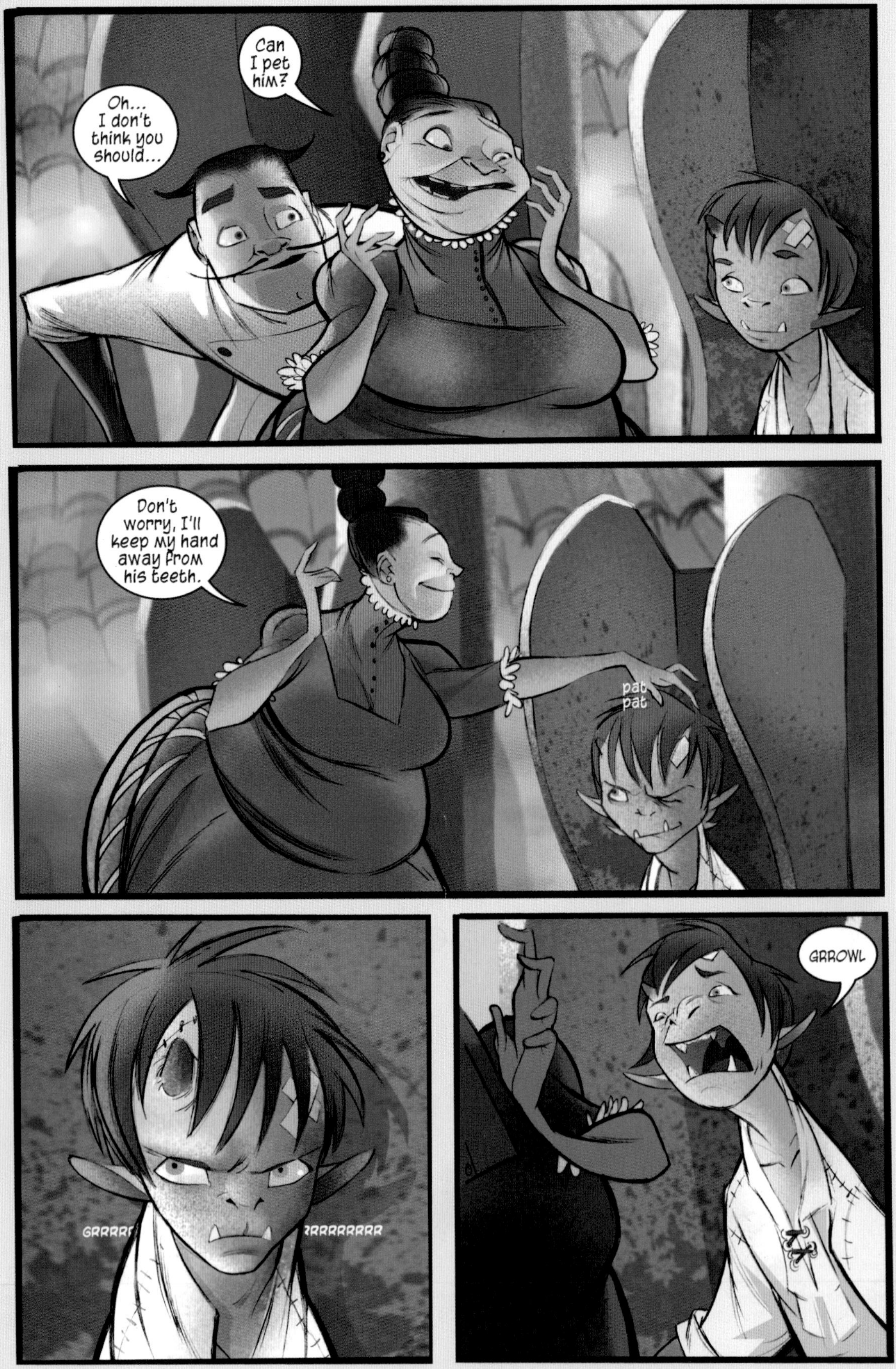
Oh... I don't think you should...
Can I pet him?
Don't worry, I'll keep my hand away from his teeth.
pat pat
GRRRRRRRRRRRRRR
GRROWL

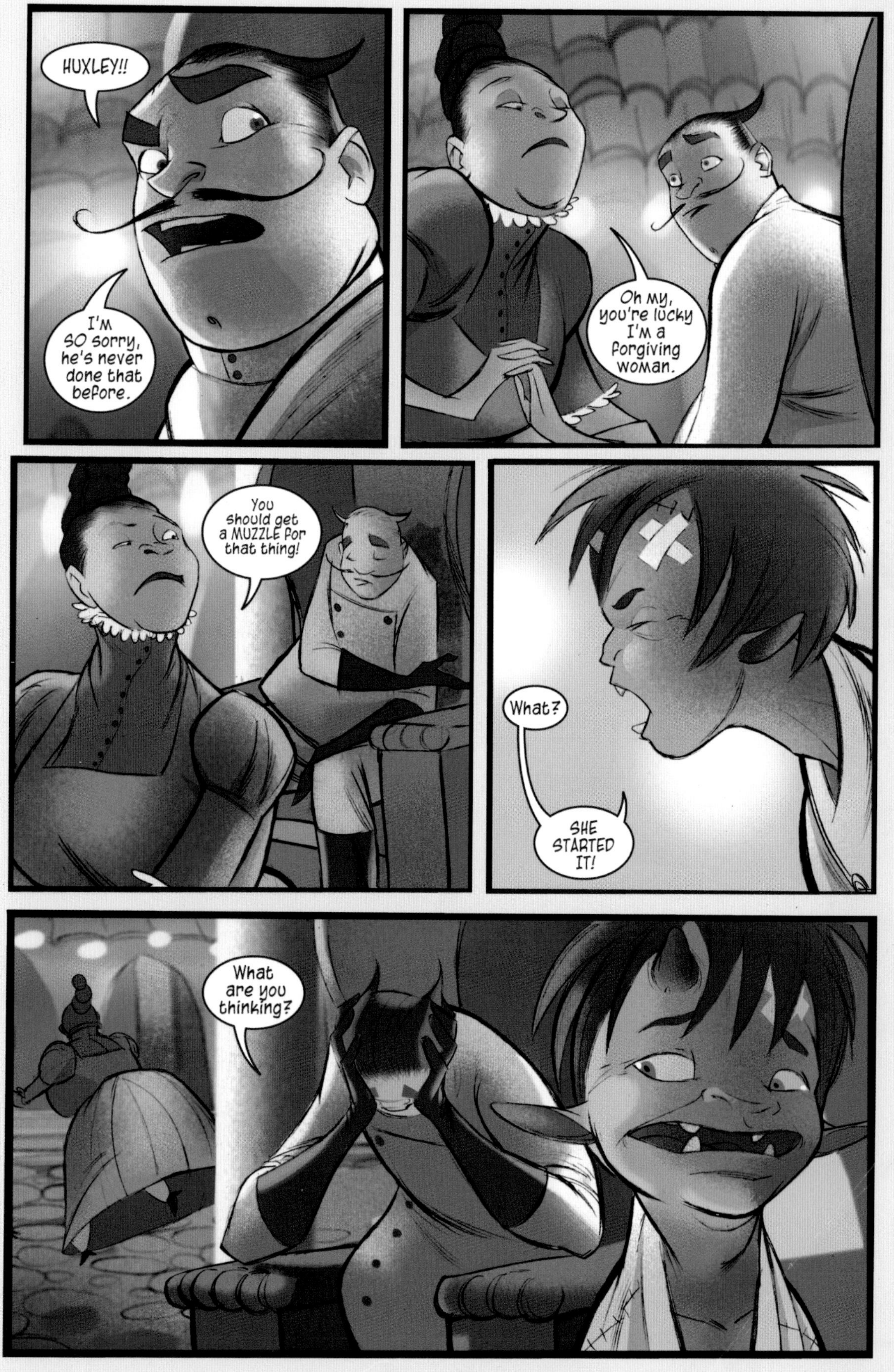
HUXLEY!!
I'M SO sorry, he's never done that before.
Oh my, you're lucky I'm a forgiving woman.
You should get a MUZZLE for that thing!
What?
SHE STARTED IT!
What are you thinking?

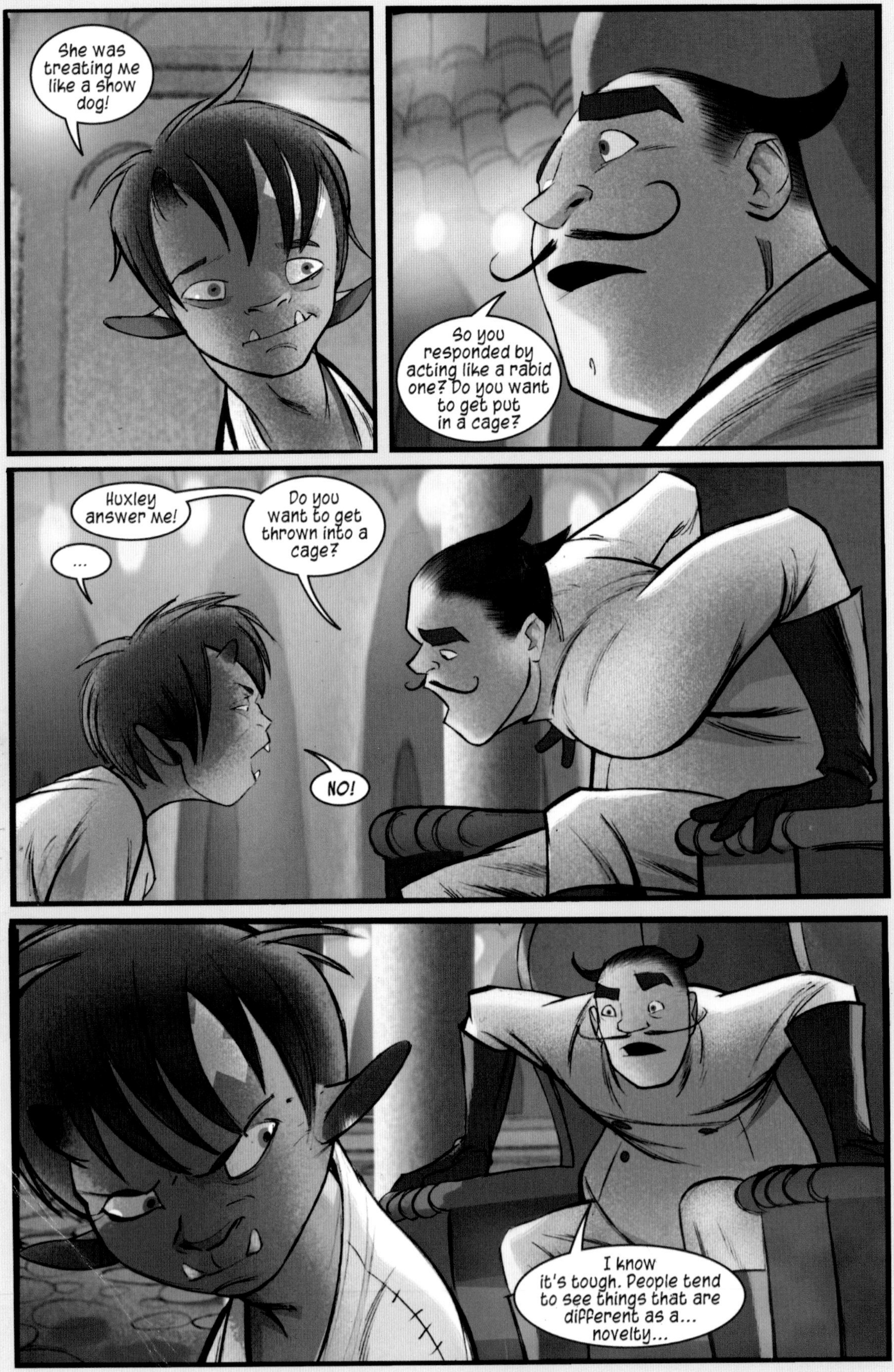
She was treating me like a show dog!
So you responded by acting like a rabid one? Do you want to get put in a cage?
Huxley answer me!
Do you want to get thrown into a cage?
...
NO!
I know it's tough. People tend to see things that are different as a... novelty...

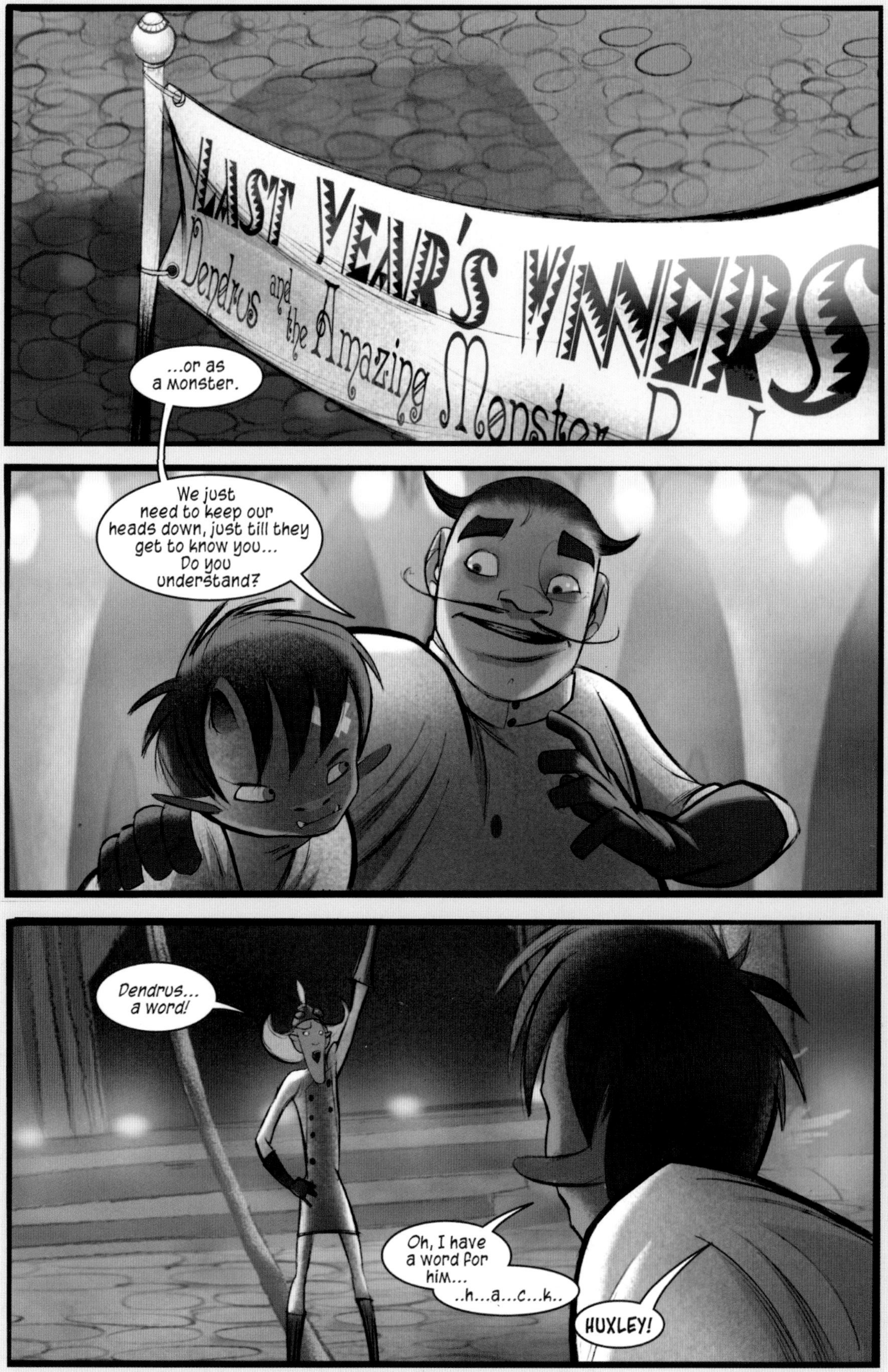
LAST YEAR'S WINNERS
Dendrus and the Amazing Monster
...or as a monster.
We just need to keep our heads down, just till they get to know you... Do you understand?
Dendrus... a word!
Oh, I have a word for him... ..h...a...c...k..
HUXLEY!

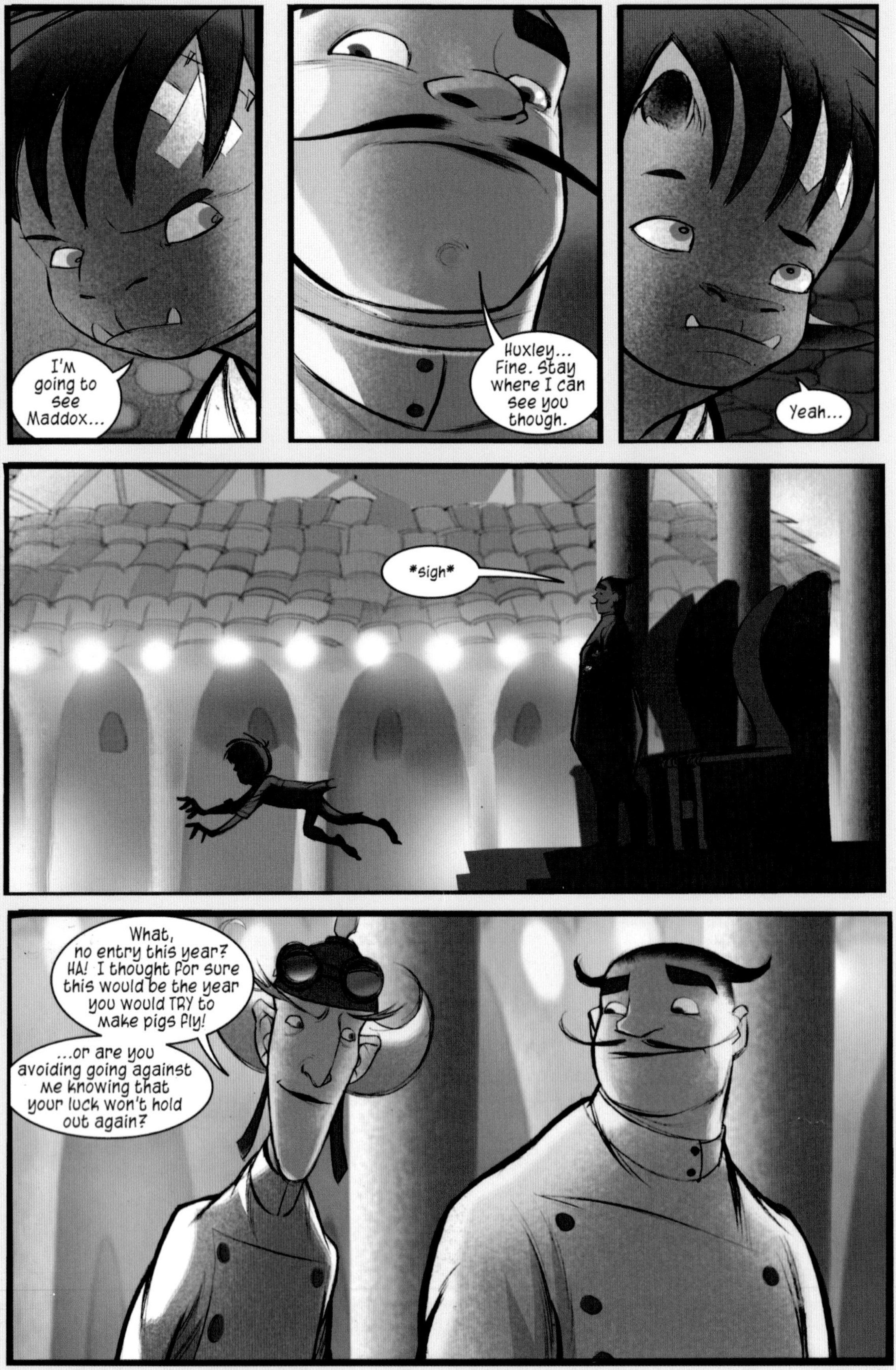
I'M going to see Maddox...
Huxley... Fine. Stay where I can see you though.
Yeah...
sigh
What, no entry this year? HA! I thought for sure this would be the year you would TRY to make pigs fly!
...or are you avoiding going against me knowing that your luck won't hold out again?

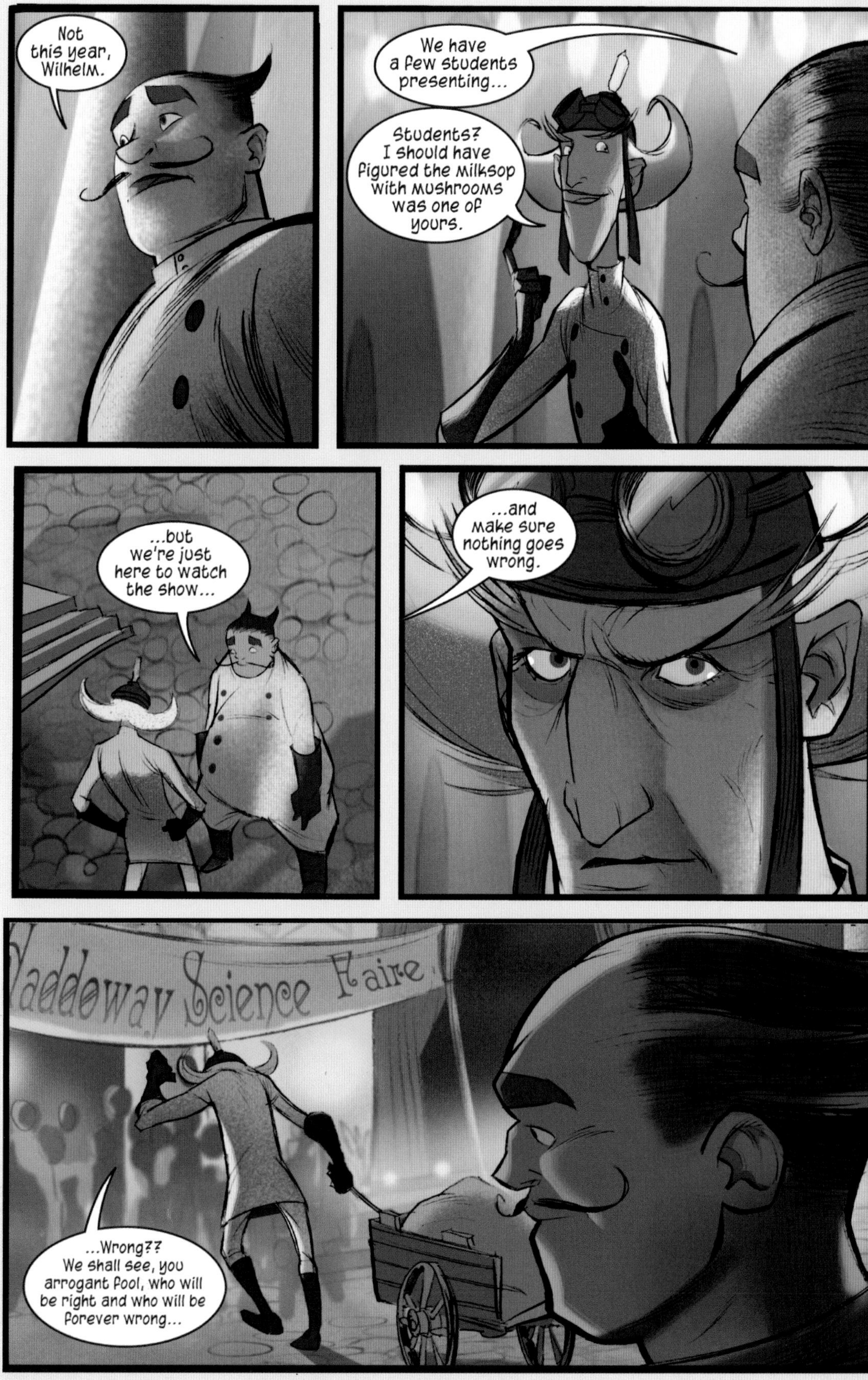
Not this year, Wilhelm.
We have a few students presenting...
Students? I should have figured the milksop with mushrooms was one of yours.
...but we're just here to watch the show...
...and make sure nothing goes wrong.
Waddoway Science Faire
...Wrong?? We shall see, you arrogant fool, who will be right and who will be forever wrong...

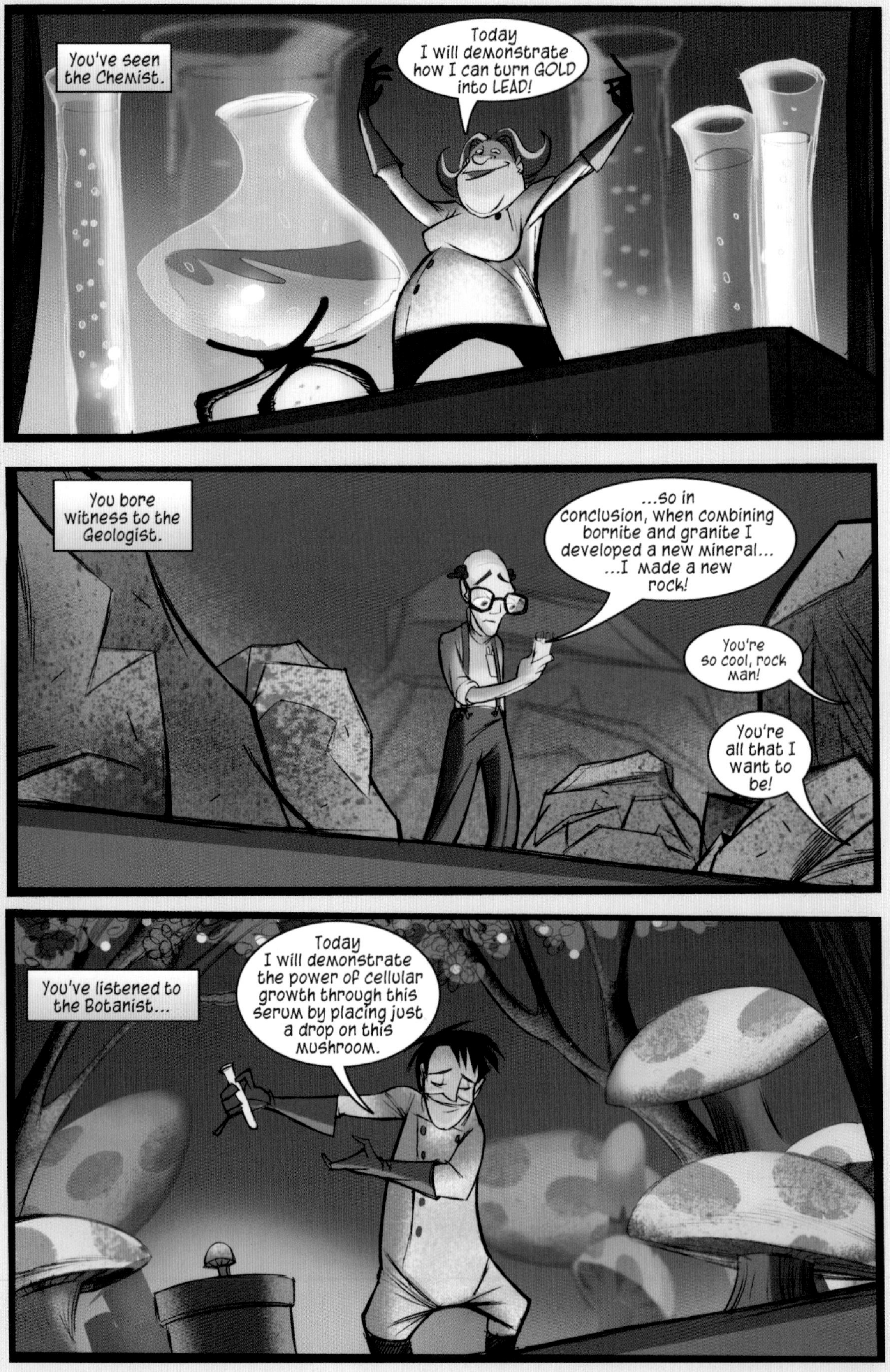
You've seen the Chemist.
Today I will demonstrate how I can turn GOLD into LEAD!
You bore witness to the Geologist.
...so in conclusion, when combining bornite and granite I developed a new mineral... ...I made a new rock!
You're so cool, rock man!
You're all that I want to be!
You've listened to the Botanist...
Today I will demonstrate the power of cellular growth through this serum by placing just a drop on this mushroom.

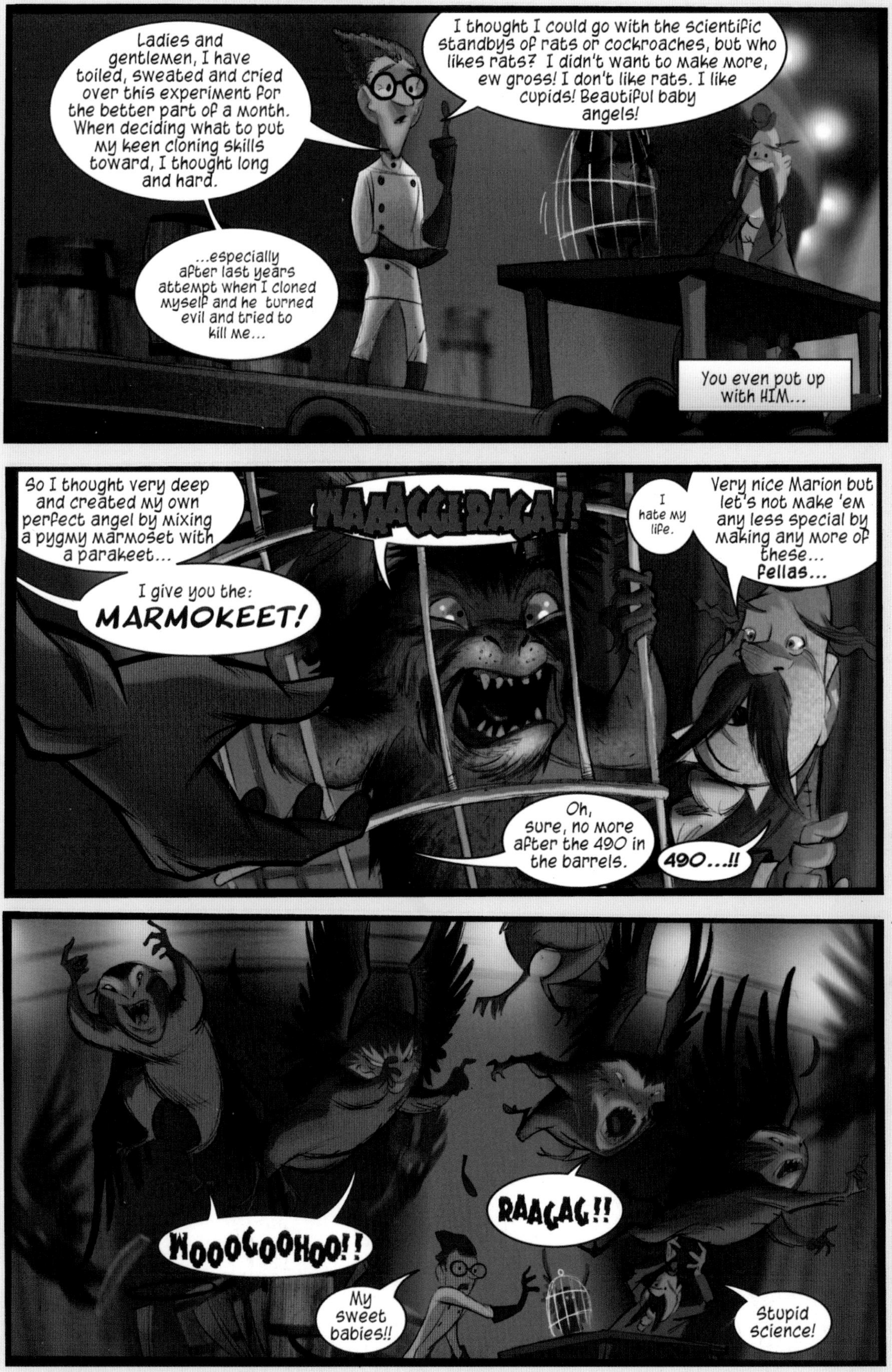

Ladies and gentlemen, I have toiled, sweated and cried over this experiment for the better part of a month. When deciding what to put my keen cloning skills toward, I thought long and hard.
...especially after last years attempt when I cloned myself and he turned evil and tried to kill me...
I thought I could go with the scientific standbys of rats or cockroaches, but who likes rats? I didn't want to make more, ew gross! I don't like rats. I like cupids! Beautiful baby angels!
You even put up with HIM...
So I thought very deep and created my own perfect angel by mixing a pygmy marmoset with a parakeet...
I give you the: MARMOKEET!
WAAAGGERAGA!!
I hate my life.
Very nice Marion but let's not make 'em any less special by making any more of these... fellas...
Oh, sure, no more after the 490 in the barrels.
490...!!
WOOOGOOHOO!!
RAAGAG!!
My sweet babies!!
Stupid science!

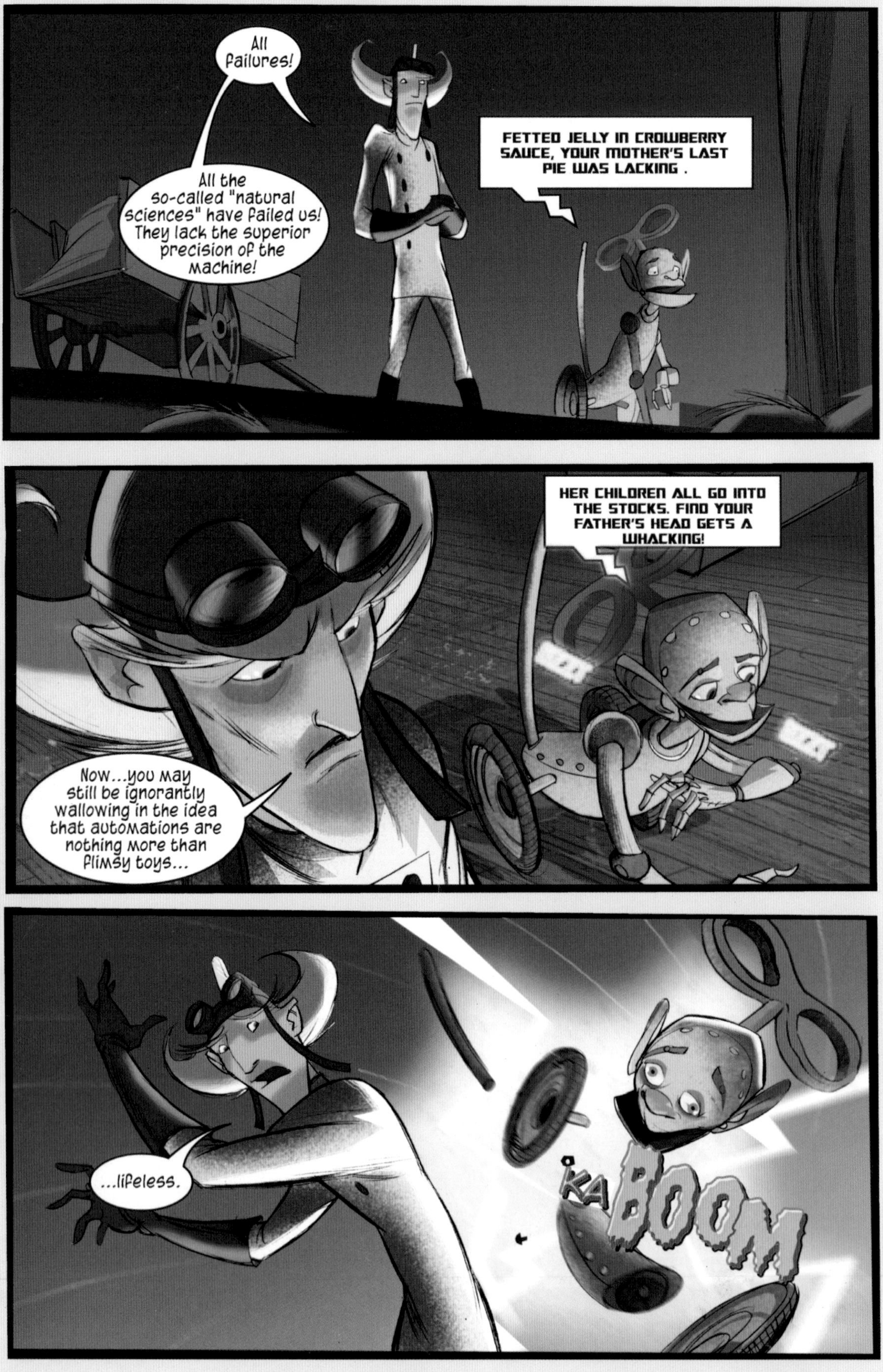
All failures!
All the so-called "natural sciences" have failed us! They lack the superior precision of the machine!
FETTED JELLY IN CROWBERRY SAUCE, YOUR MOTHER'S LAST PIE WAS LACKING .
HER CHILDREN ALL GO INTO THE STOCKS. FIND YOUR FATHER'S HEAD GETS A WHACKING!
Now…you may still be ignorantly wallowing in the idea that automations are nothing more than flimsy toys…
…lifeless.
KA BOOM

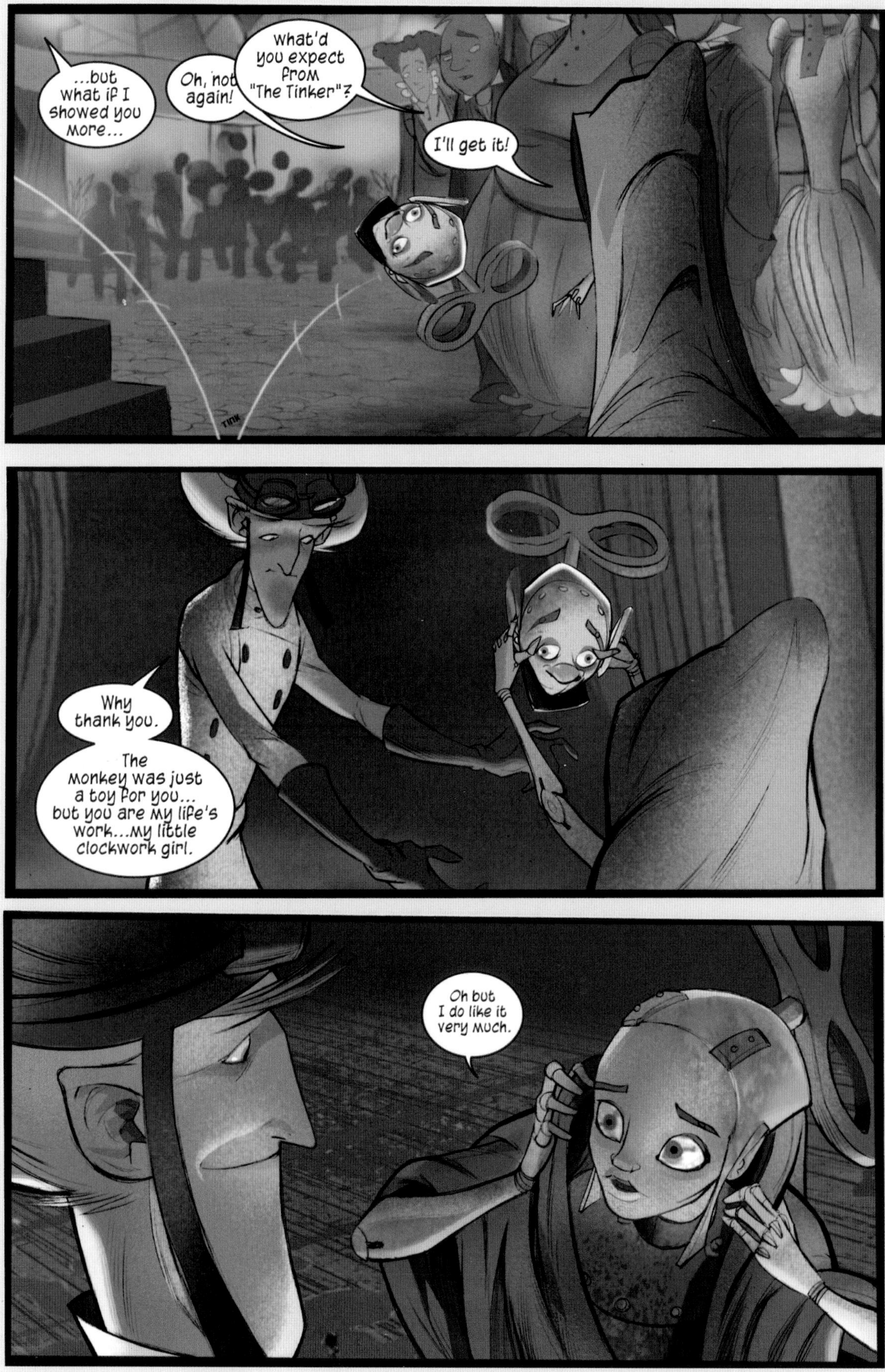
...but what if I showed you more...
Oh, not again!
What'd you expect from "The Tinker"?
I'll get it!
TINK
Why thank you.
The Monkey was just a toy for you... but you are my life's work...my little clockwork girl.
Oh but I do like it very much.

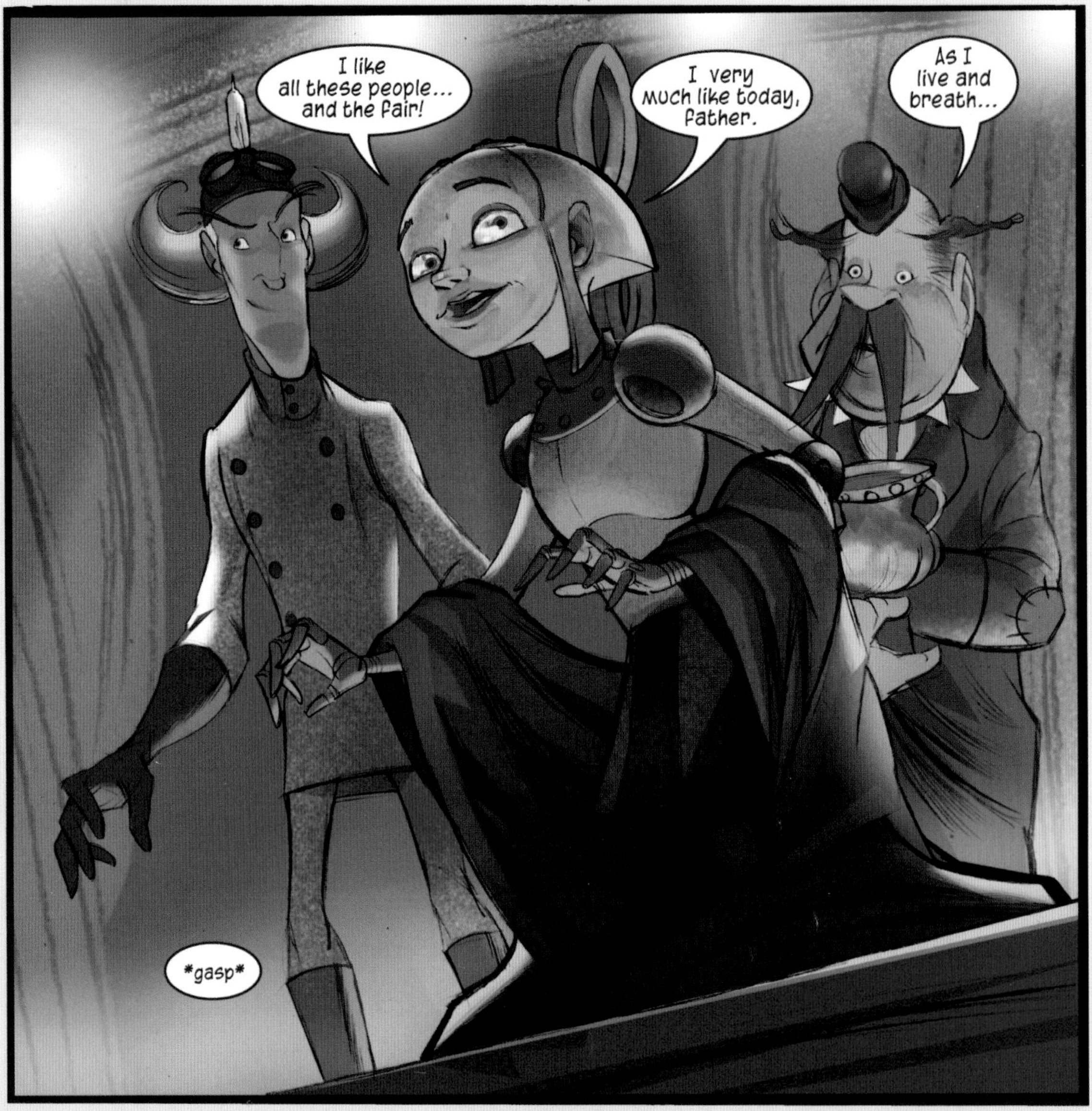
I like all these people... and the fair!
I very much like today, father.
As I live and breath...
gasp

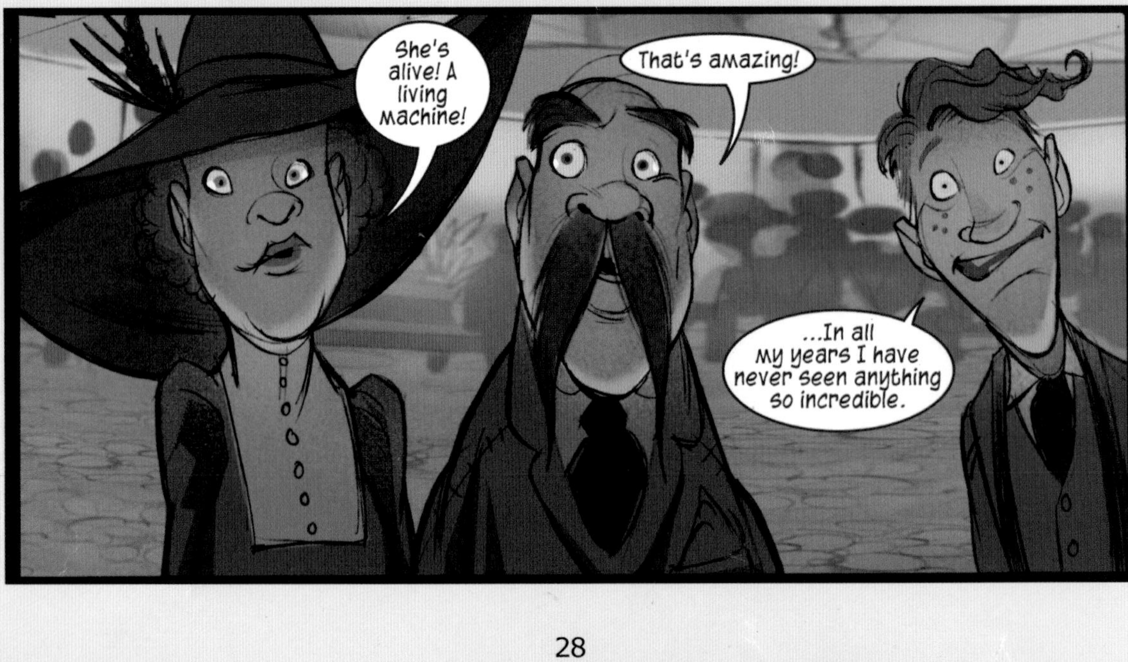
She's alive! A living machine!
That's amazing!
...In all my years I have never seen anything so incredible.

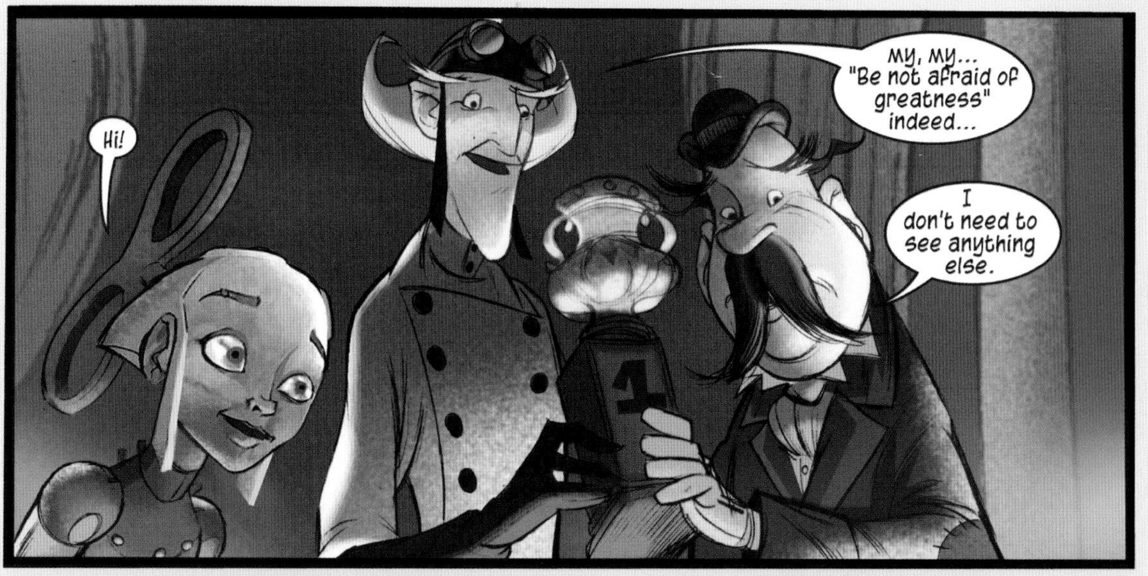
Hi!
My, my... "Be not afraid of greatness" indeed...
I don't need to see anything else.

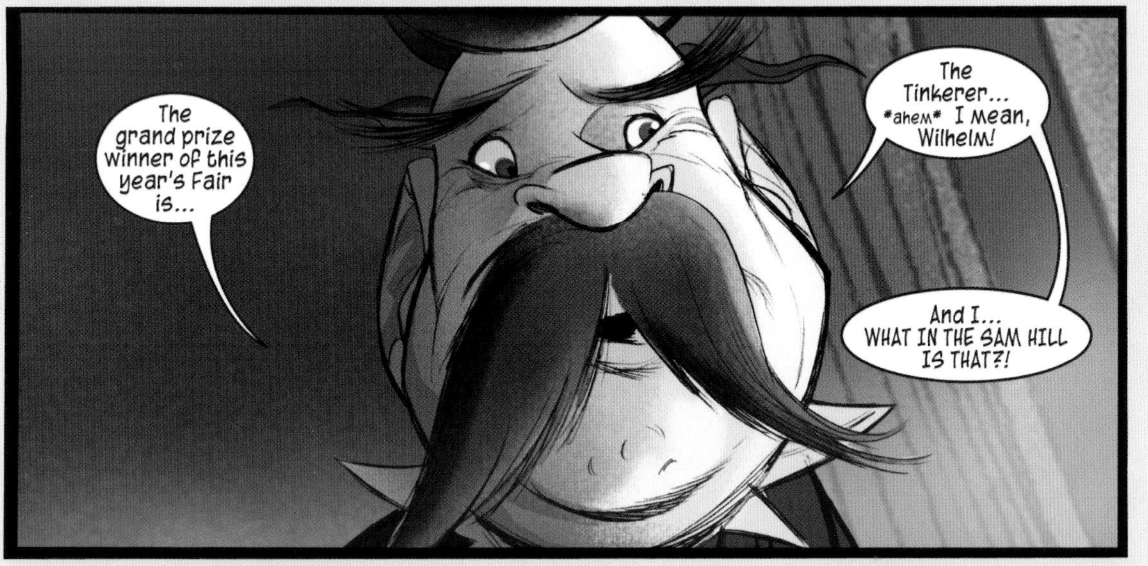
The grand prize winner of this year's Fair is...
The Tinkerer... *ahem* I mean, Wilhelm!
And I... WHAT IN THE SAM HILL IS THAT?!

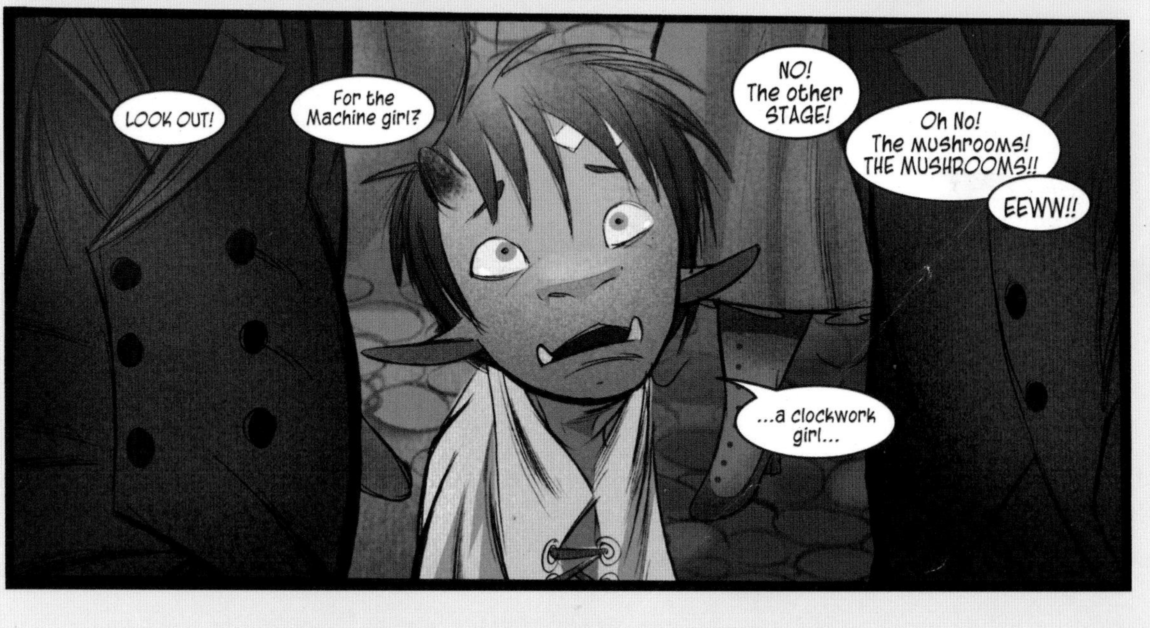
LOOK OUT!
For the Machine girl?
NO! The other STAGE!
Oh No! The MUSHROOMS! THE MUSHROOMS!!
EEWW!!
...a clockwork girl...

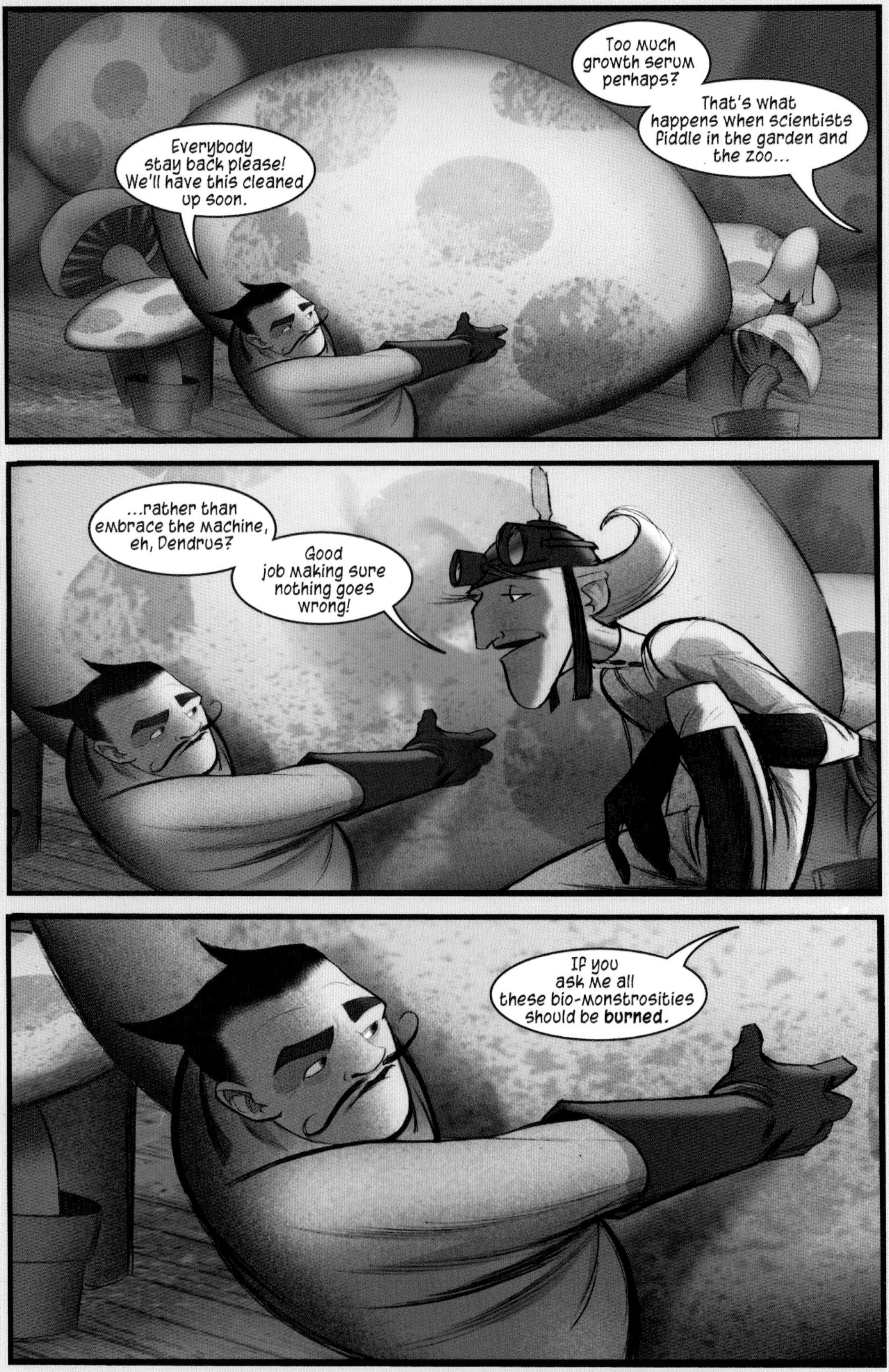
Everybody stay back please! We'll have this cleaned up soon.
Too much growth serum perhaps?
That's what happens when scientists fiddle in the garden and the zoo...
...rather than embrace the machine, eh, Dendrus?
Good job making sure nothing goes wrong!
If you ask me all these bio-monstrosities should be **burned**.

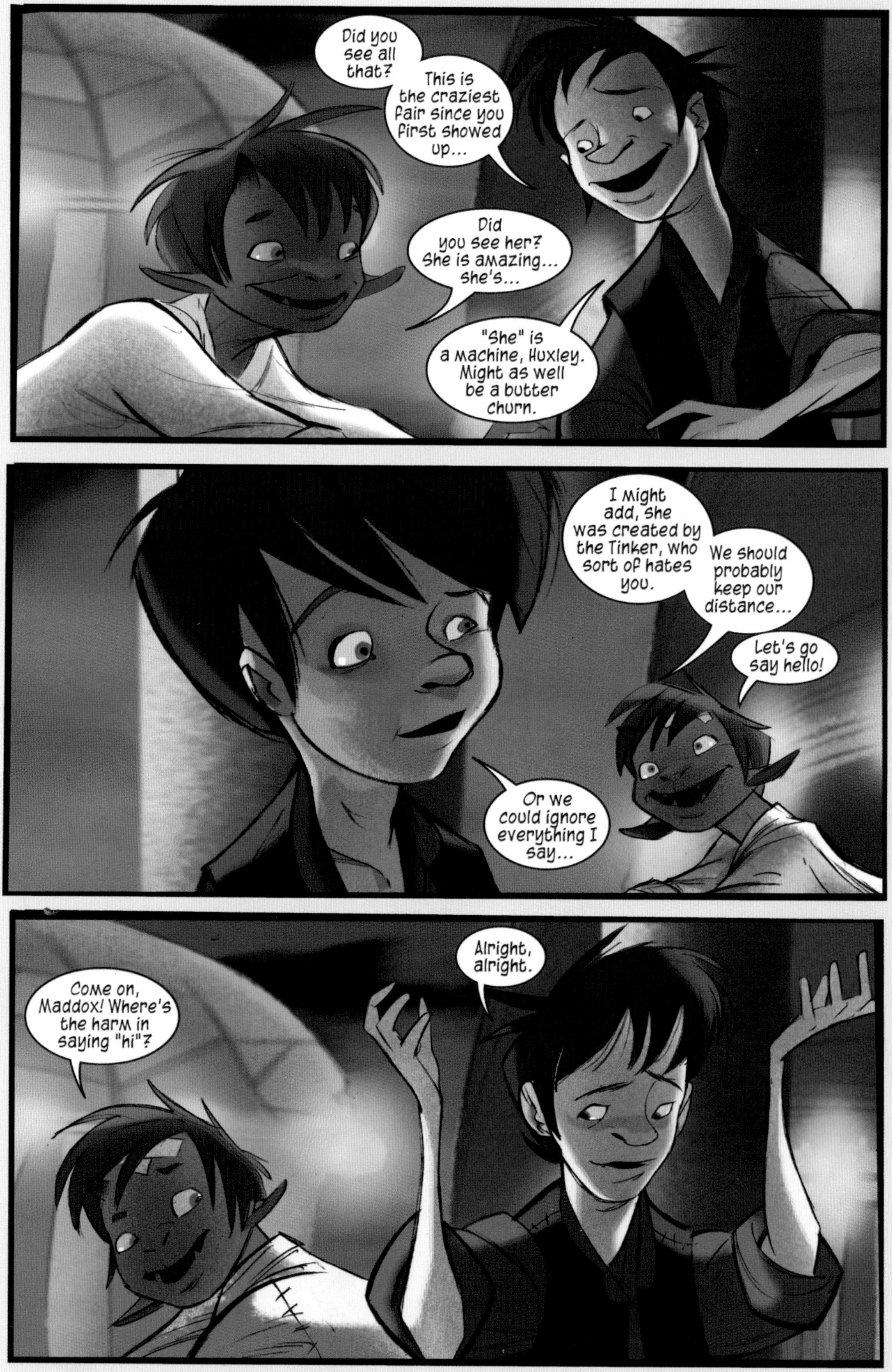
Did you see all that?
This is the craziest fair since you first showed up...
Did you see her? She is amazing... she's...
"She" is a machine, Huxley. Might as well be a butter churn.
I might add, she was created by the Tinker, who sort of hates you.
We should probably keep our distance...
Let's go say hello!
Or we could ignore everything I say...
Alright, alright.
Come on, Maddox! Where's the harm in saying "hi"?

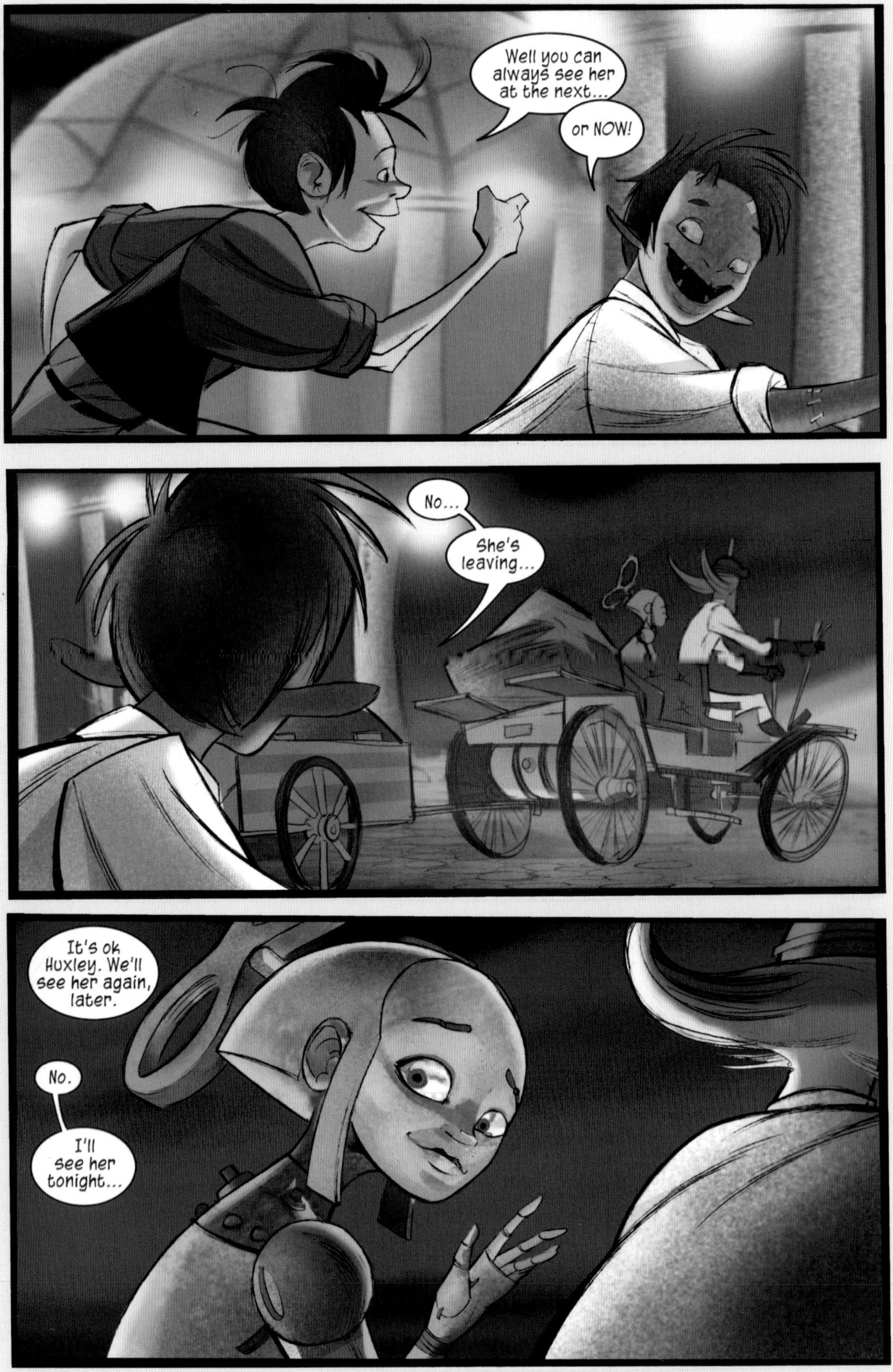
Well you can always see her at the next...
or NOW!
No...
She's leaving...
It's ok Huxley. We'll see her again, later.
No.
I'll see her tonight...

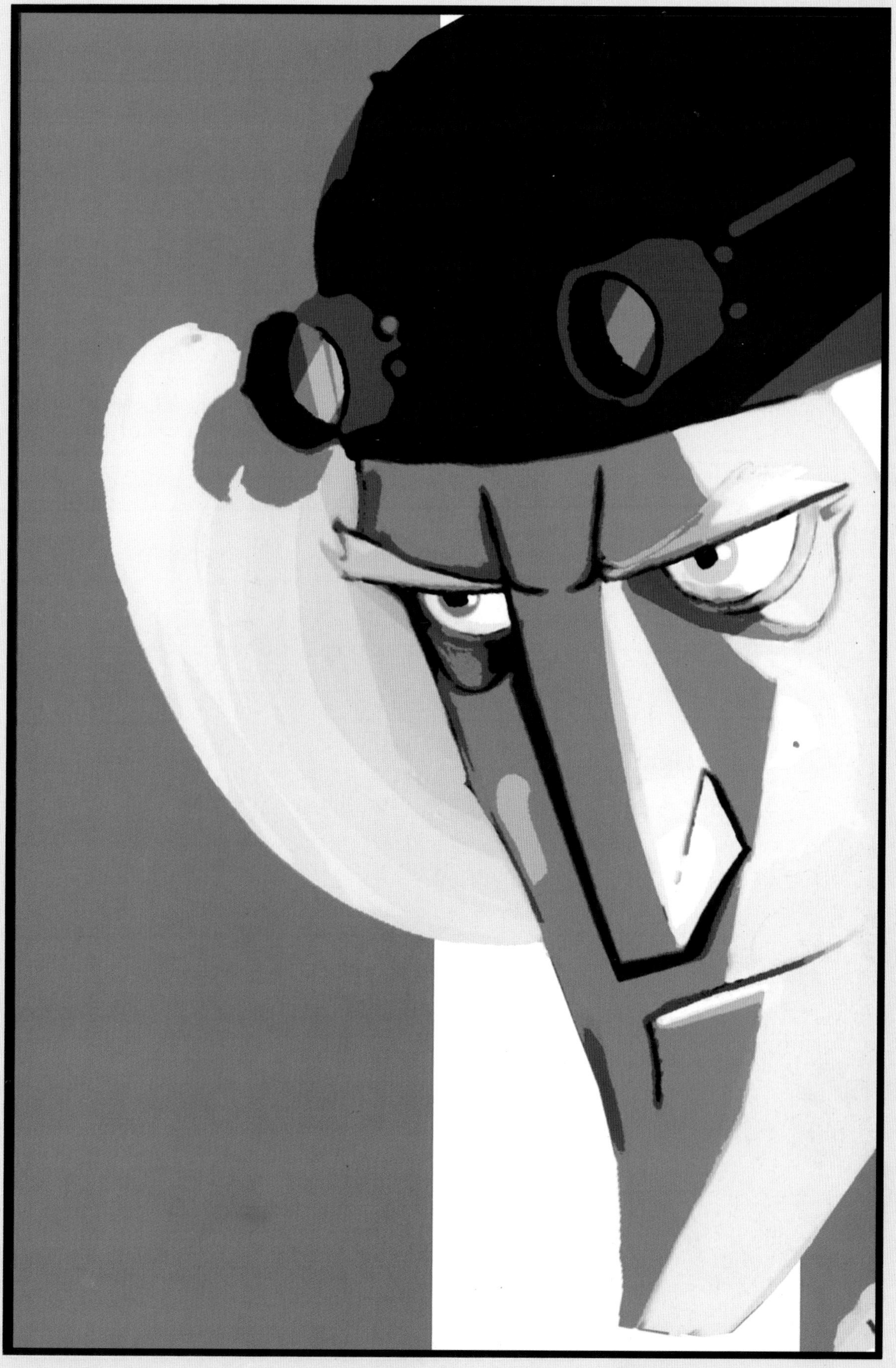

Chapter 2

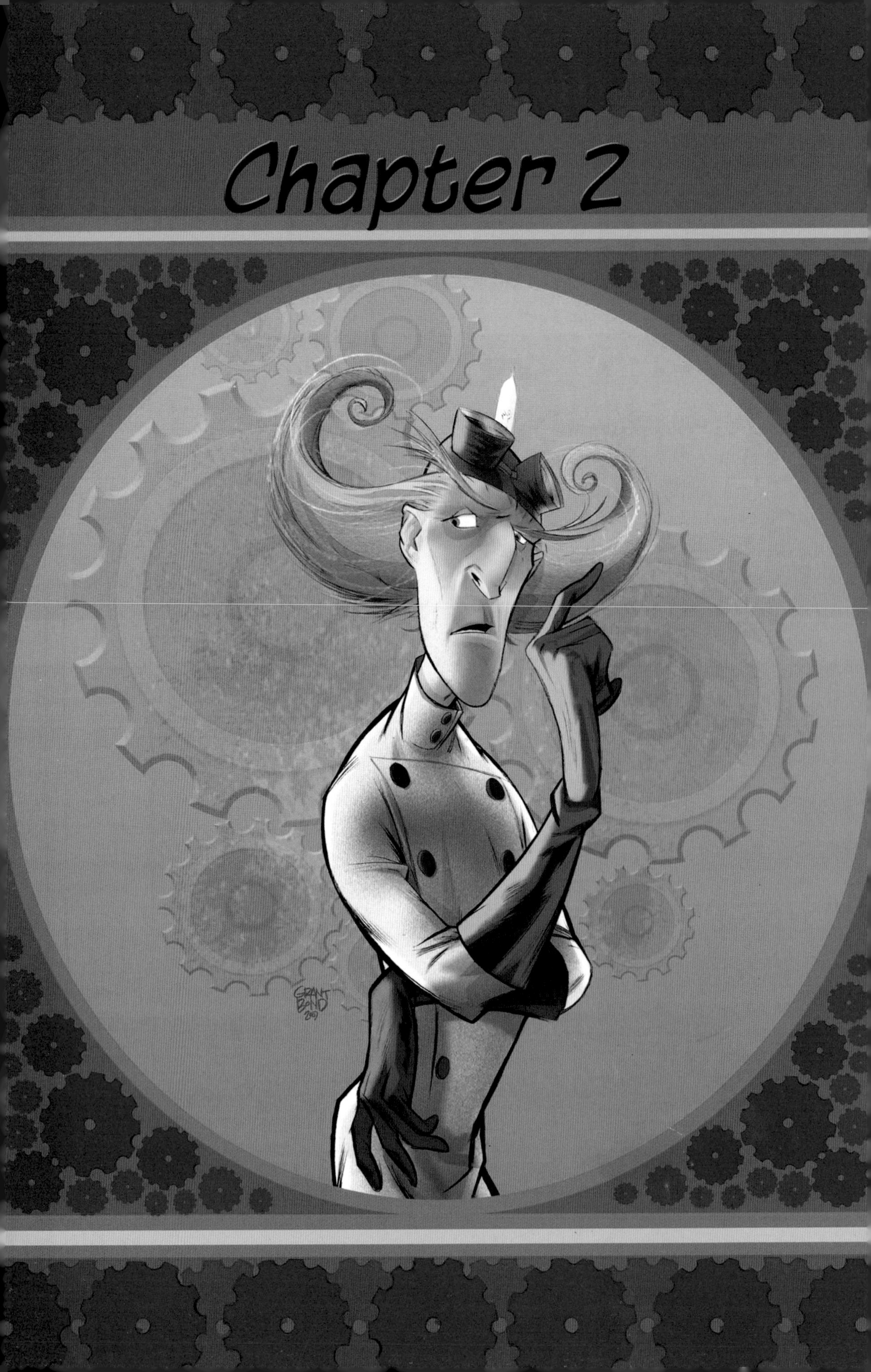

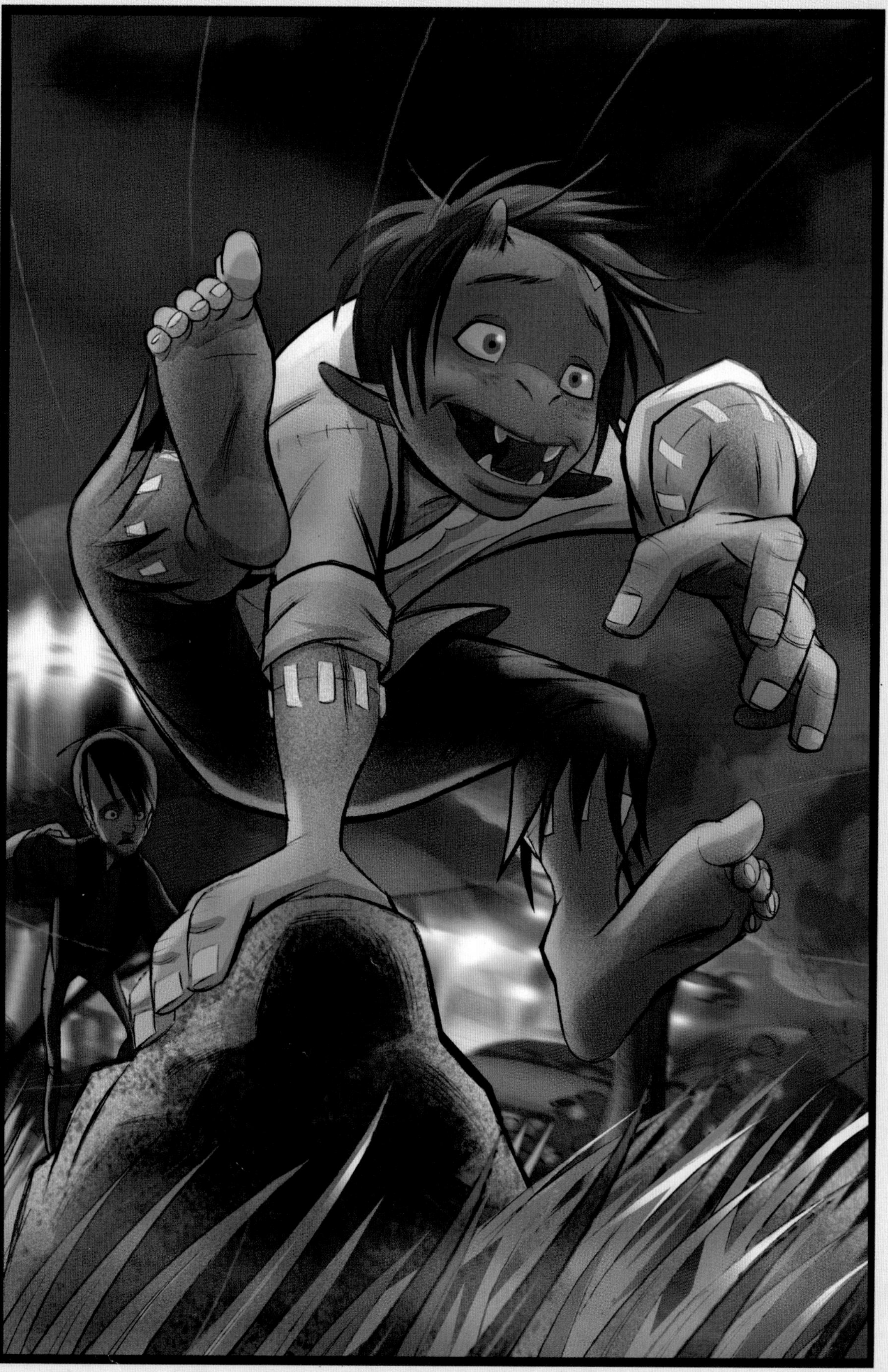

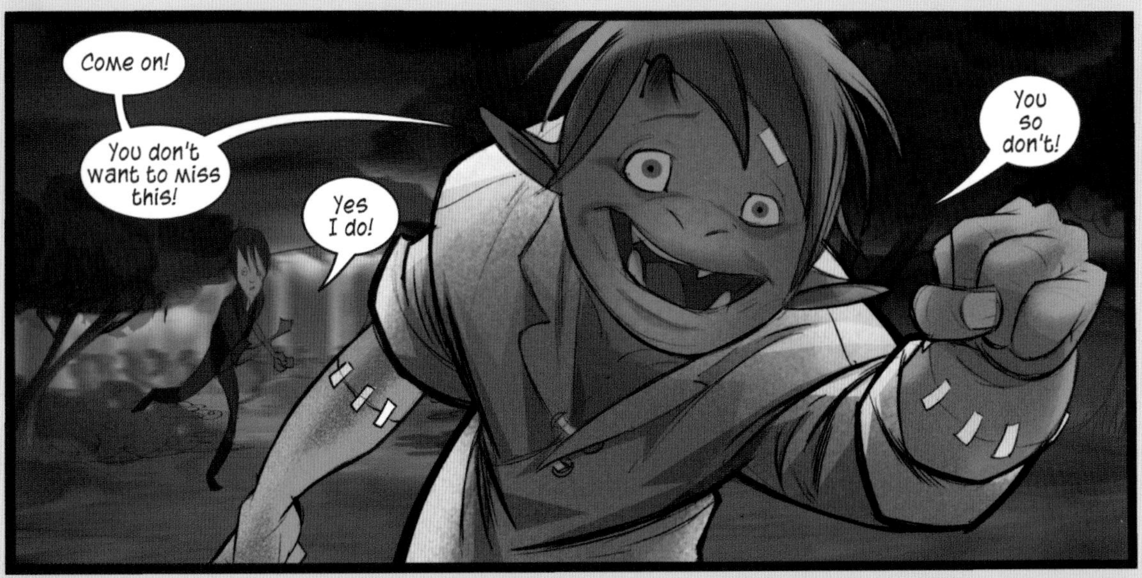
Come on!
You don't want to miss this!
Yes I do!
You so don't!

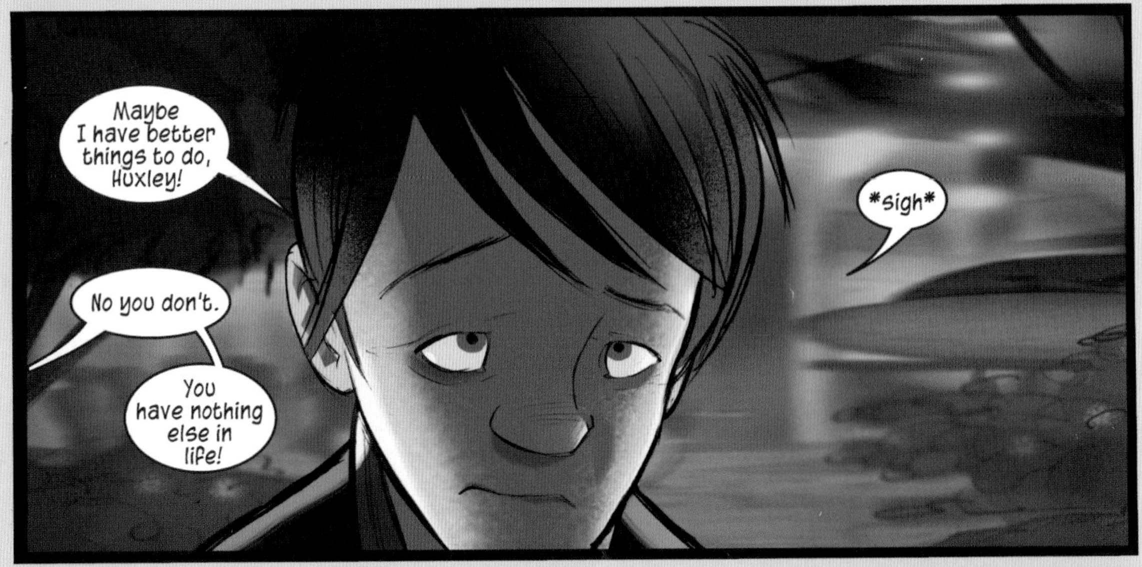
Maybe I have better things to do, Huxley!
sigh
No you don't.
You have nothing else in life!

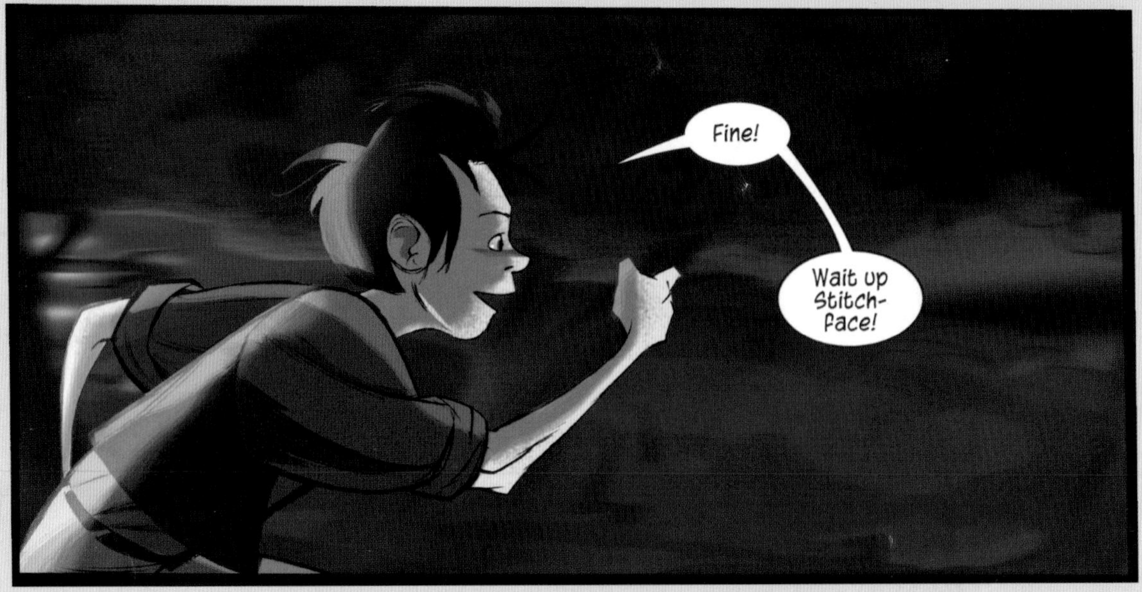
Fine!
Wait up Stitch-face!

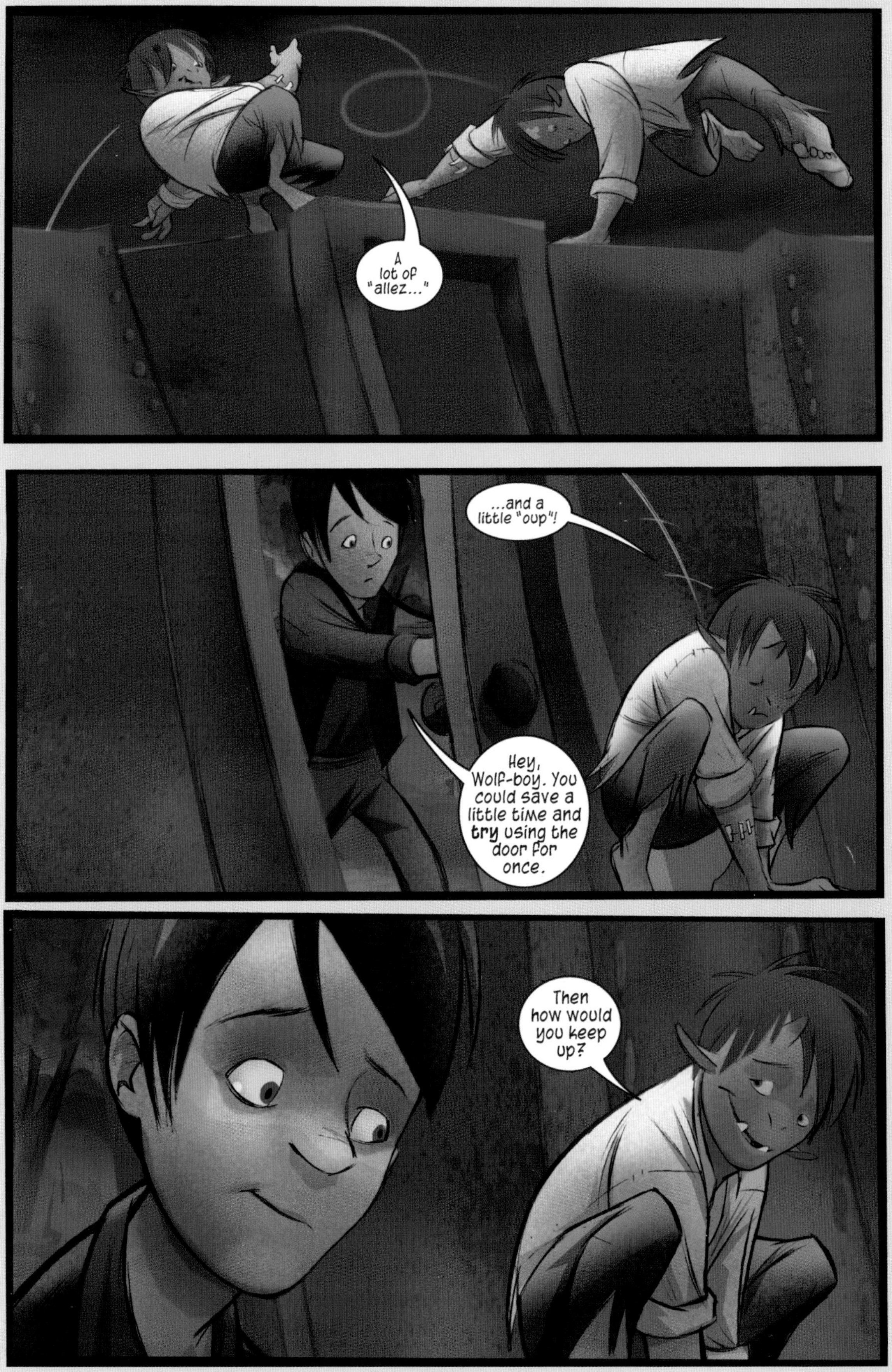
A lot of "allez..."
...and a little "oup"!
Hey, Wolf-boy. You could save a little time and **try** using the door for once.
Then how would you keep up?

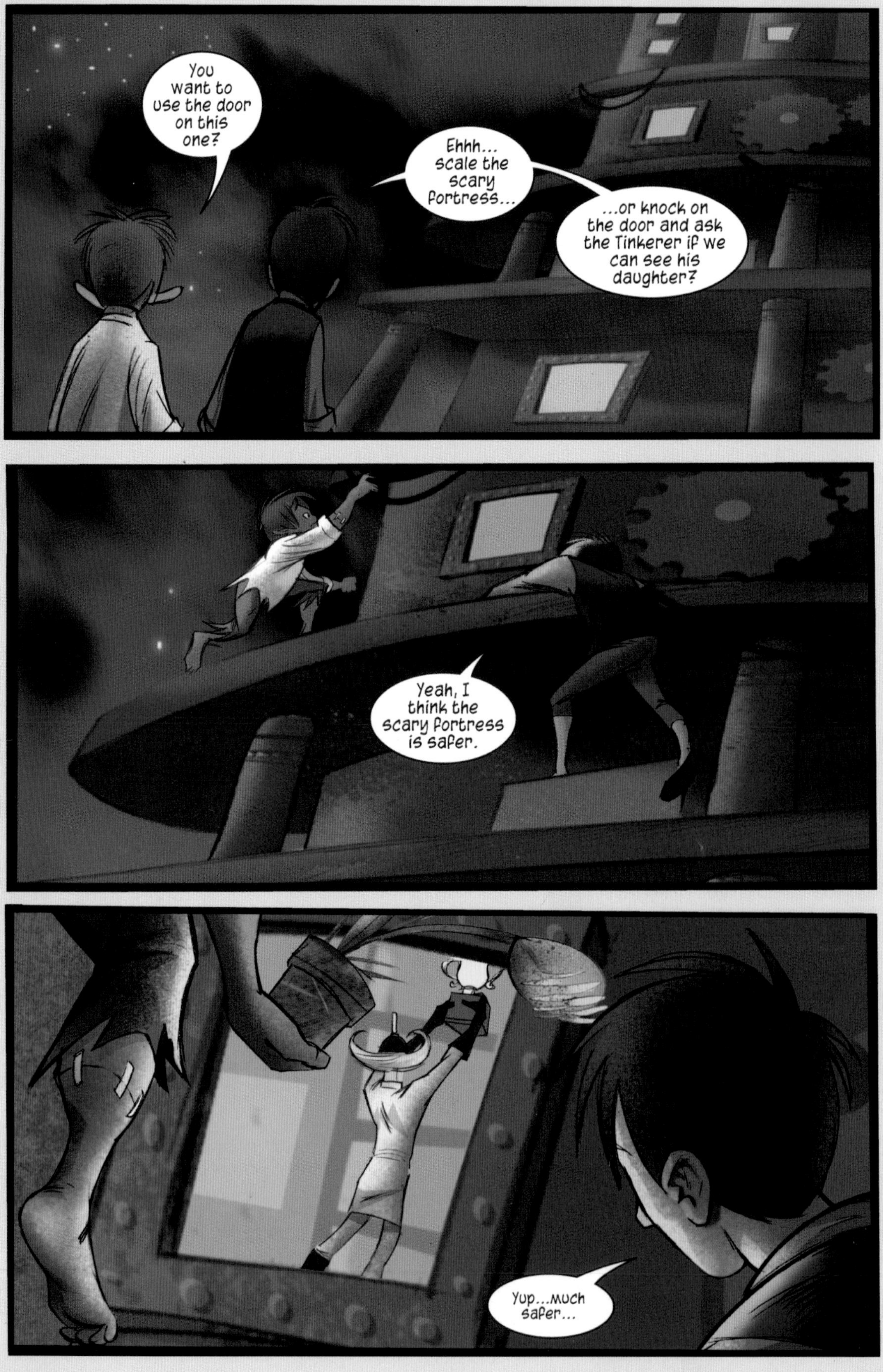
You want to use the door on this one?
Ehhh... scale the scary fortress...
...or knock on the door and ask the Tinkerer if we can see his daughter?
Yeah, I think the scary fortress is safer.
Yup...much safer...

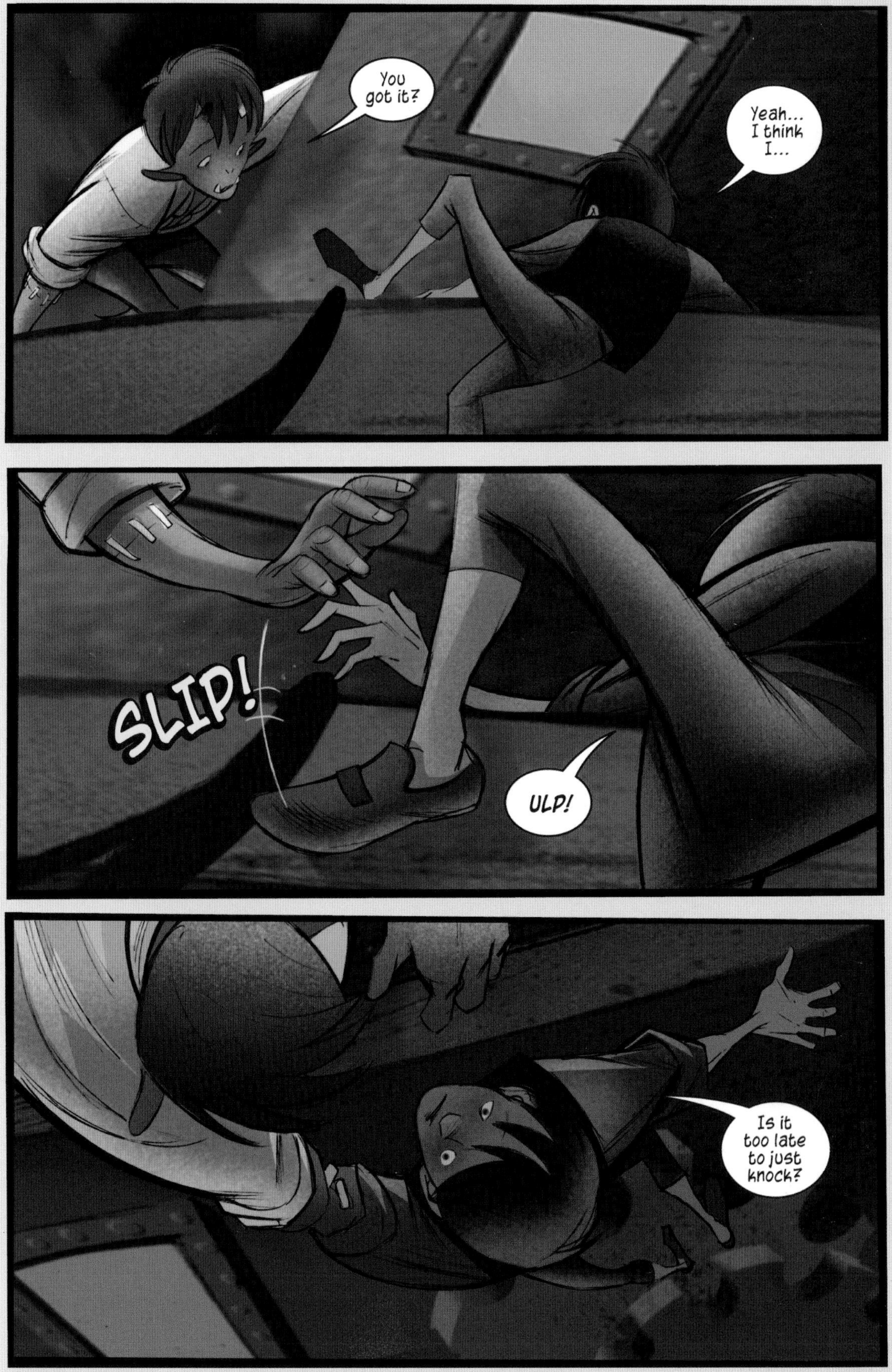
You got it?
Yeah... I think I...
SLIP!
ULP!
Is it too late to just knock?

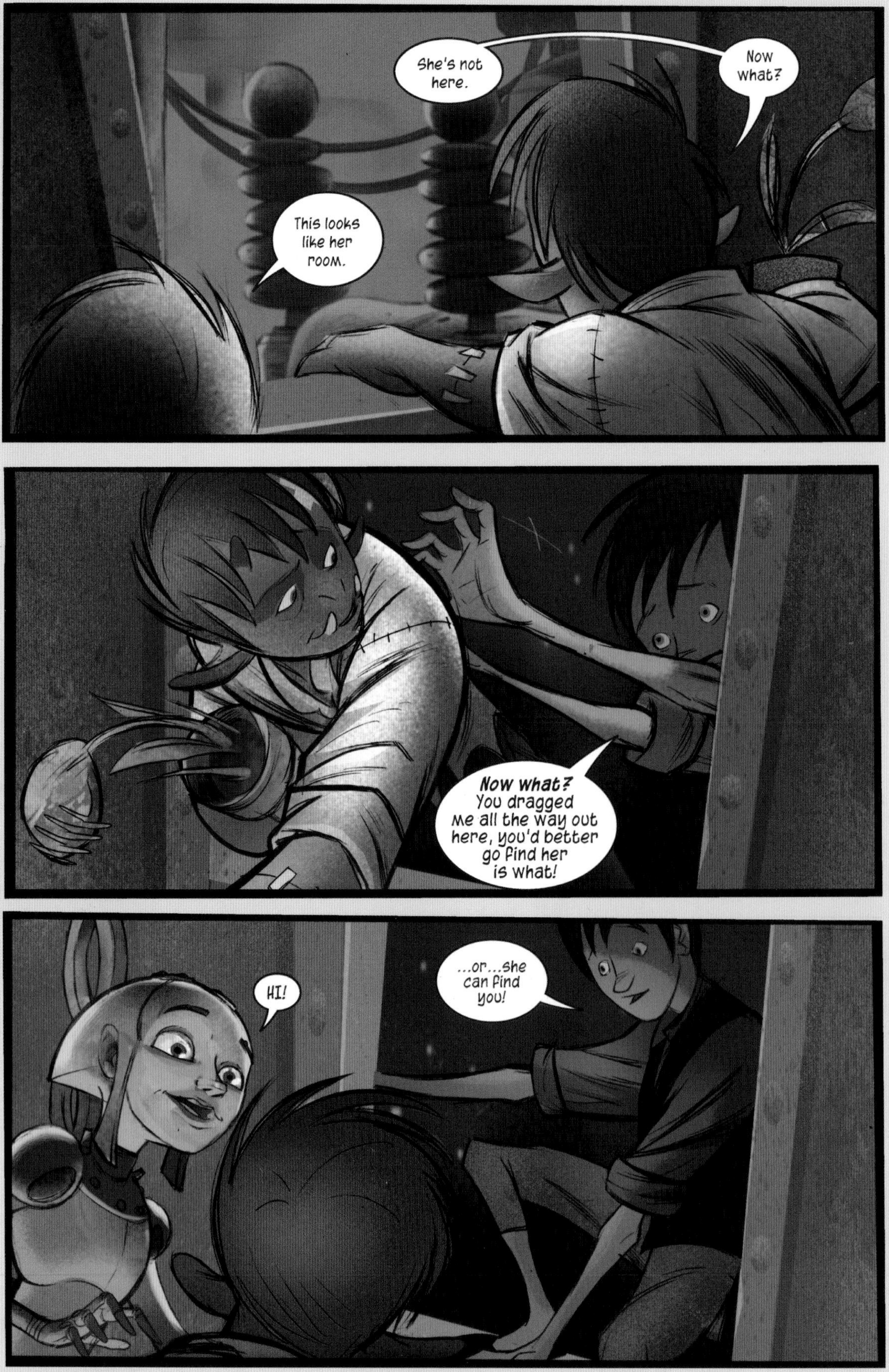

She's not here.
Now what?
This looks like her room.
Now what? You dragged me all the way out here, you'd better go find her is what!
HI!
...or...she can find you!

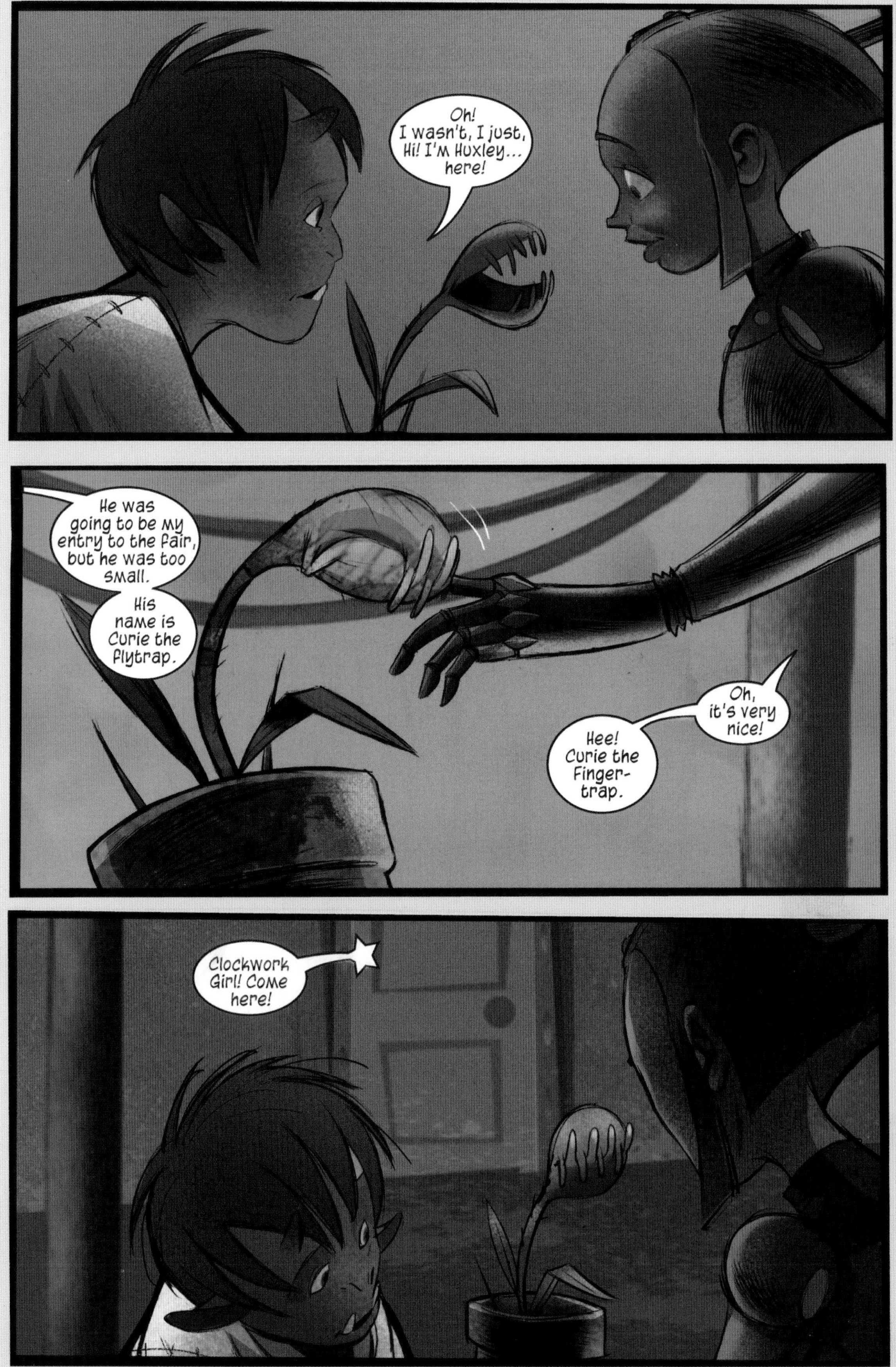
Oh! I wasn't, I just, Hi! I'm Huxley... here!
He was going to be my entry to the fair, but he was too small.
His name is Curie the flytrap.
Oh, it's very nice!
Hee! Curie the Finger-trap.
Clockwork Girl! Come here!

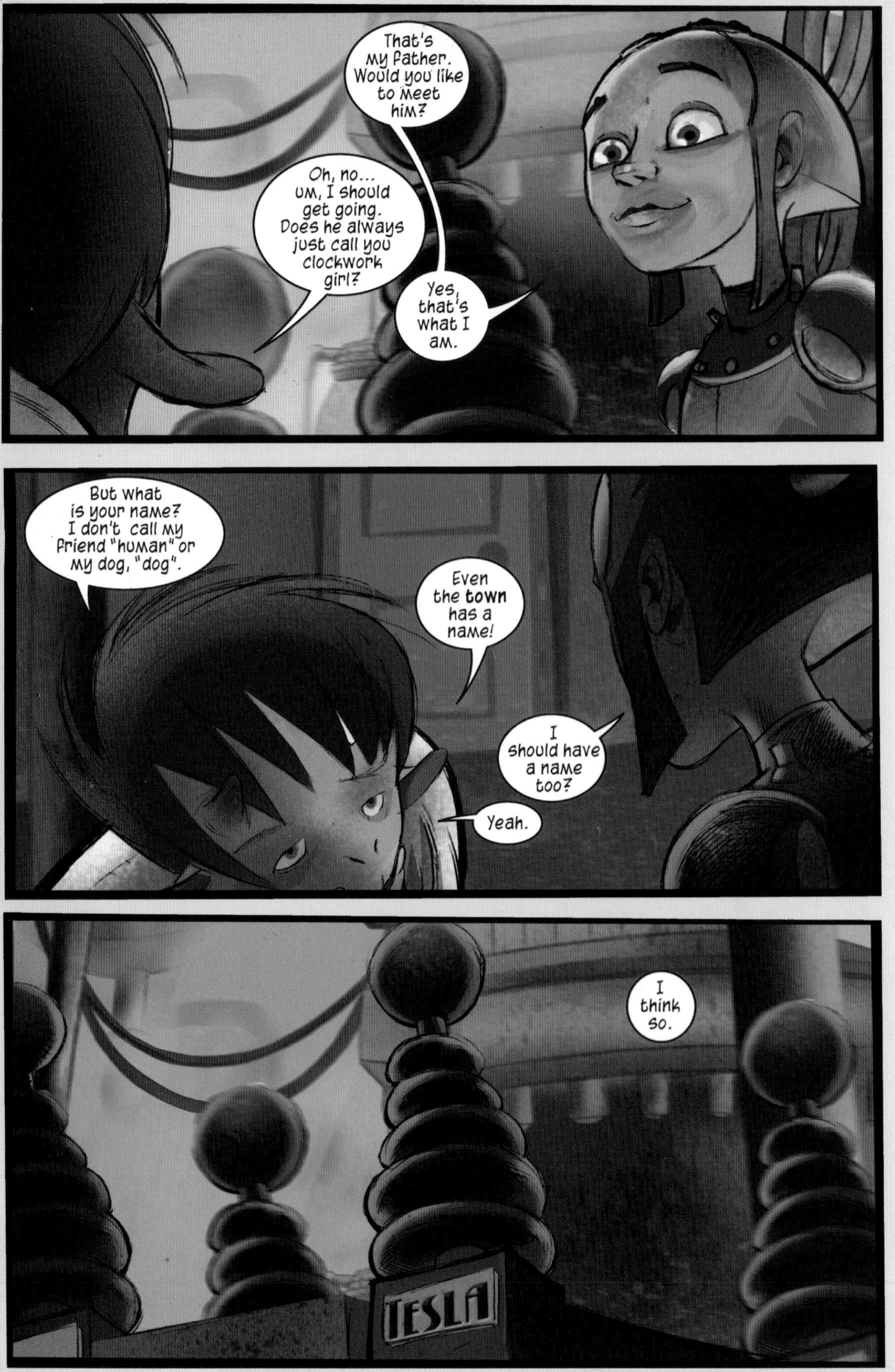
That's my father. Would you like to meet him?
Oh, no... um, I should get going. Does he always just call you clockwork girl?
Yes, that's what I am.
But what is your name? I don't call my friend "human" or my dog, "dog".
Even the **town** has a name!
I should have a name too?
Yeah.
I think so.
TESLA

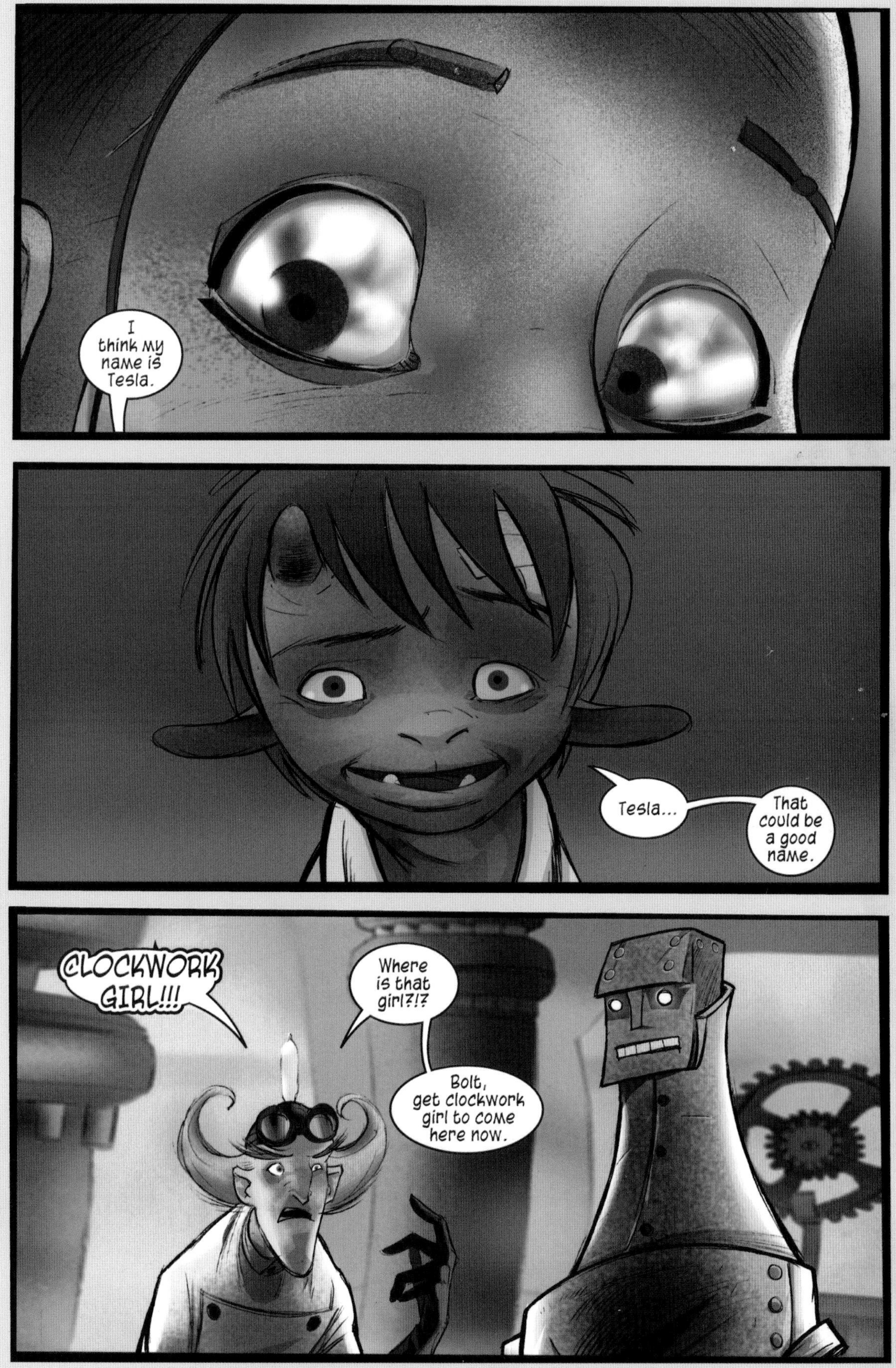
I think my name is Tesla.
Tesla...
That could be a good name.
CLOCKWORK GIRL!!!
Where is that girl?!?
Bolt, get clockwork girl to come here now.

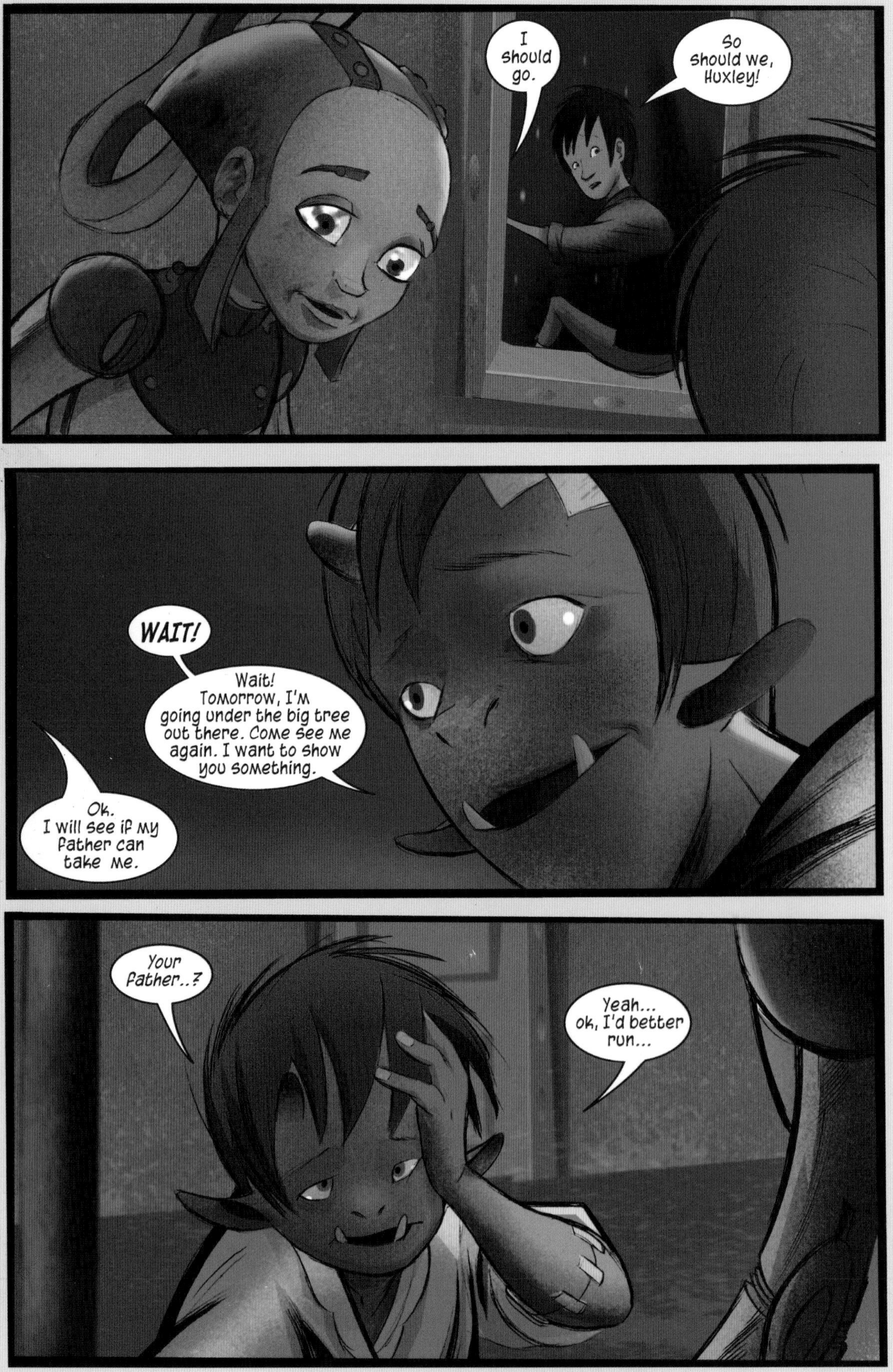

I should go.
So should we, Huxley!
WAIT!
Wait! Tomorrow, I'M going under the big tree out there. Come see me again. I want to show you something.
Ok. I will see if my father can take me.
Your father..?
Yeah... ok, I'd better run...

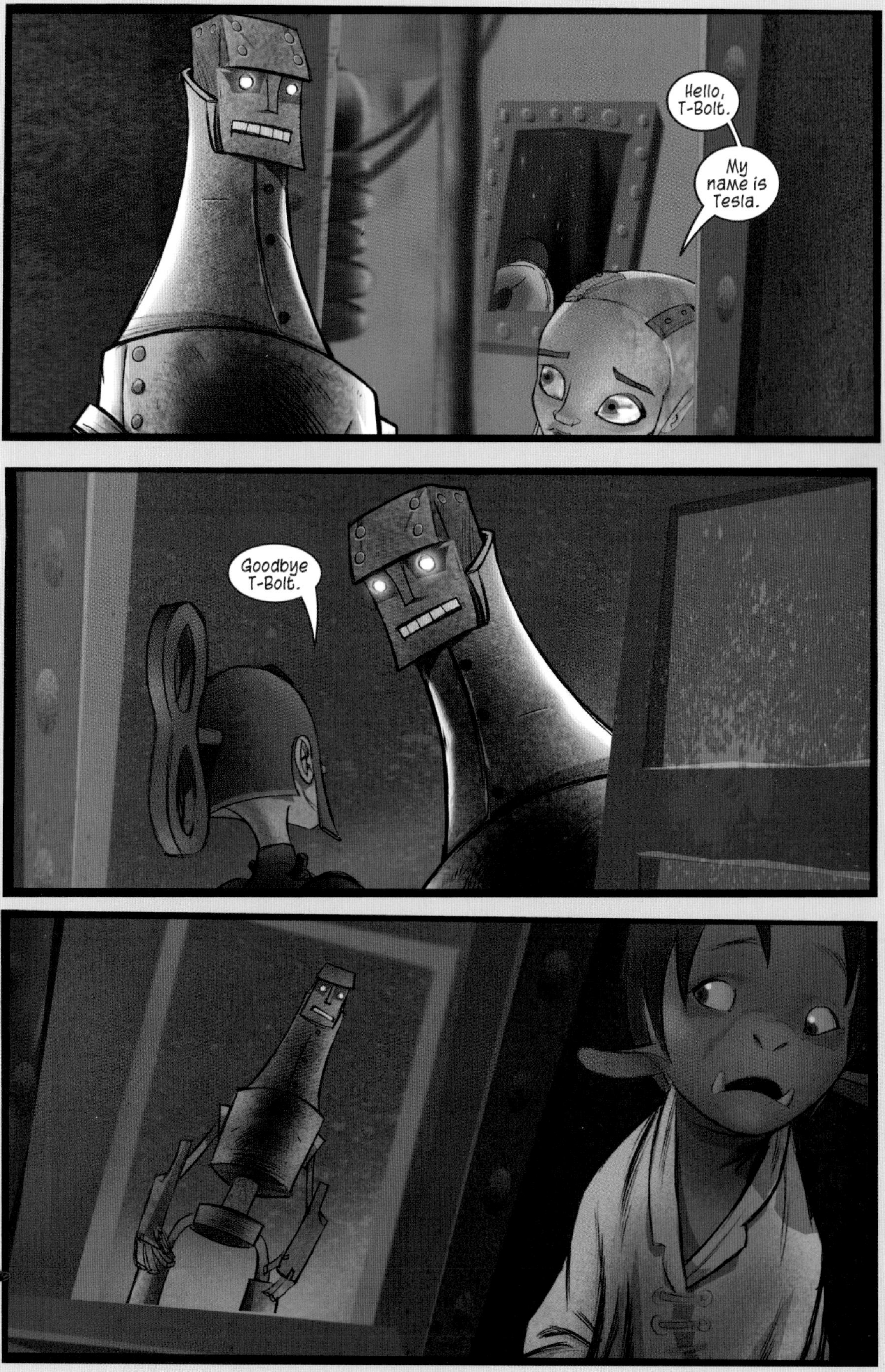
Hello, T-Bolt.
My name is Tesla.
Goodbye T-Bolt.

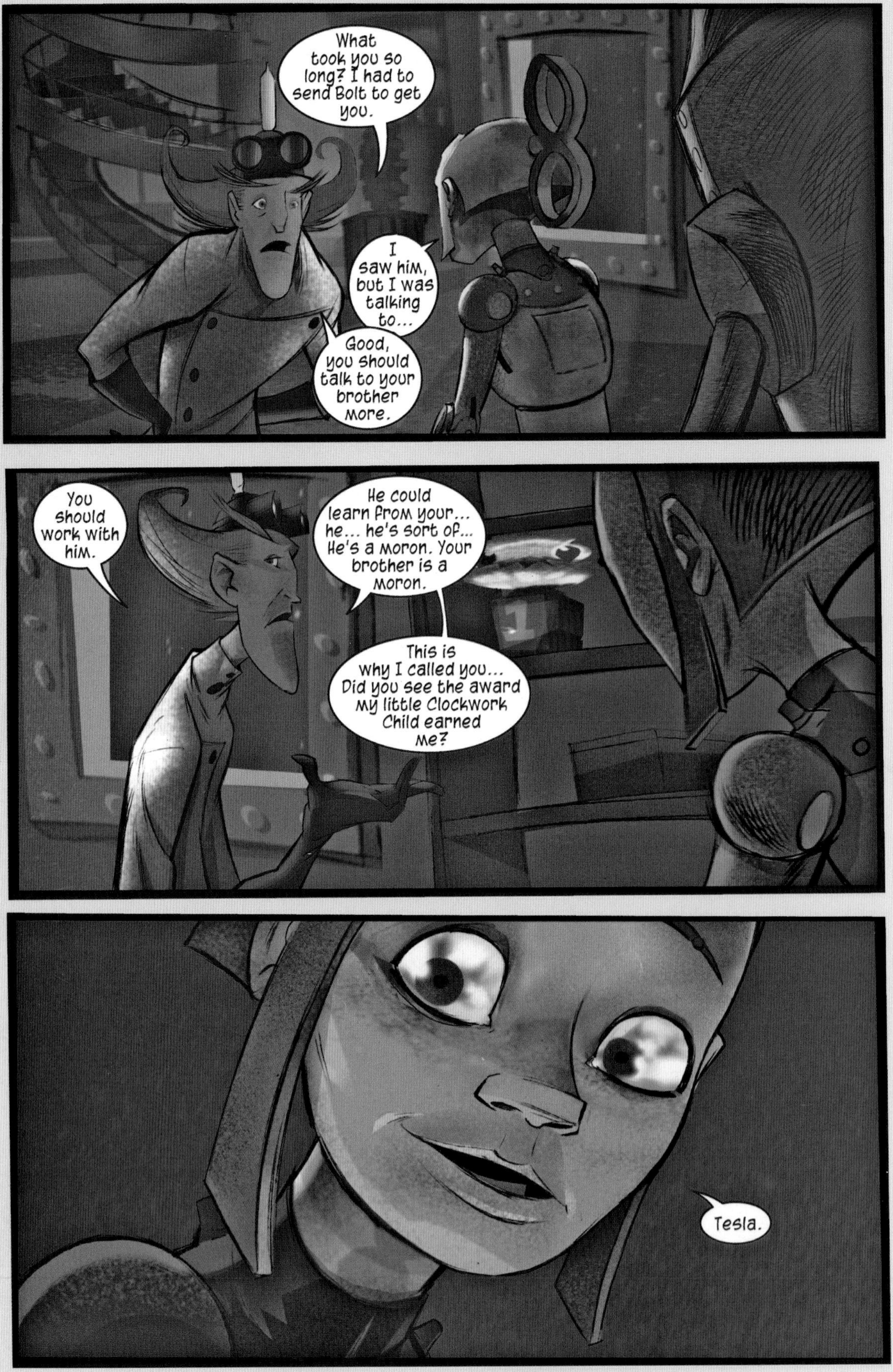
What took you so long? I had to send Bolt to get you.
I saw him, but I was talking to...
Good, you should talk to your brother more.
You should work with him.
He could learn from your... he... he's sort of... He's a moron. Your brother is a moron.
This is why I called you... Did you see the award my little Clockwork Child earned me?
Tesla.

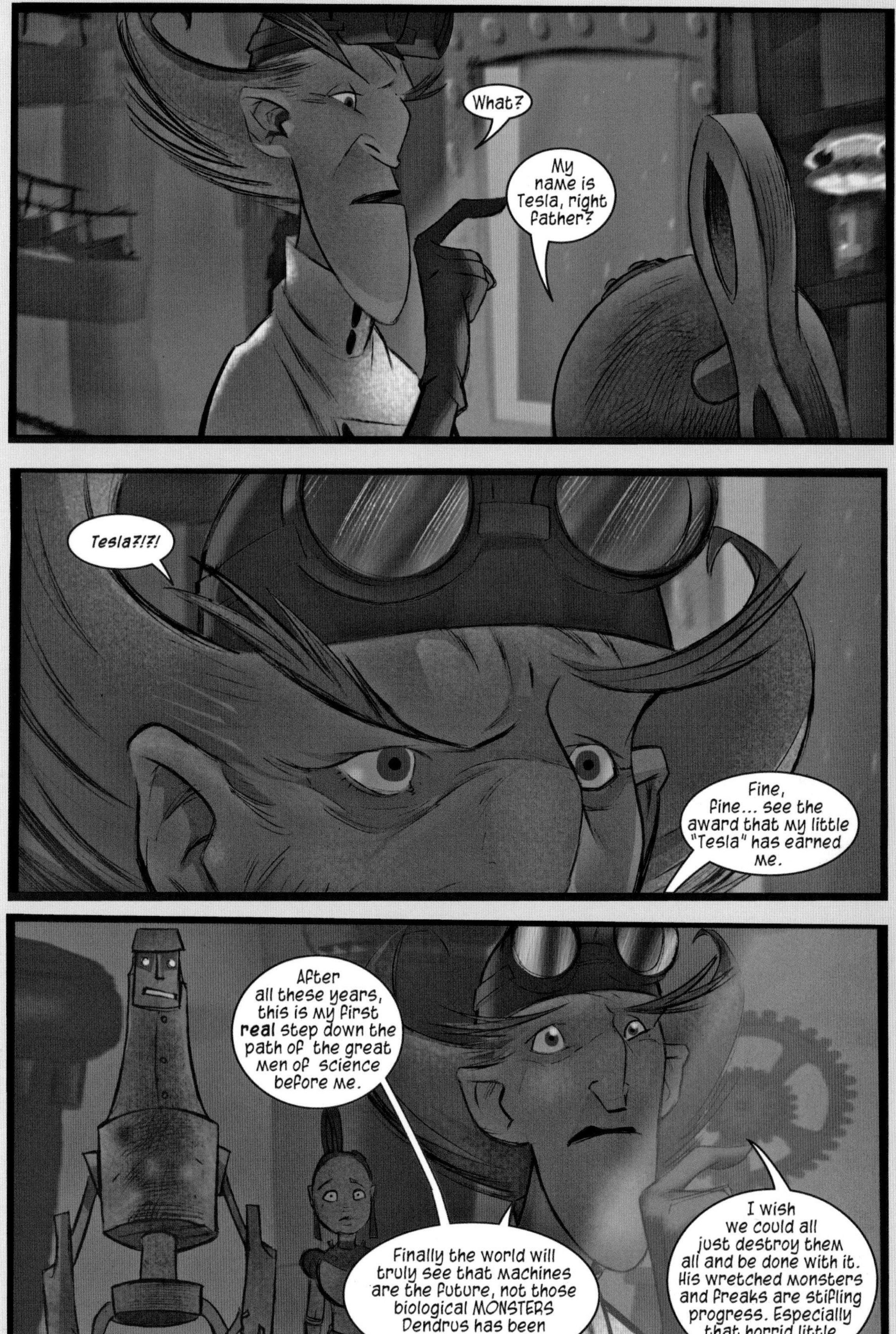
What?
My name is Tesla, right father?
Tesla?!?!
Fine, fine... see the award that my little "Tesla" has earned me.
After all these years, this is my first **real** step down the path of the great men of science before me.
Finally the world will truly see that machines are the future, not those biological MONSTERS Dendrus has been kludging together.
I wish we could all just destroy them all and be done with it. His wretched monsters and freaks are stifling progress. Especially that horrid little mutant boy.

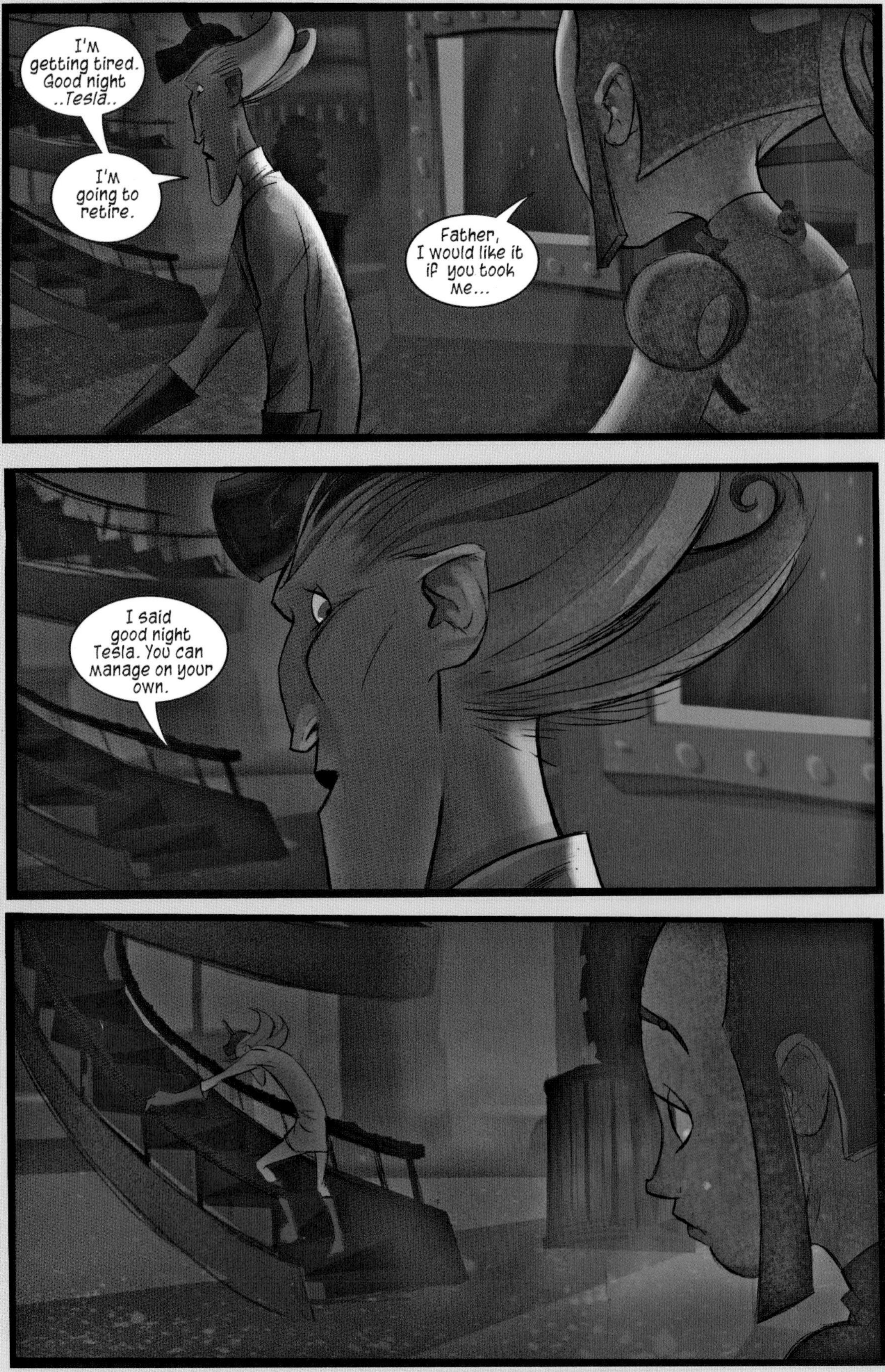
I'M getting tired. Good night ..Tesla..
I'M going to retire.
Father, I would like it if you took me...
I said good night Tesla. You can manage on your own.

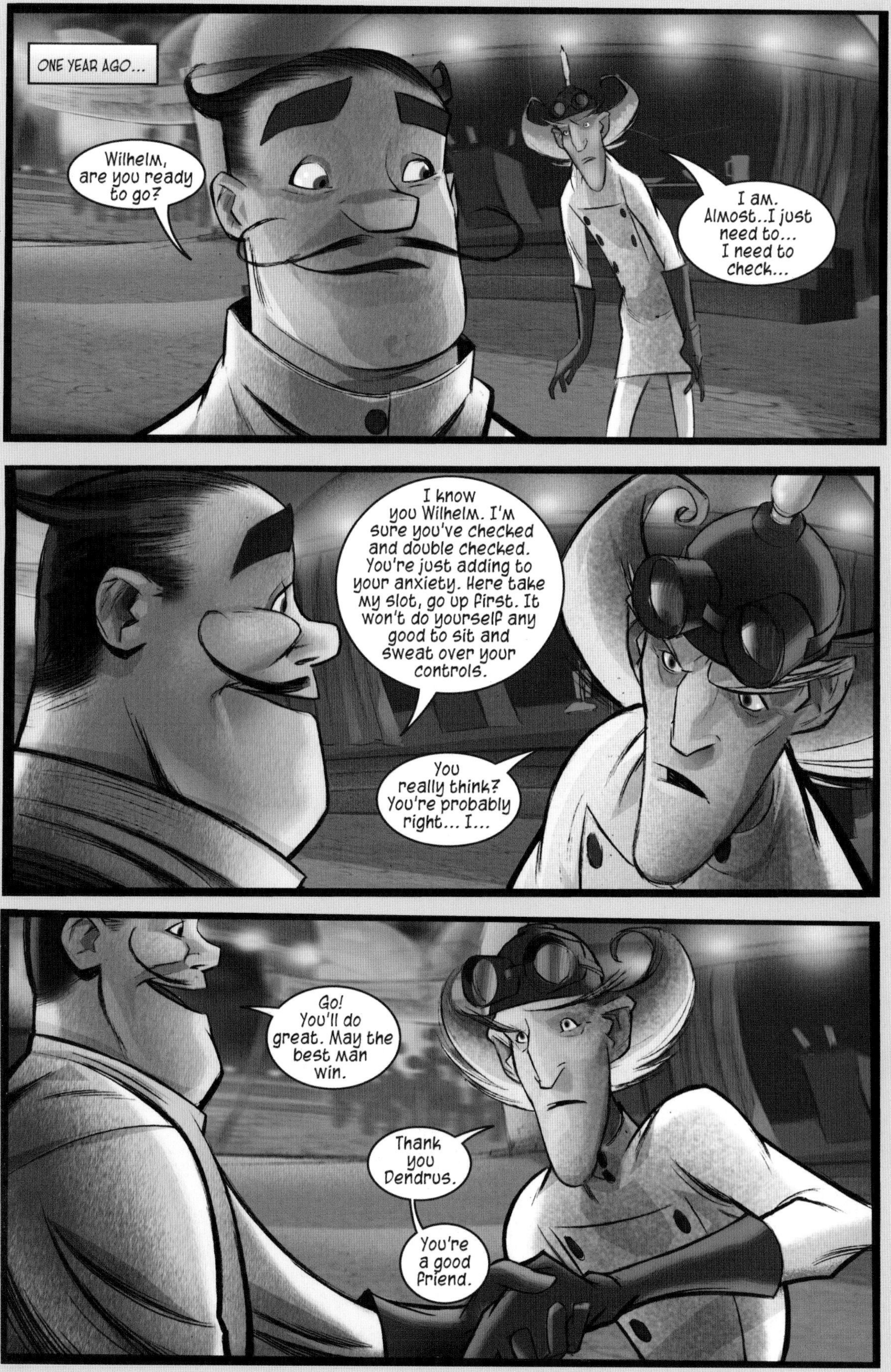
ONE YEAR AGO...
Wilhelm, are you ready to go?
I am. Almost..I just need to... I need to check...
I know you Wilhelm. I'm sure you've checked and double checked. You're just adding to your anxiety. Here take my slot, go up first. It won't do yourself any good to sit and sweat over your controls.
You really think? You're probably right... I...
Go! You'll do great. May the best man win.
Thank you Dendrus.
You're a good friend.

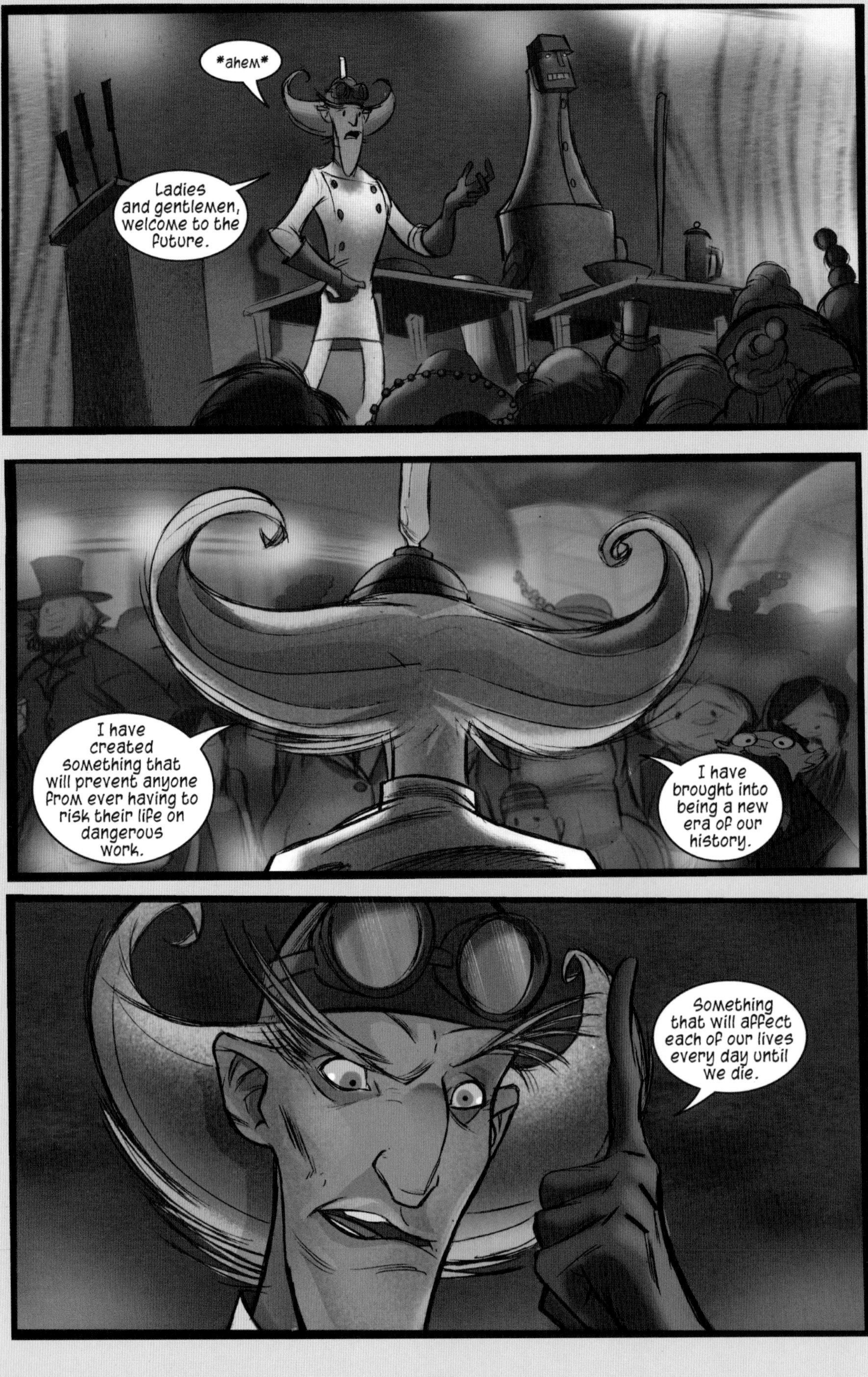
ahem
Ladies and gentlemen, welcome to the future.
I have created something that will prevent anyone from ever having to risk their life on dangerous work.
I have brought into being a new era of our history.
Something that will affect each of our lives every day until we die.

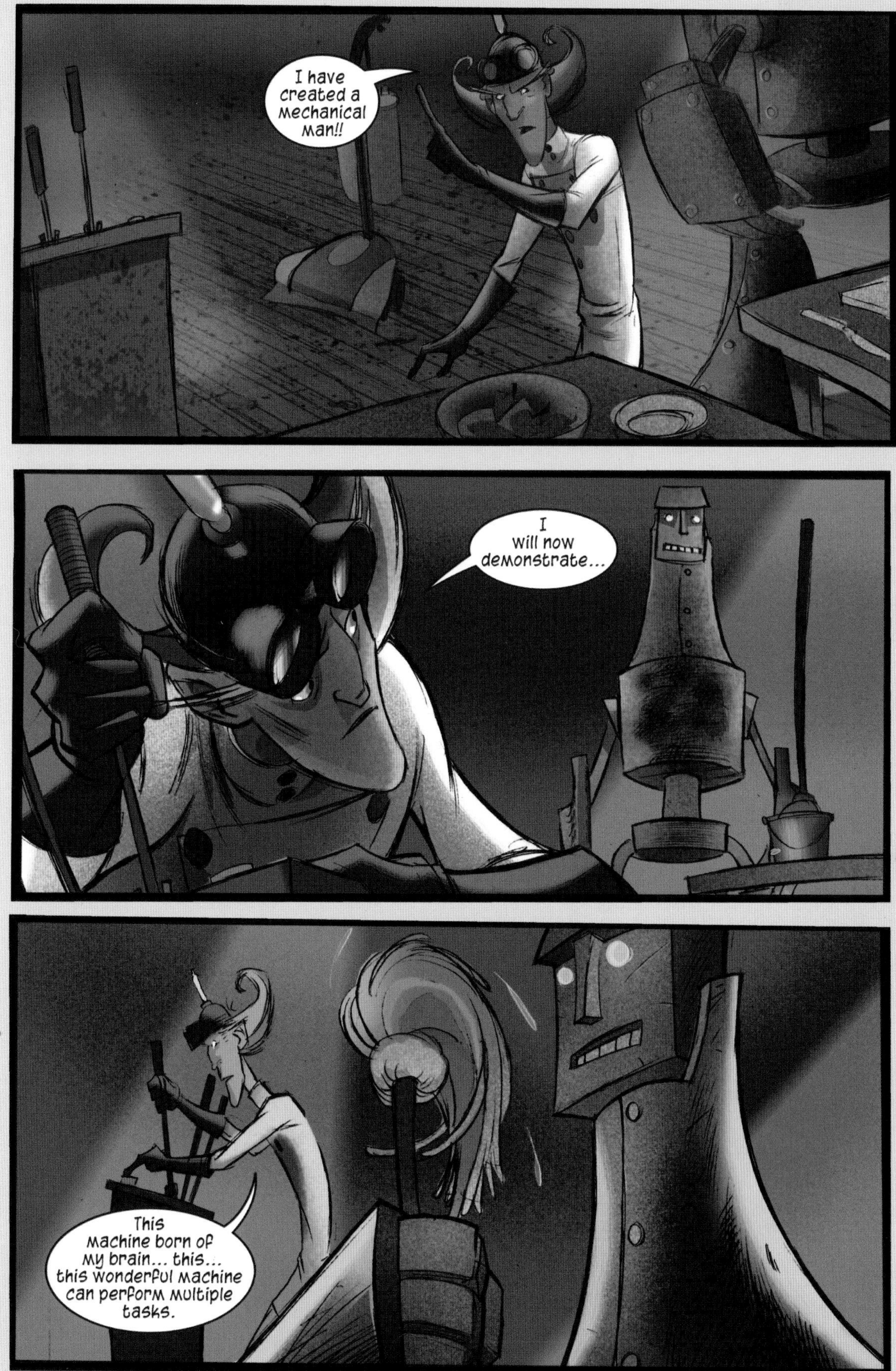
I have created a Mechanical Man!!
I will now demonstrate...
This Machine born of my brain... this... this wonderful machine can perform multiple tasks.

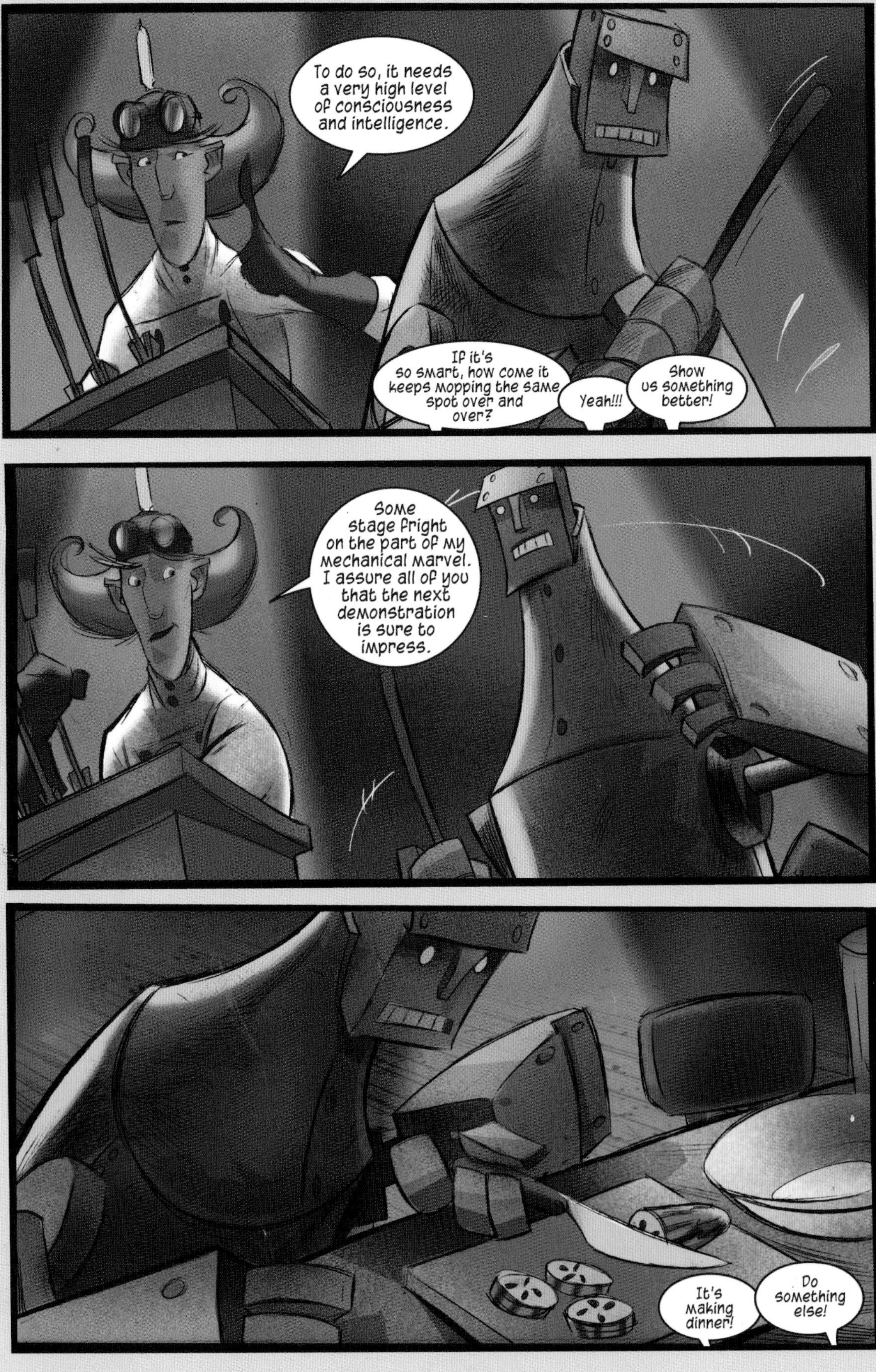
To do so, it needs a very high level of consciousness and intelligence.
If it's so smart, how come it keeps mopping the same spot over and over?
Yeah!!!
Show us something better!
Some stage fright on the part of my mechanical marvel. I assure all of you that the next demonstration is sure to impress.
It's making dinner!
Do something else!

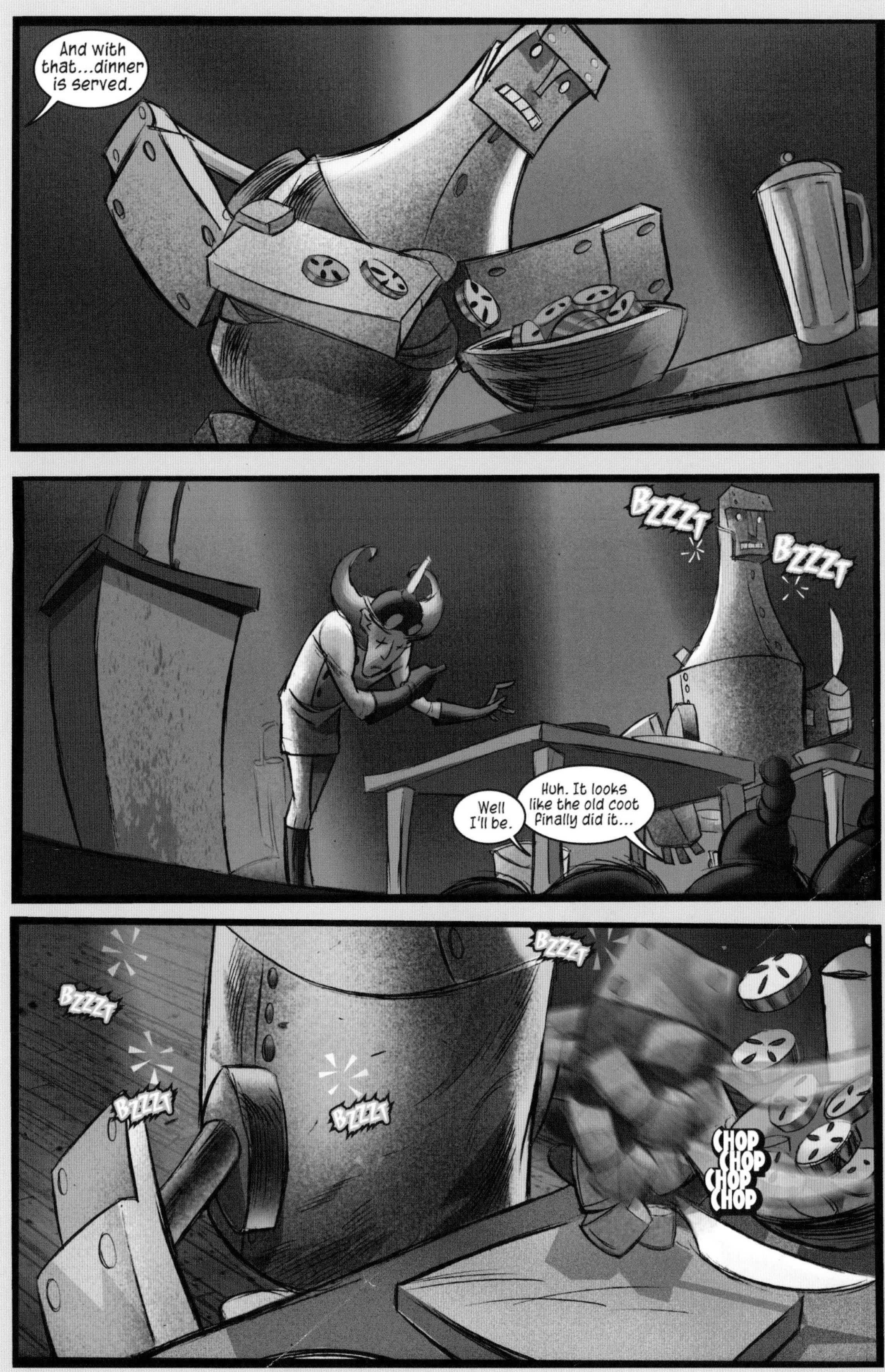
And with that...dinner is served.
BZZZT
BZZZT
Huh. It looks like the old coot finally did it...
Well I'll be.
BZZZT
BZZZT
BZZZT
BZZZT
CHOP CHOP CHOP CHOP

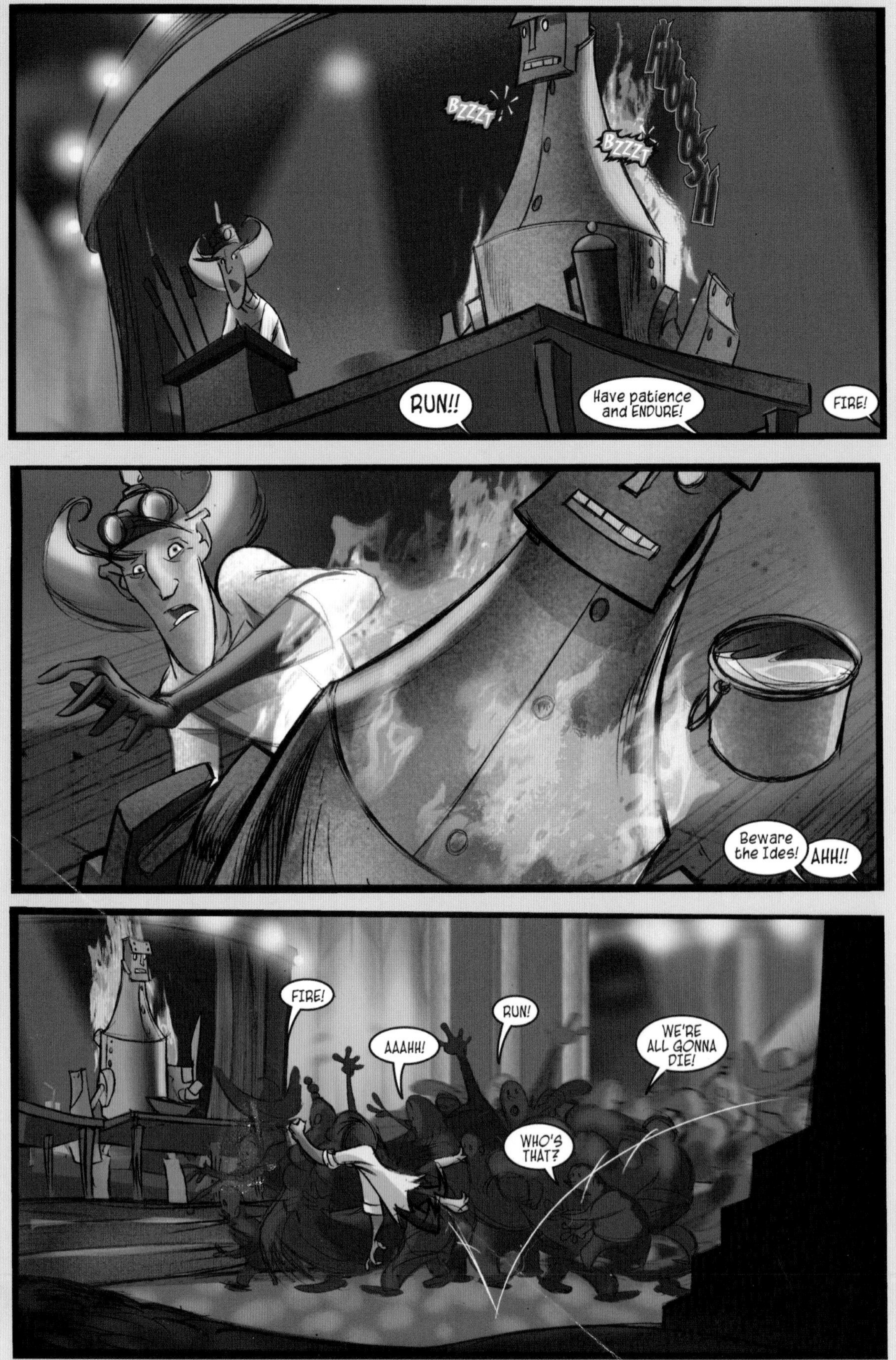
BZZZT
BZZZT
RUN!!
Have patience and ENDURE!
FIRE!
Beware the Ides!
AHH!!
FIRE!
AAAHH!
RUN!
WE'RE ALL GONNA DIE!
WHO'S THAT?

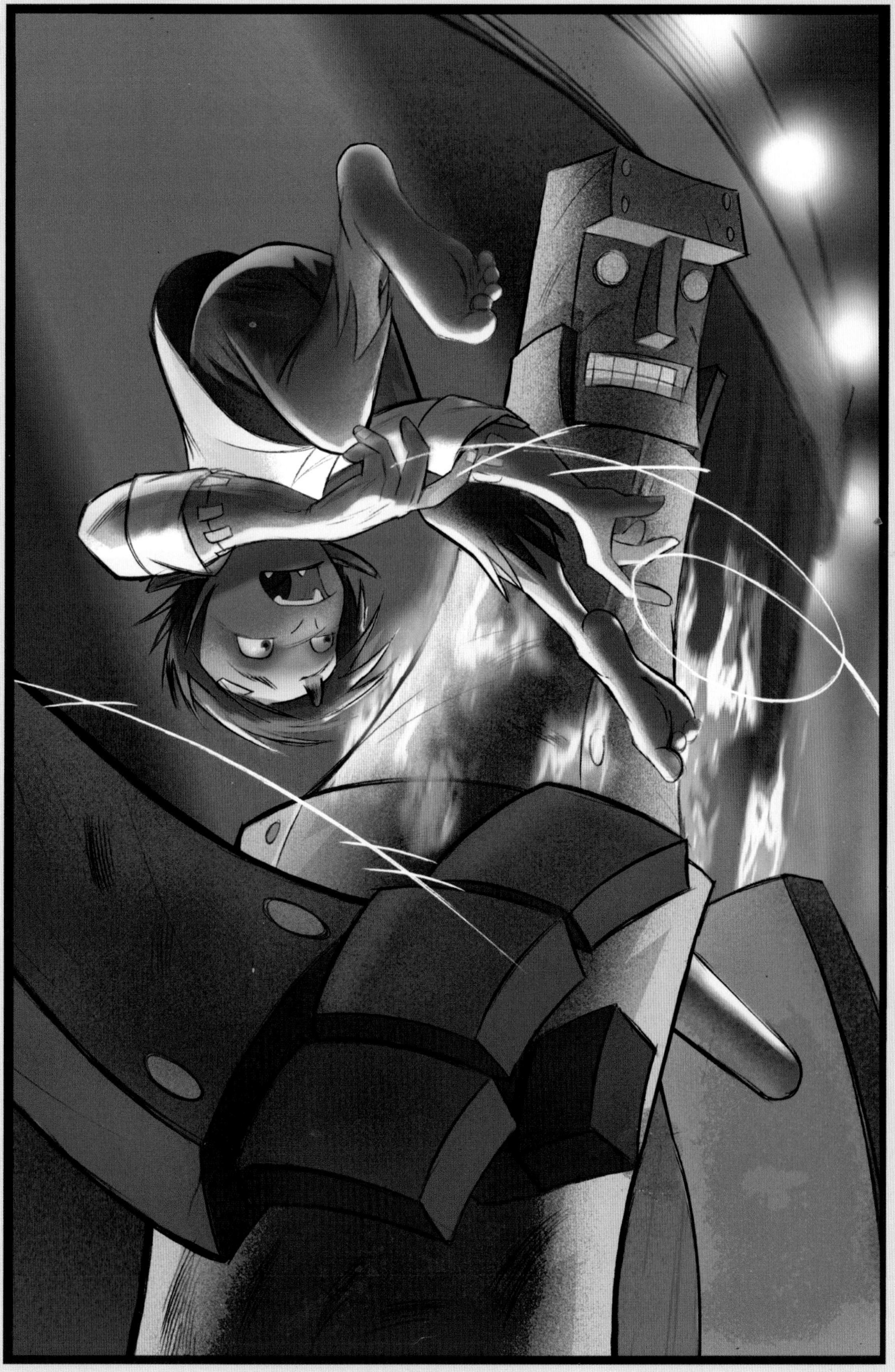

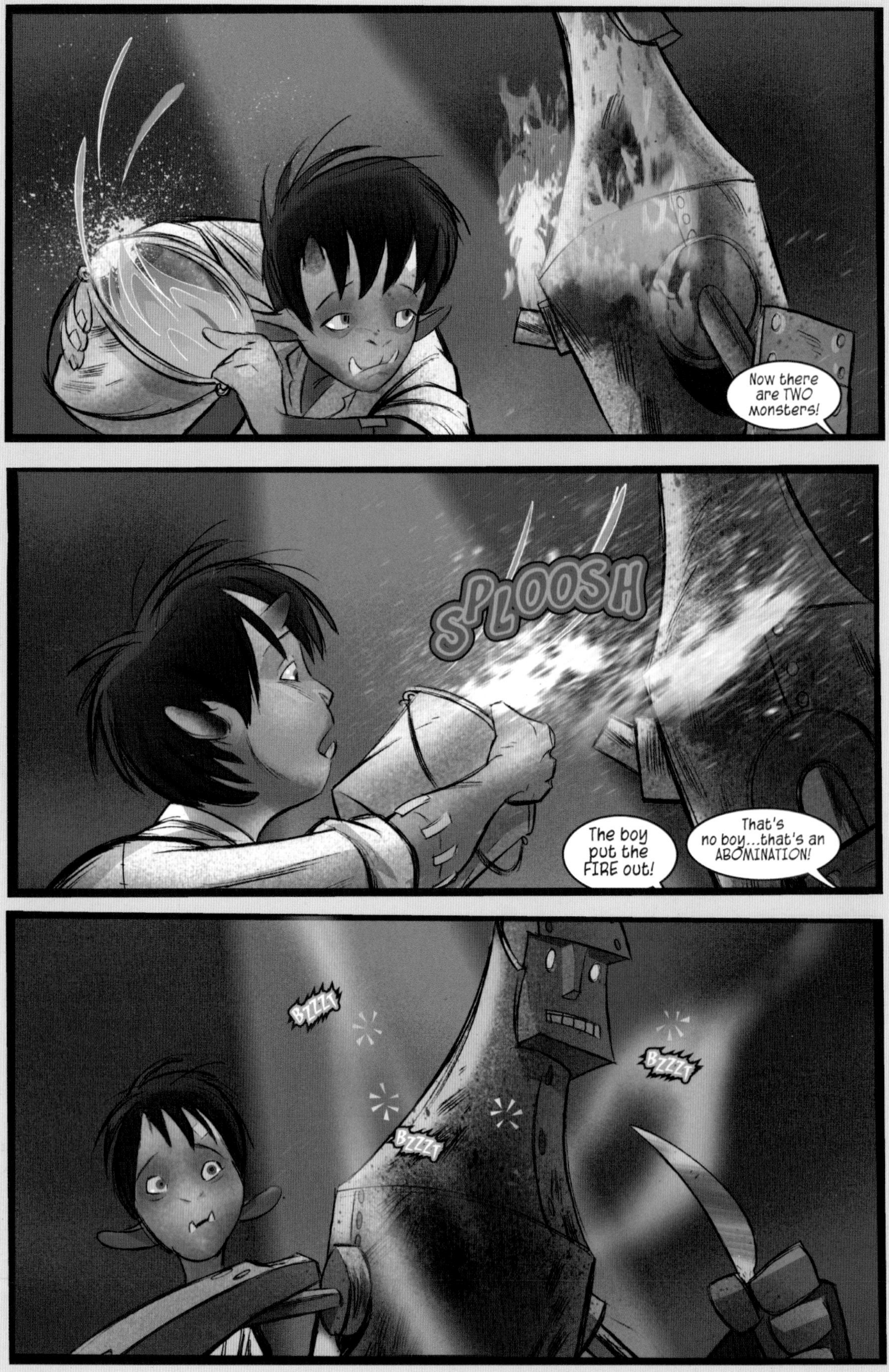
Now there are TWO monsters!
SPLOOSH
The boy put the FIRE out!
That's no boy...that's an ABOMINATION!
BZZZT
BZZZT
BZZZT

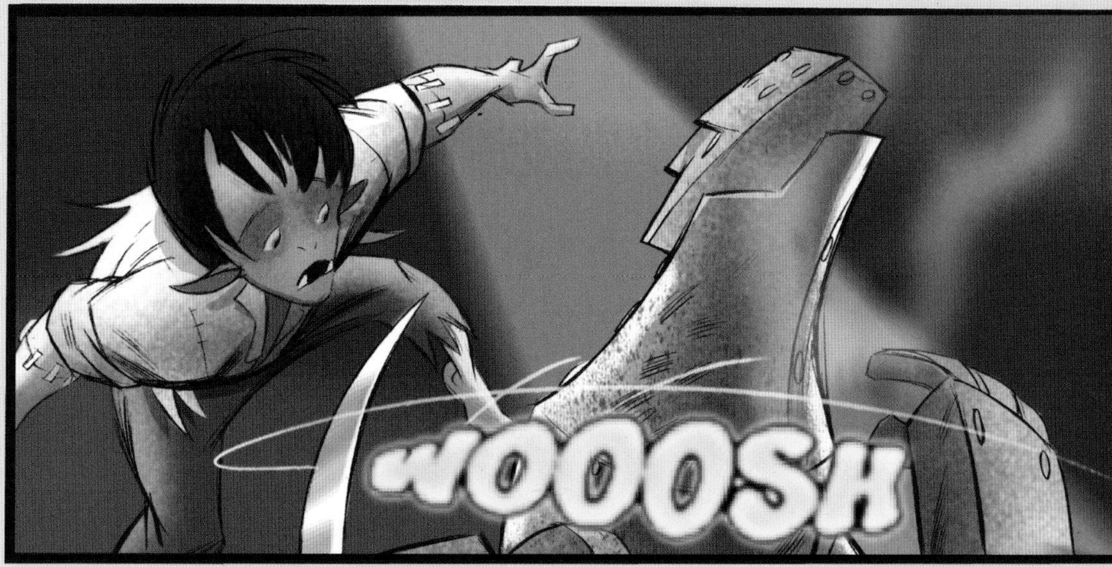
WOOOSH
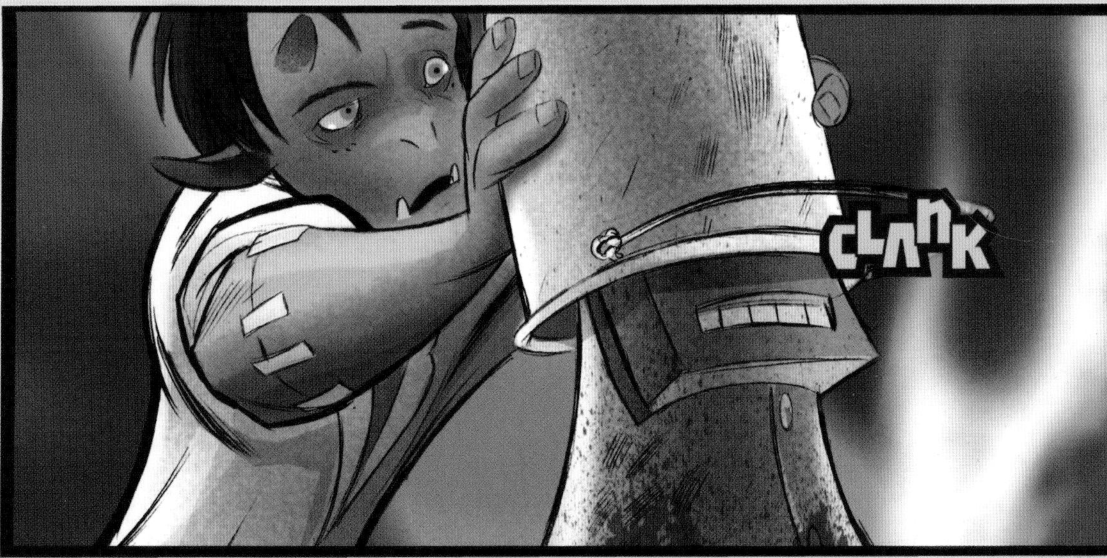
CLANK
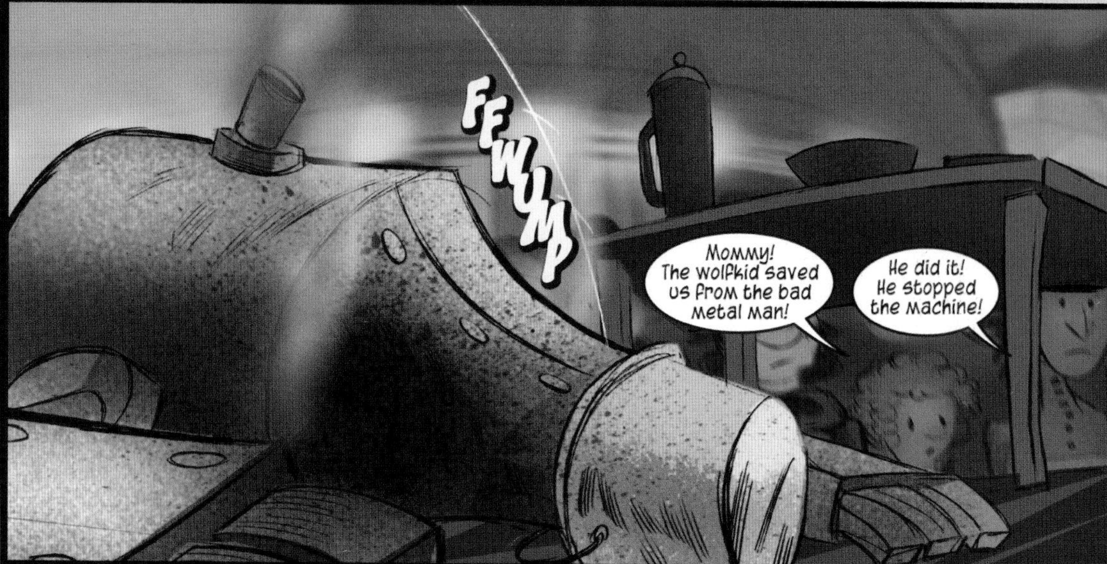
FFWUMP
Mommy! The wolfkid saved us from the bad Metal Man!
He did it! He stopped the Machine!

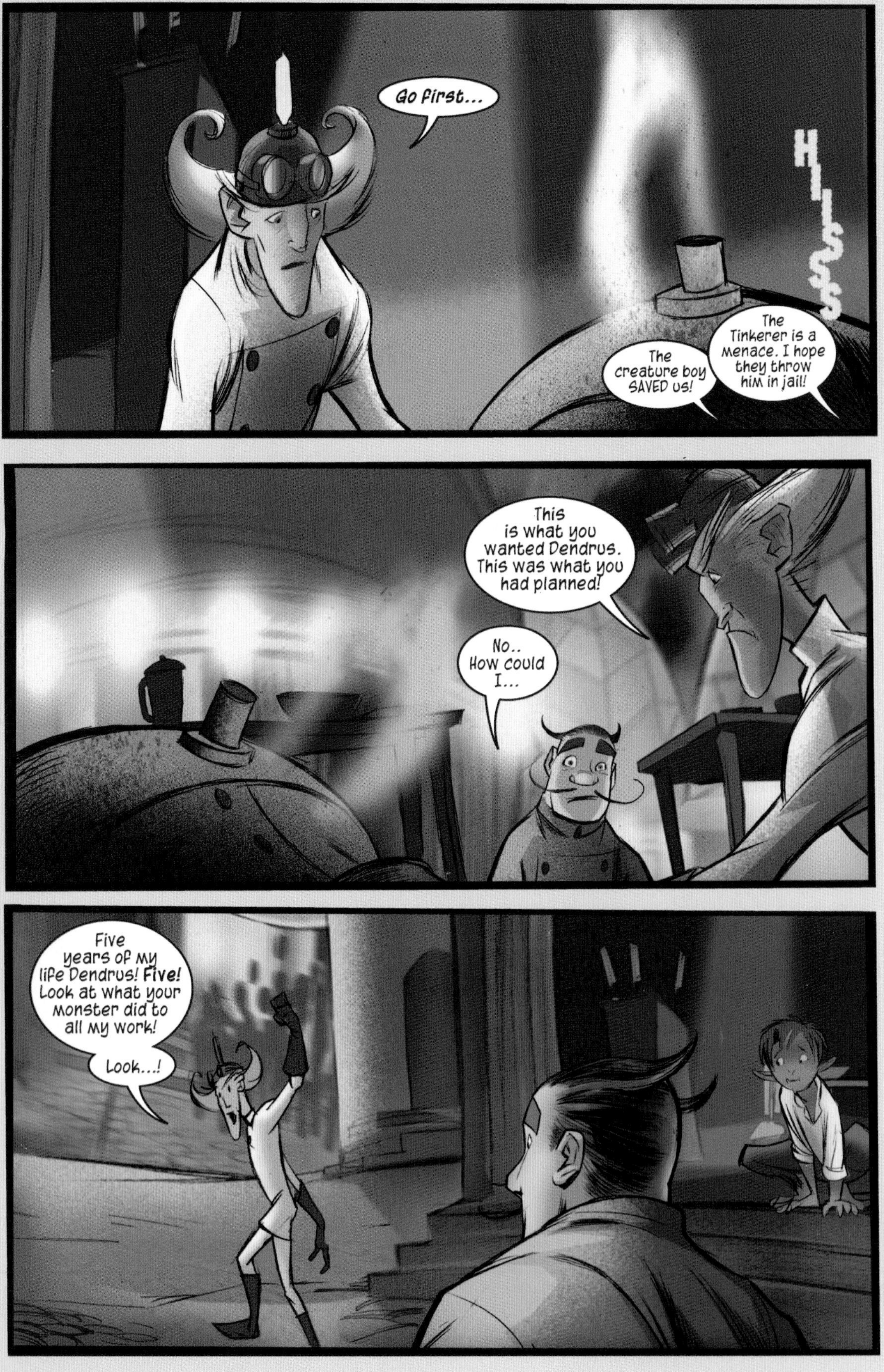
Go first...
HISSS
The creature boy SAVED us!
The Tinkerer is a menace. I hope they throw him in jail!
This is what you wanted Dendrus. This was what you had planned!
No.. How could I...
Five years of my life Dendrus! Five! Look at what your monster did to all my work!
Look...!

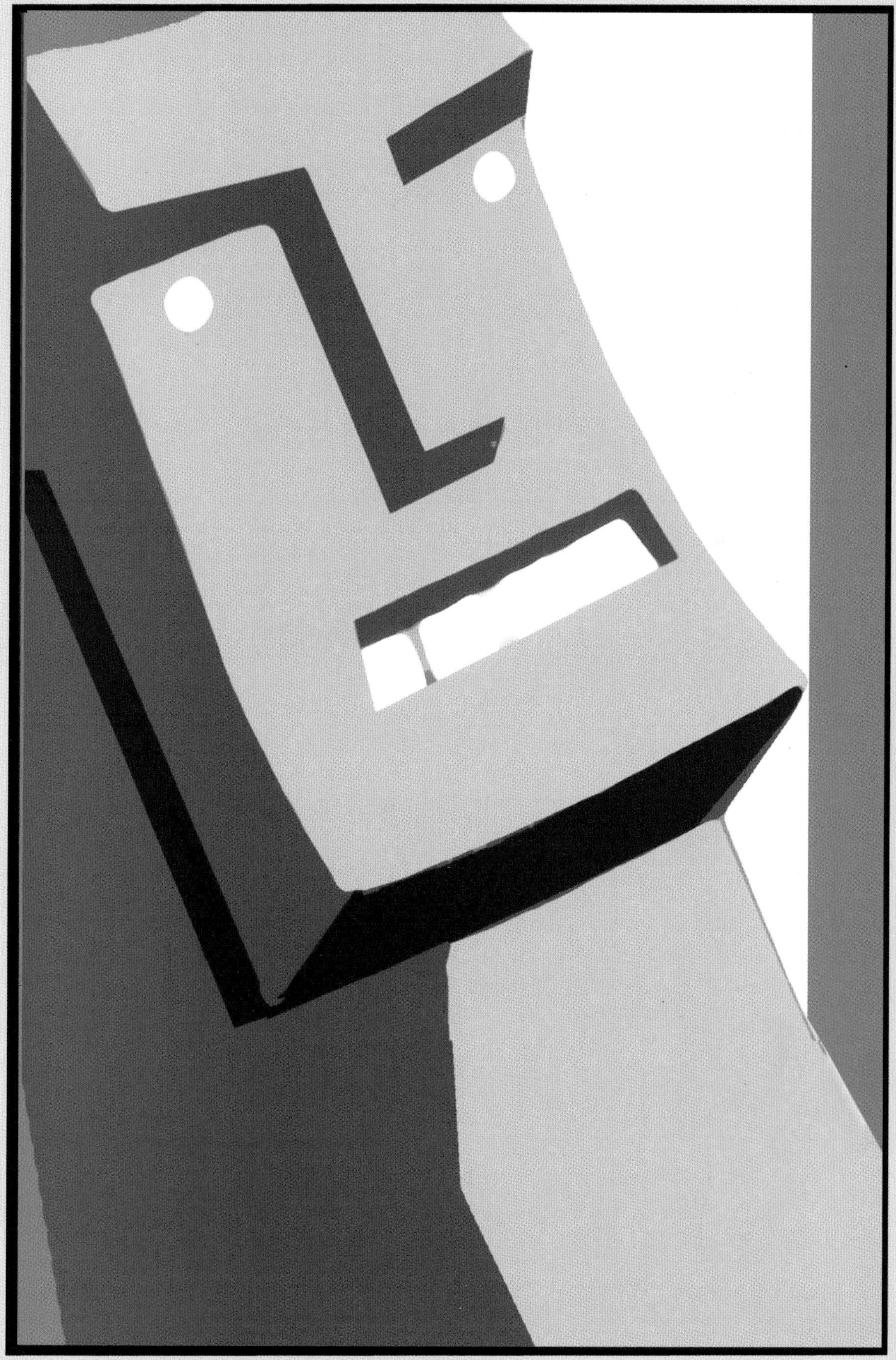

Chapter 3

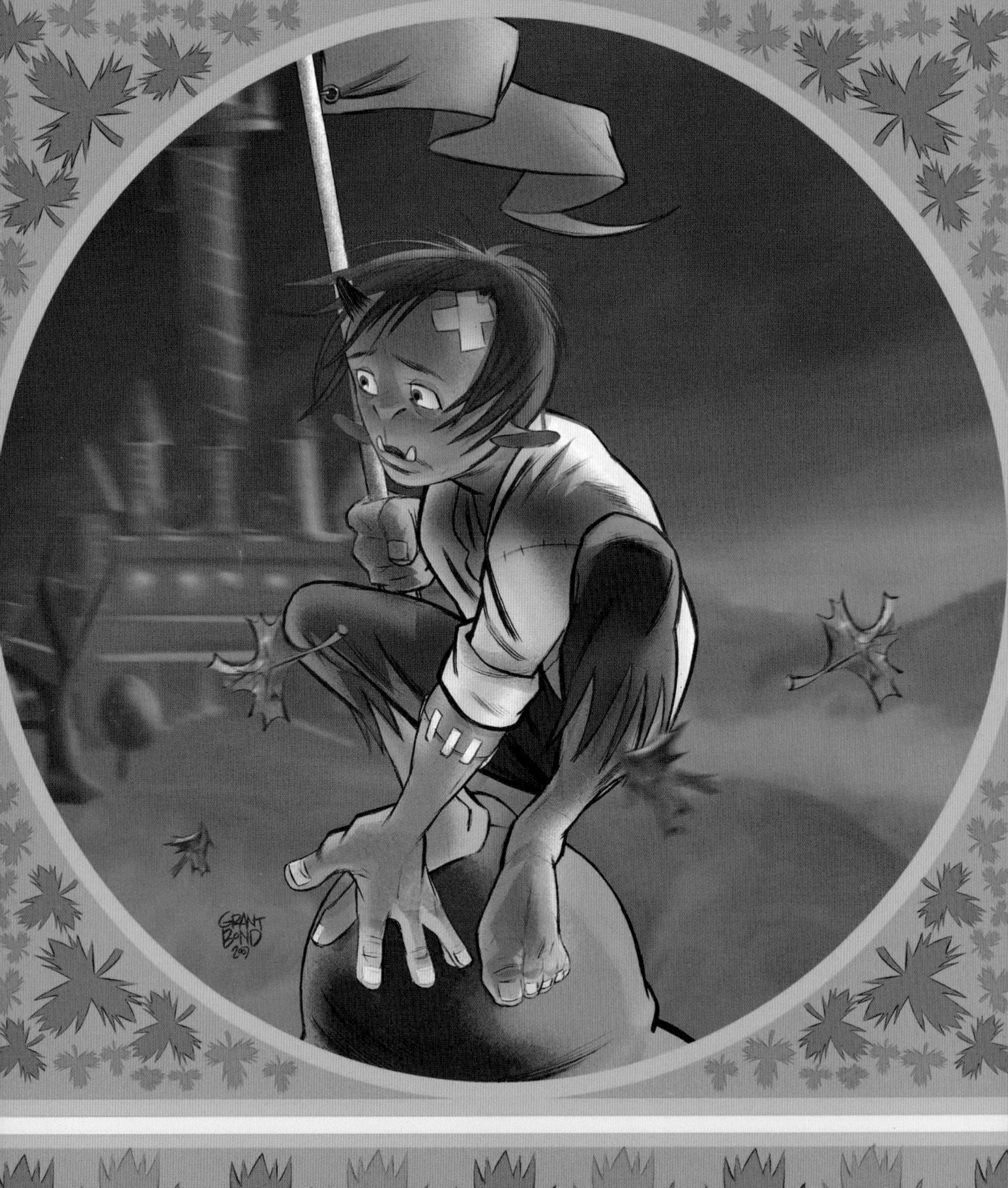

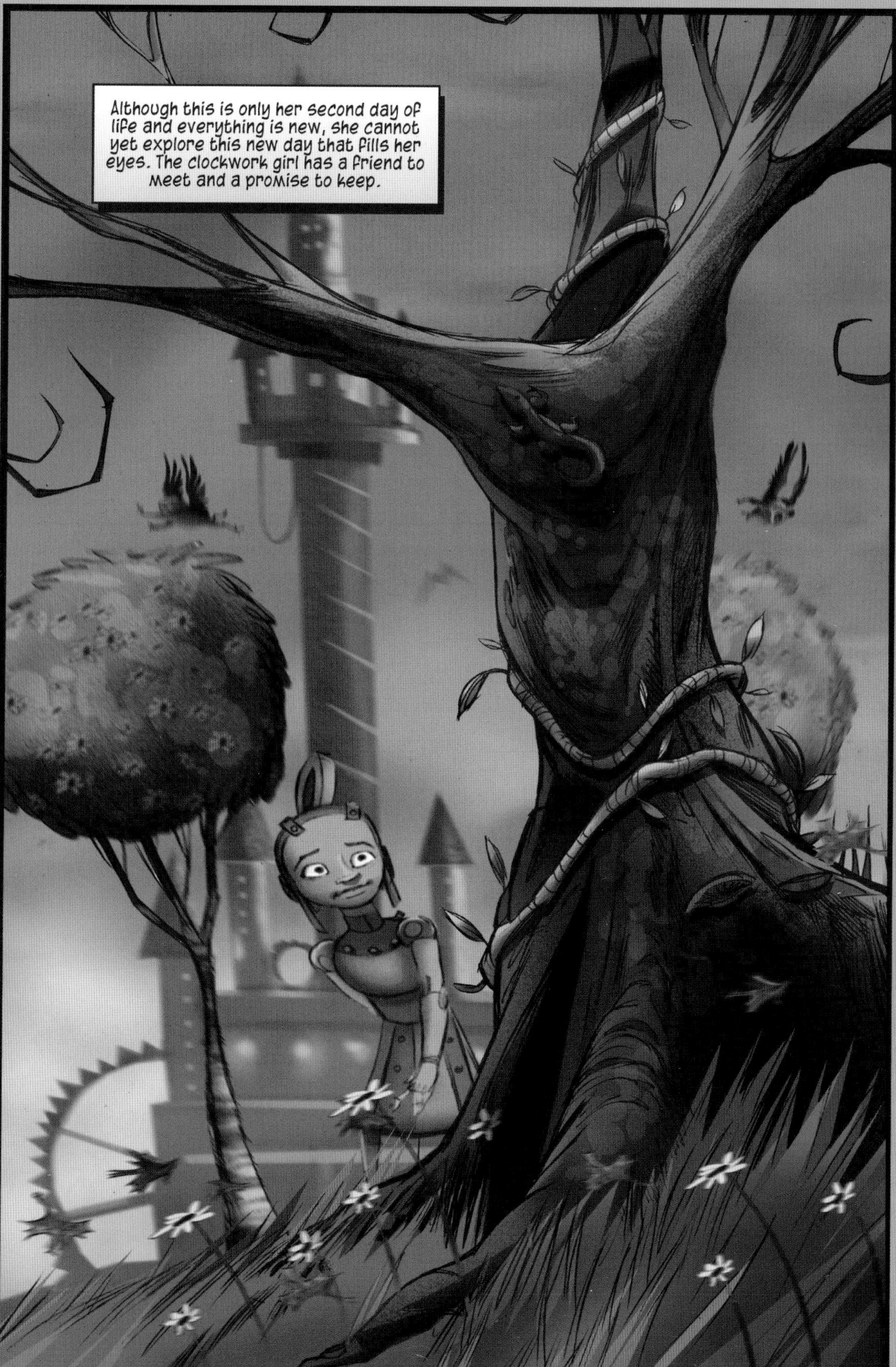
Although this is only her second day of life and everything is new, she cannot yet explore this new day that fills her eyes. The clockwork girl has a friend to meet and a promise to keep.

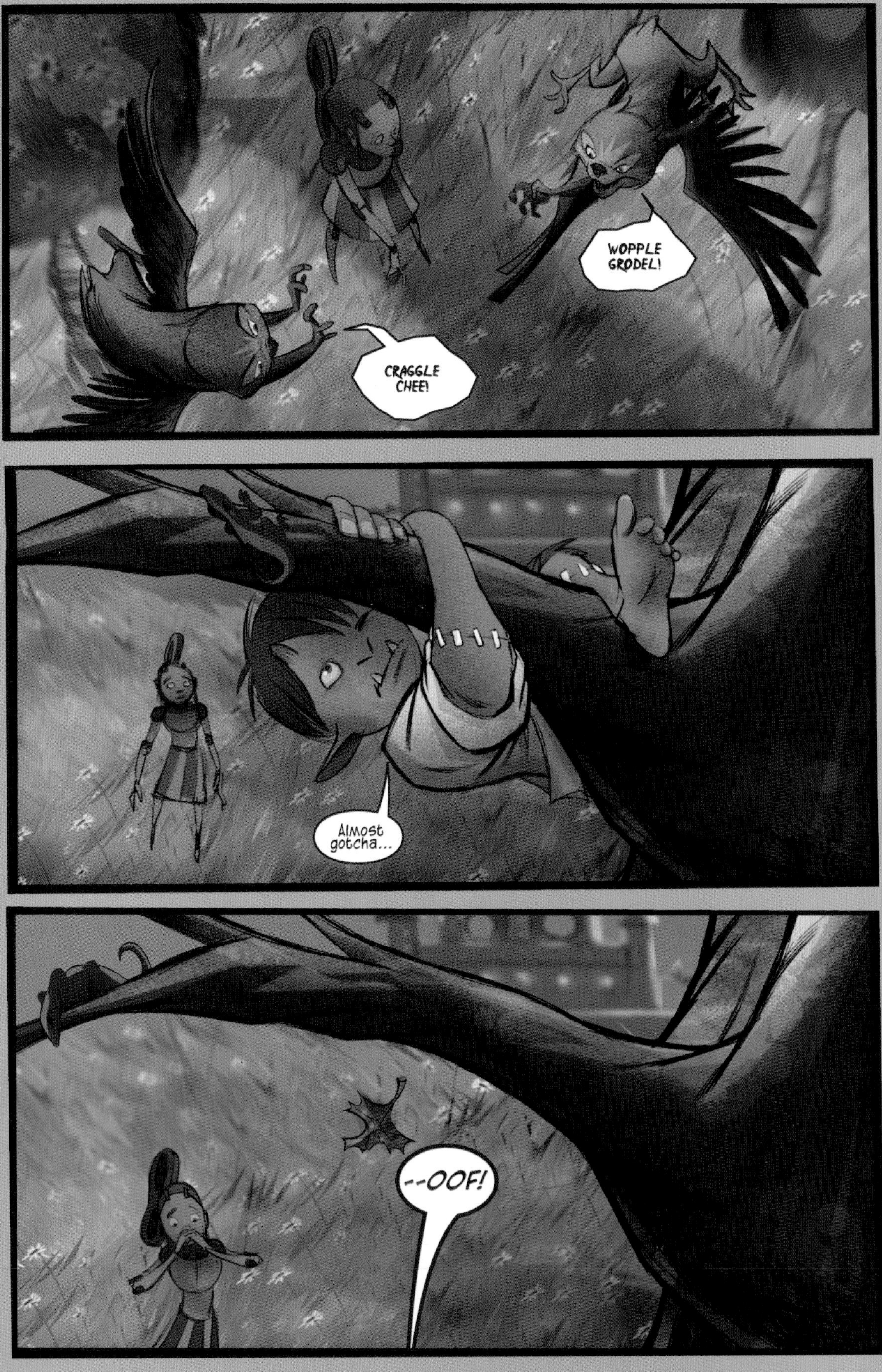
WOPPLE GRODEL!
CRAGGLE CHEE!
Almost gotcha...
--OOF!

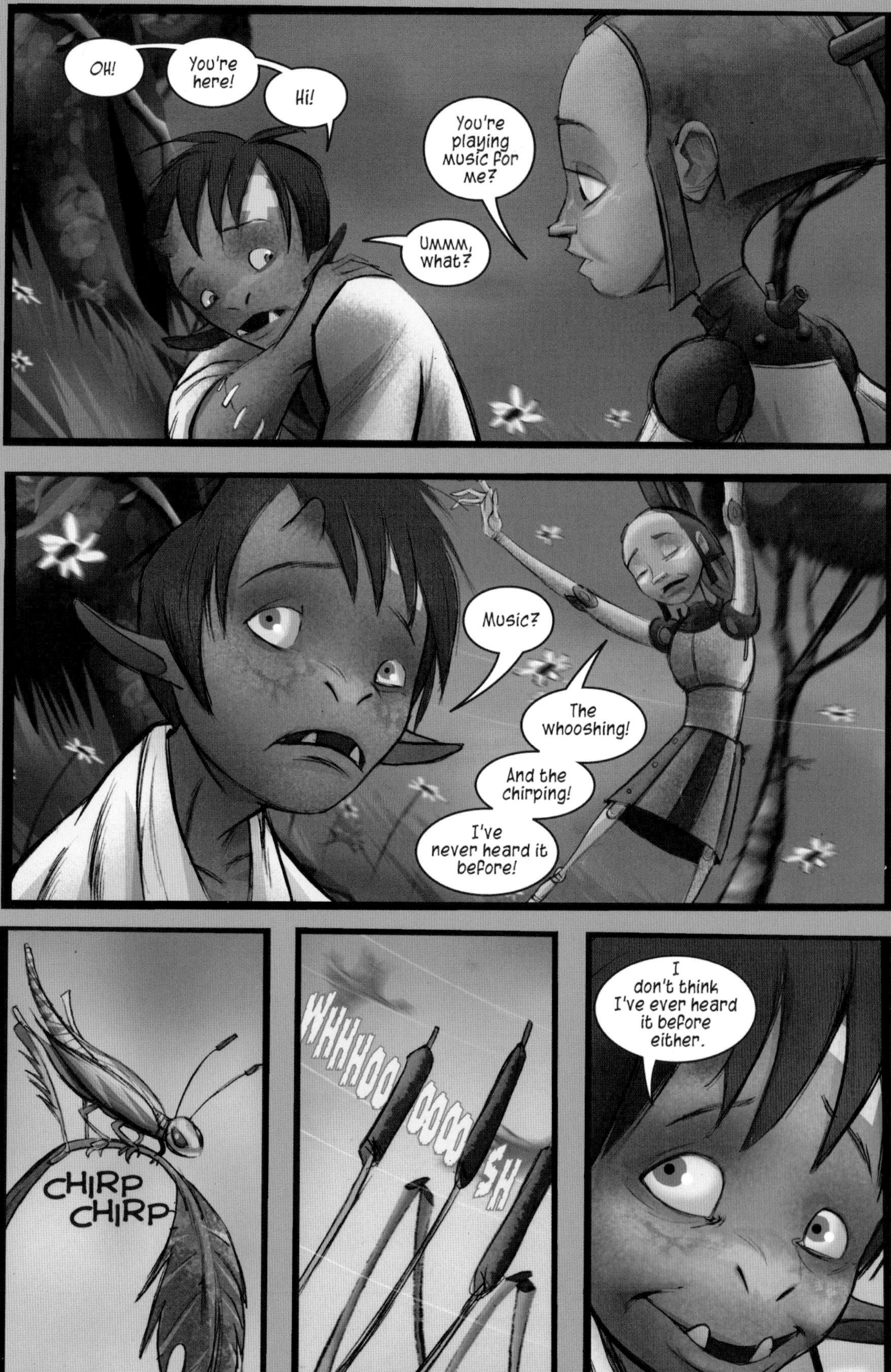
OH!
You're here!
Hi!
You're playing music for me?
UMMM, what?
Music?
The whooshing!
And the chirping!
I've never heard it before!
CHIRP CHIRP
WHHHOOOOOOOSH
I don't think I've ever heard it before either.

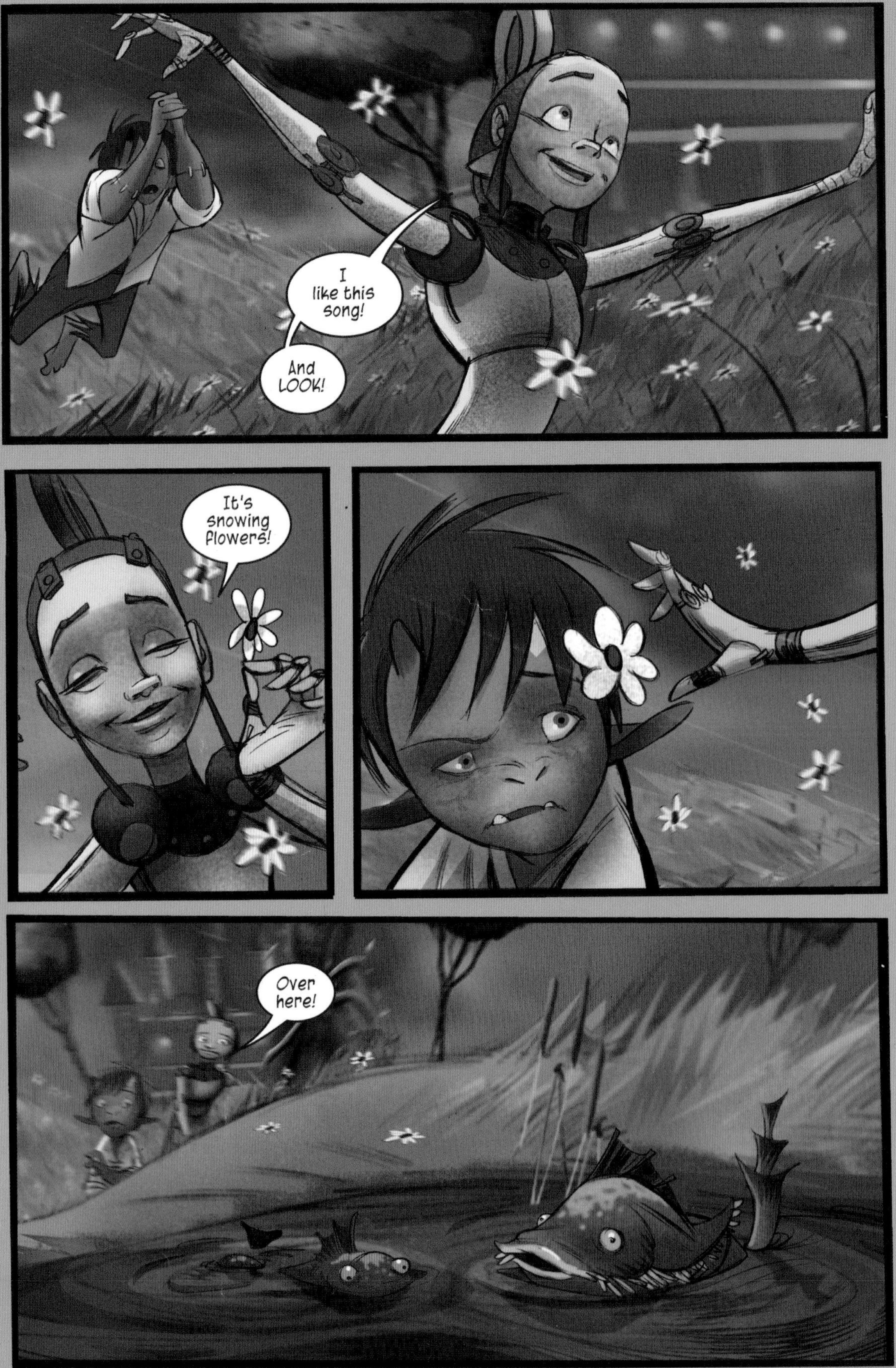
I like this song!
And LOOK!
It's snowing flowers!
Over here!

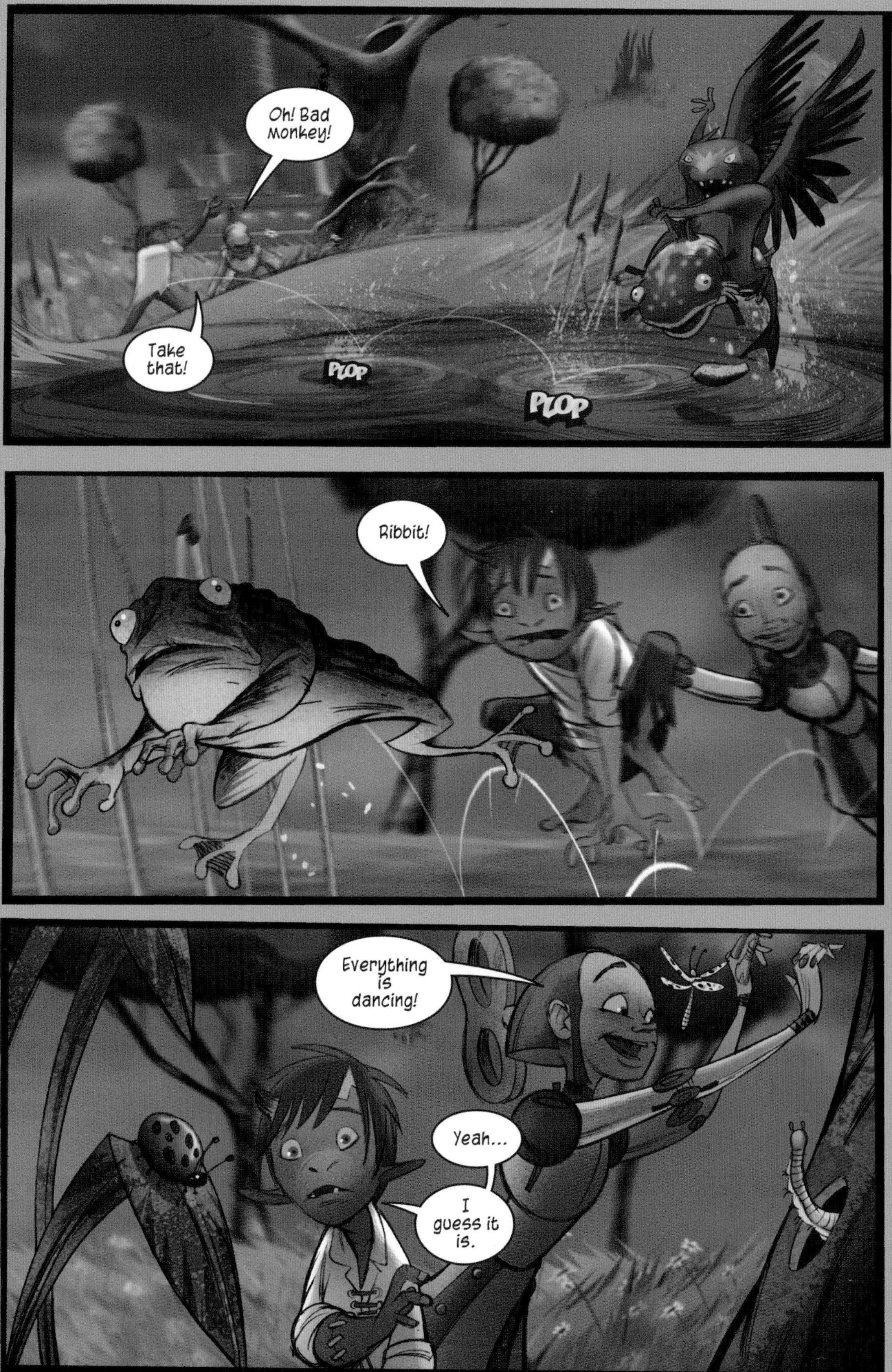
Oh! Bad Monkey!
Take that!
PLOP
PLOP
Ribbit!
Everything is dancing!
Yeah...
I guess it is.

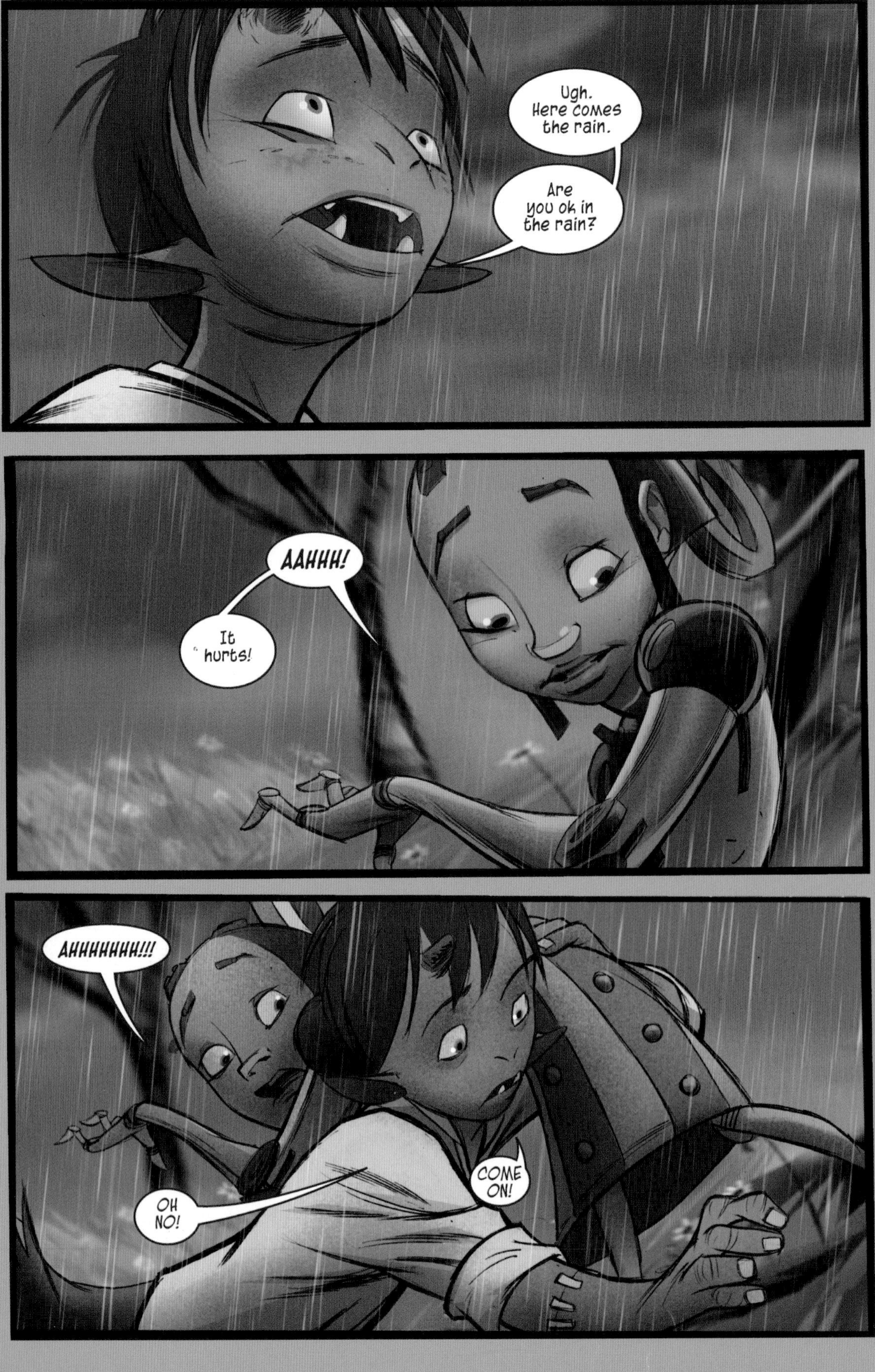

Ugh. Here comes the rain.
Are you ok in the rain?
AAHHH!
It hurts!
AHHHHHHH!!!
COME ON!
OH NO!

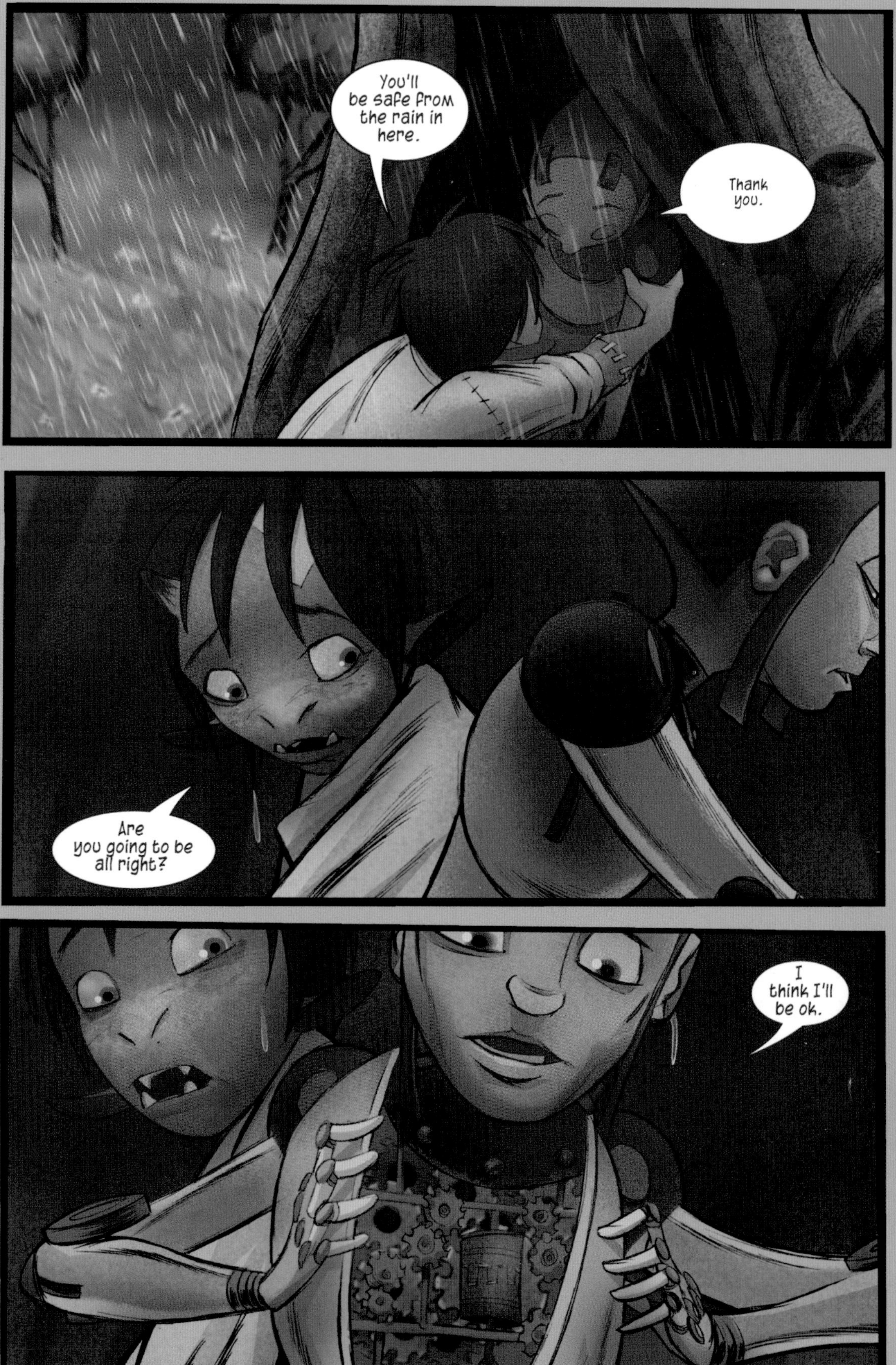
You'll be safe from the rain in here.
Thank you.
Are you going to be all right?
I think I'll be ok.

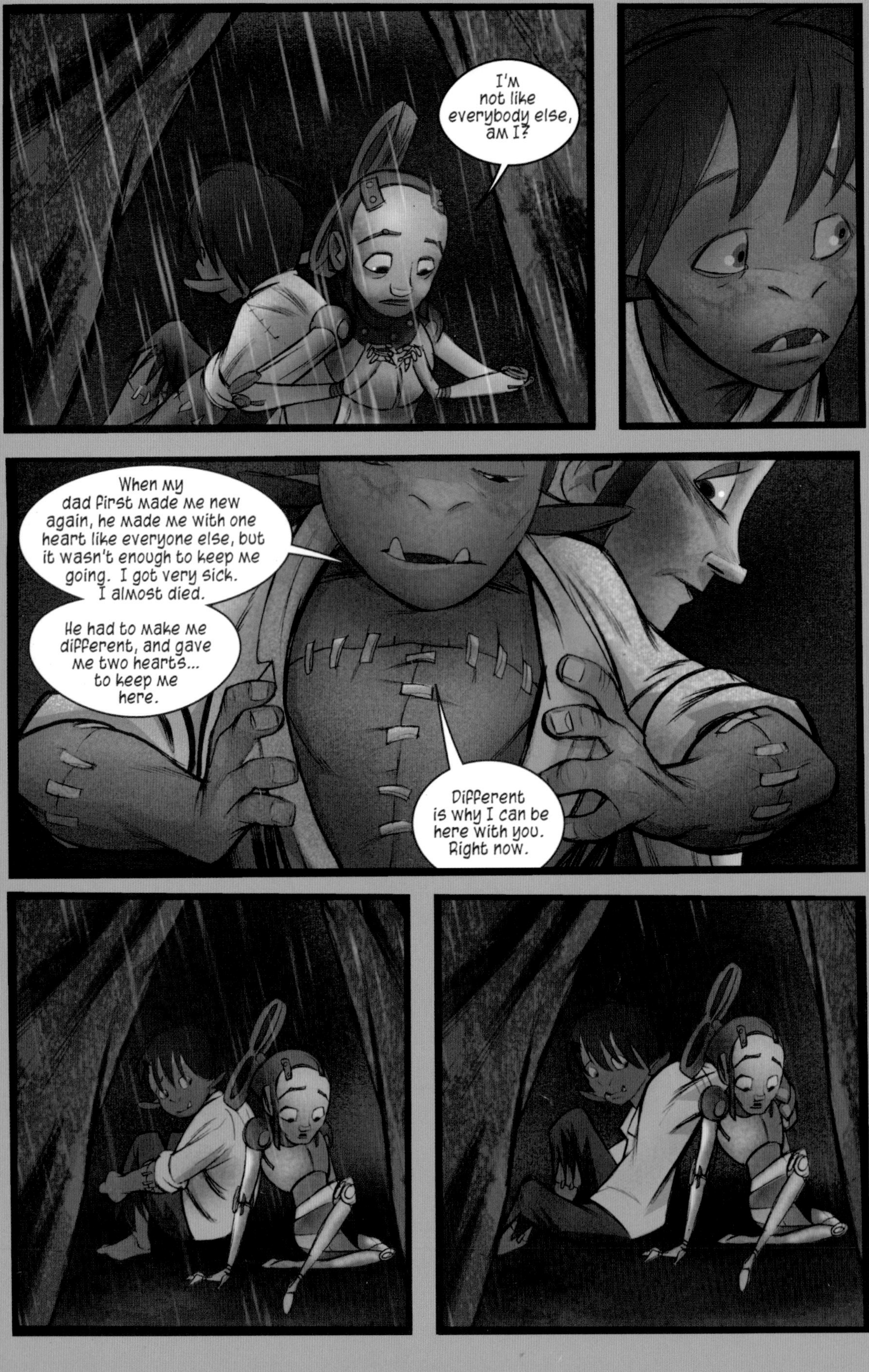
I'm not like everybody else, am I?
When my dad first made me new again, he made me with one heart like everyone else, but it wasn't enough to keep me going. I got very sick. I almost died.
He had to make me different, and gave me two hearts... to keep me here.
Different is why I can be here with you. Right now.

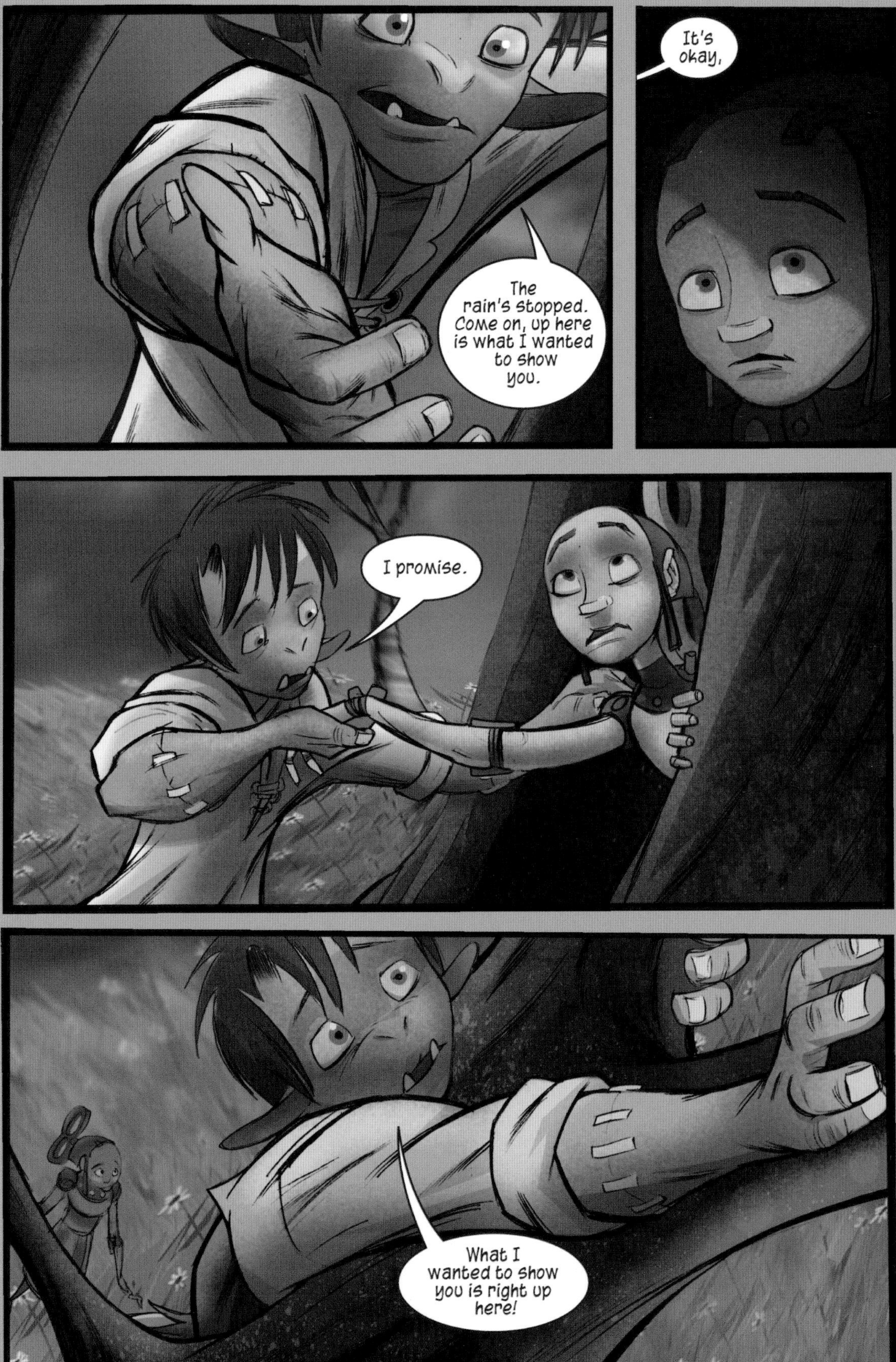
The rain's stopped. Come on, up here is what I wanted to show you.
It's okay,
I promise.
What I wanted to show you is right up here!

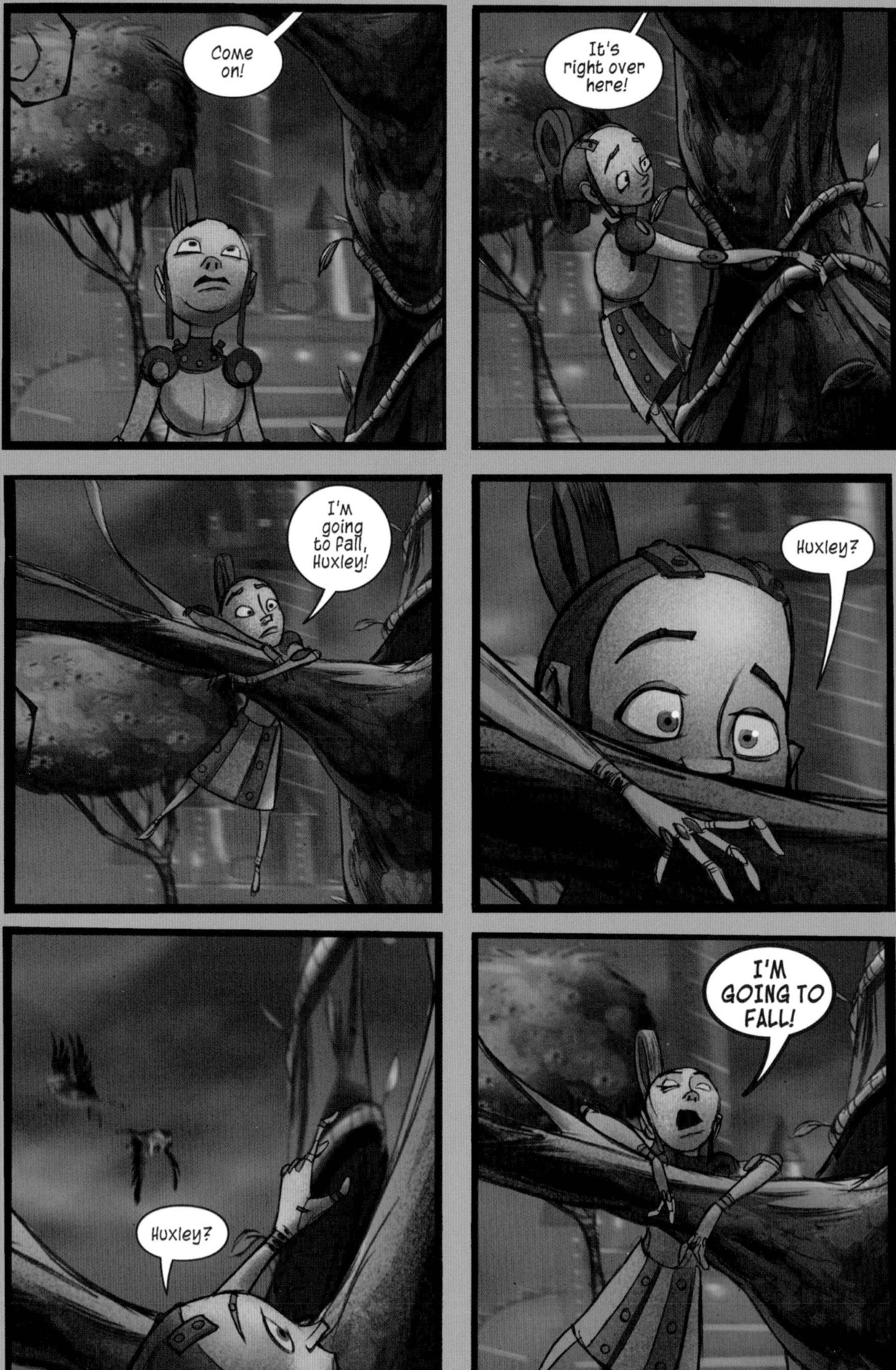
Come on!
It's right over here!
I'm going to fall, Huxley!
Huxley?
Huxley?
I'M GOING TO FALL!

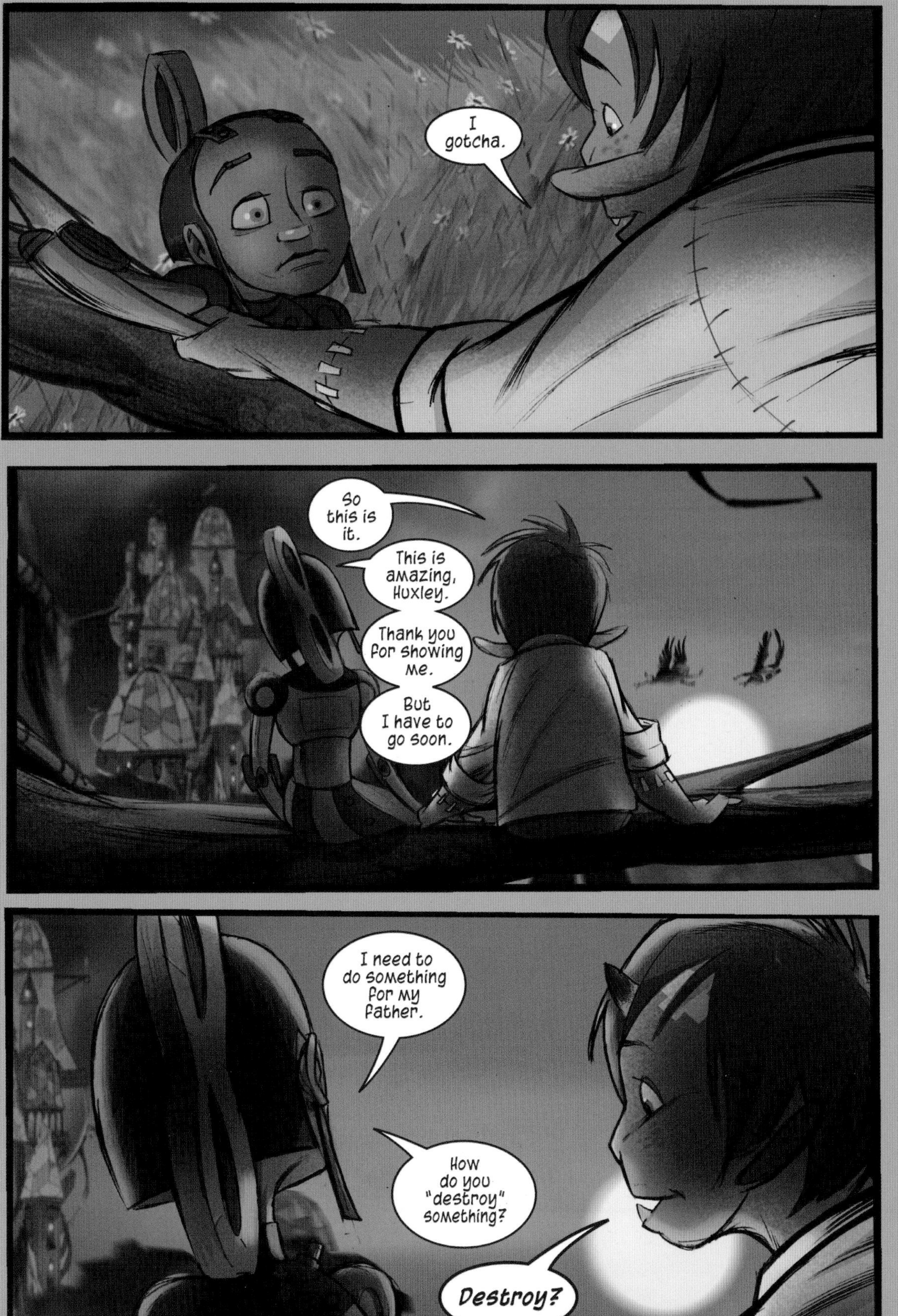
I gotcha.
So this is it.
This is amazing, Huxley.
Thank you for showing me.
But I have to go soon.
I need to do something for my father.
How do you "destroy" something?
Destroy?

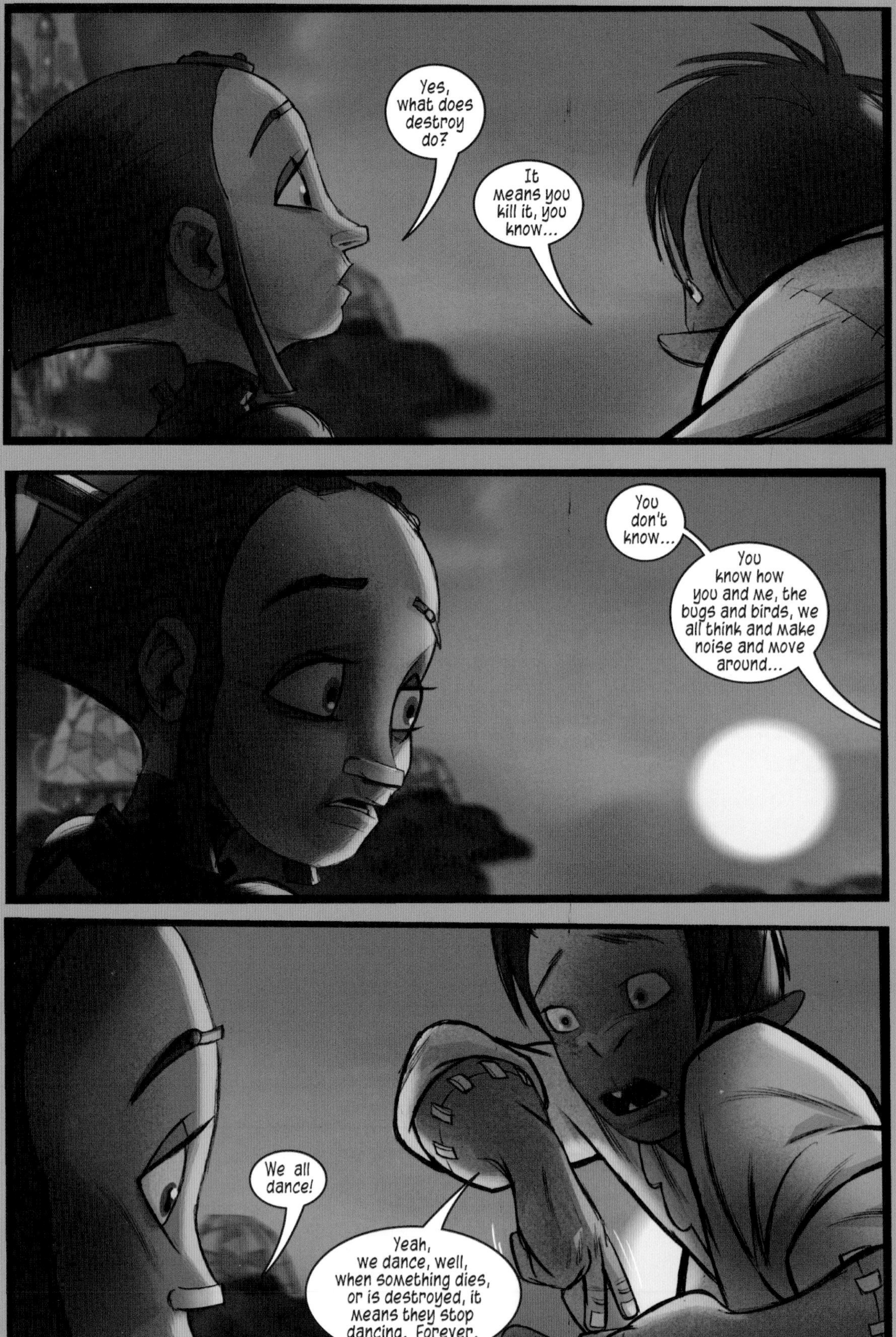
Yes, what does destroy do?
It means you kill it, you know...
You don't know...
You know how you and me, the bugs and birds, we all think and make noise and move around...
We all dance!
Yeah, we dance, well, when something dies, or is destroyed, it means they stop dancing. Forever.

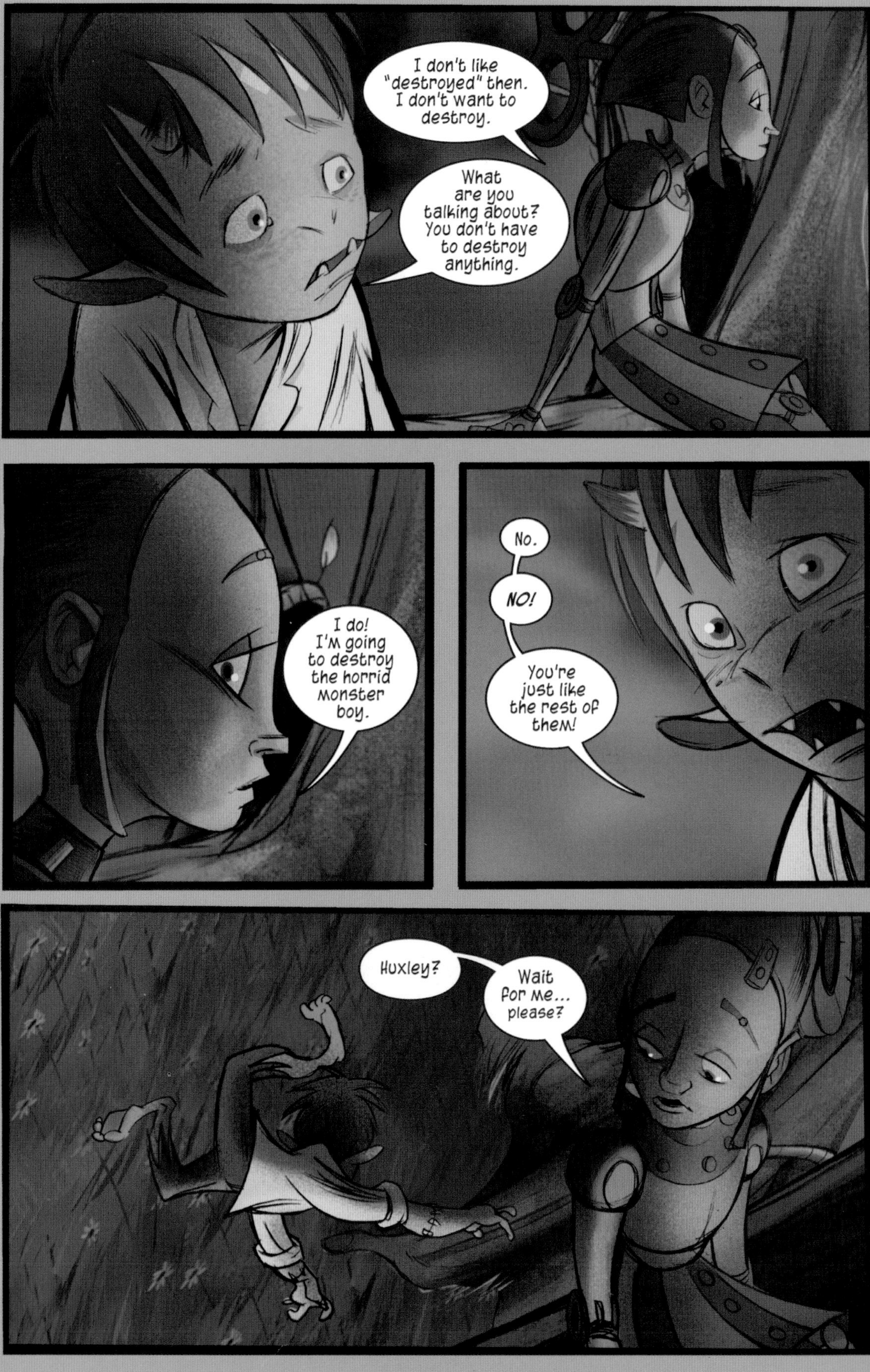
I don't like "destroyed" then. I don't want to destroy.
What are you talking about? You don't have to destroy anything.
I do! I'm going to destroy the horrid monster boy.
No.
NO!
You're just like the rest of them!
Huxley?
Wait for me... please?

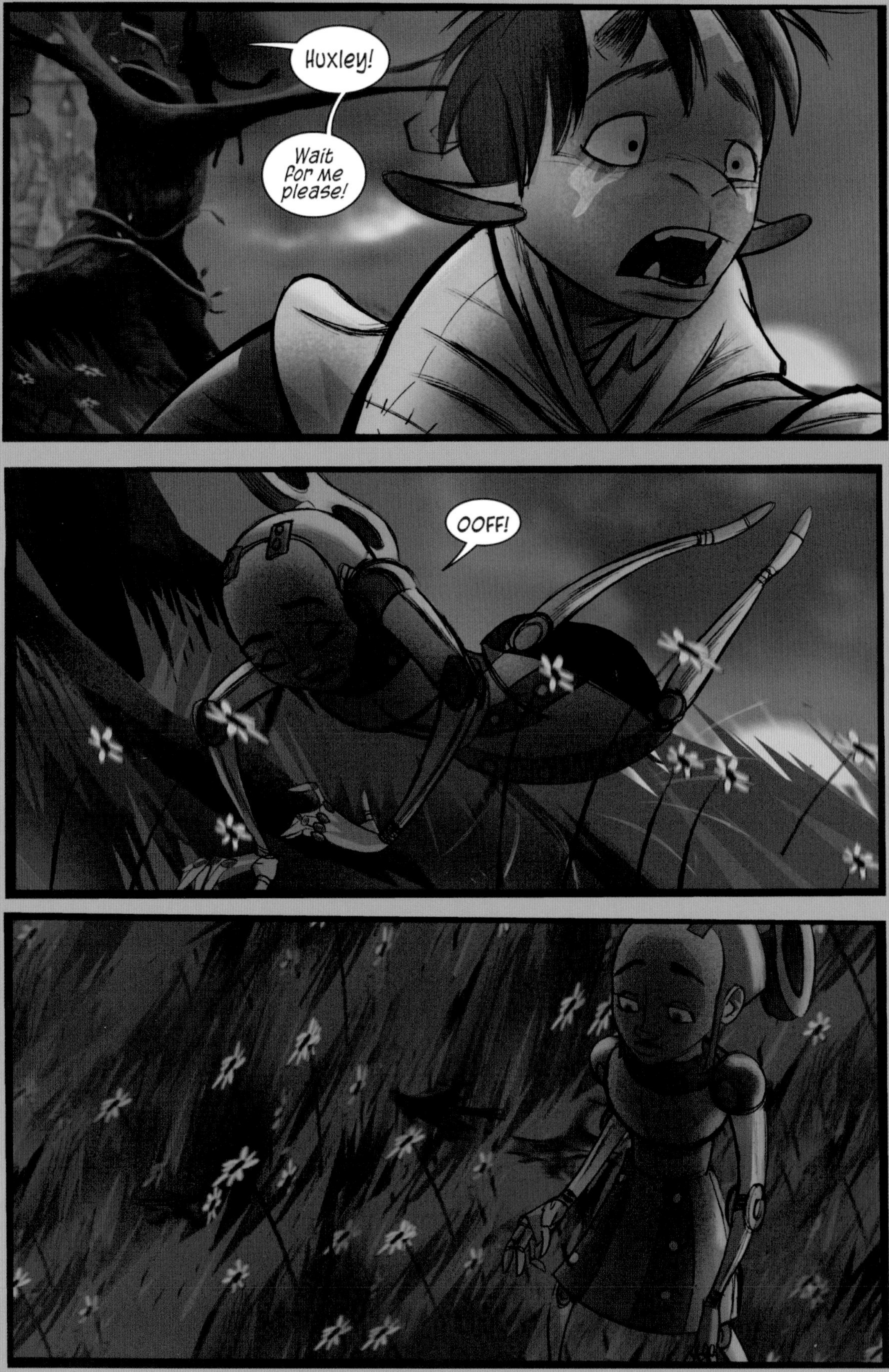
Huxley!
Wait for me please!
OOFF!

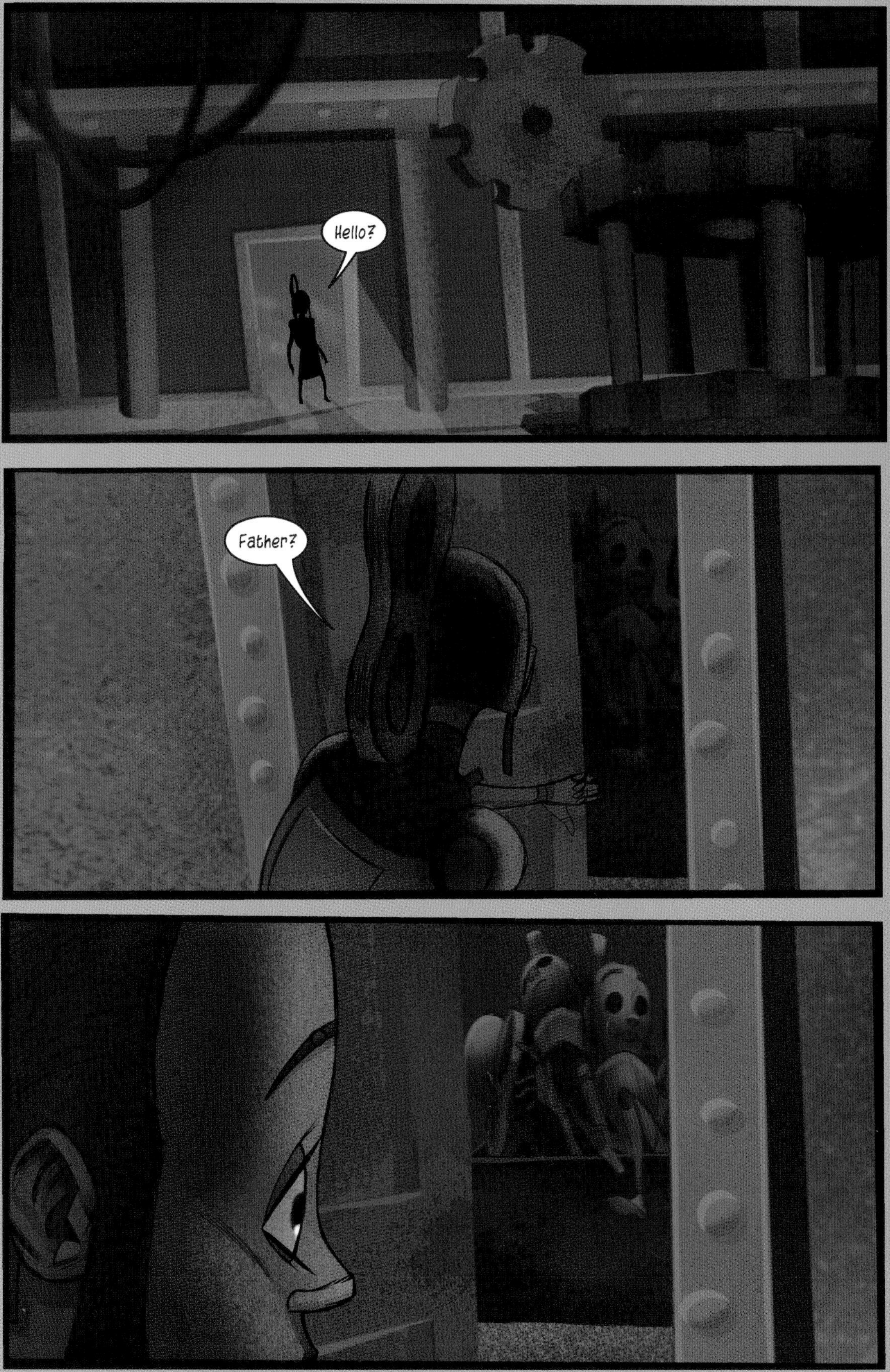
Hello?
Father?

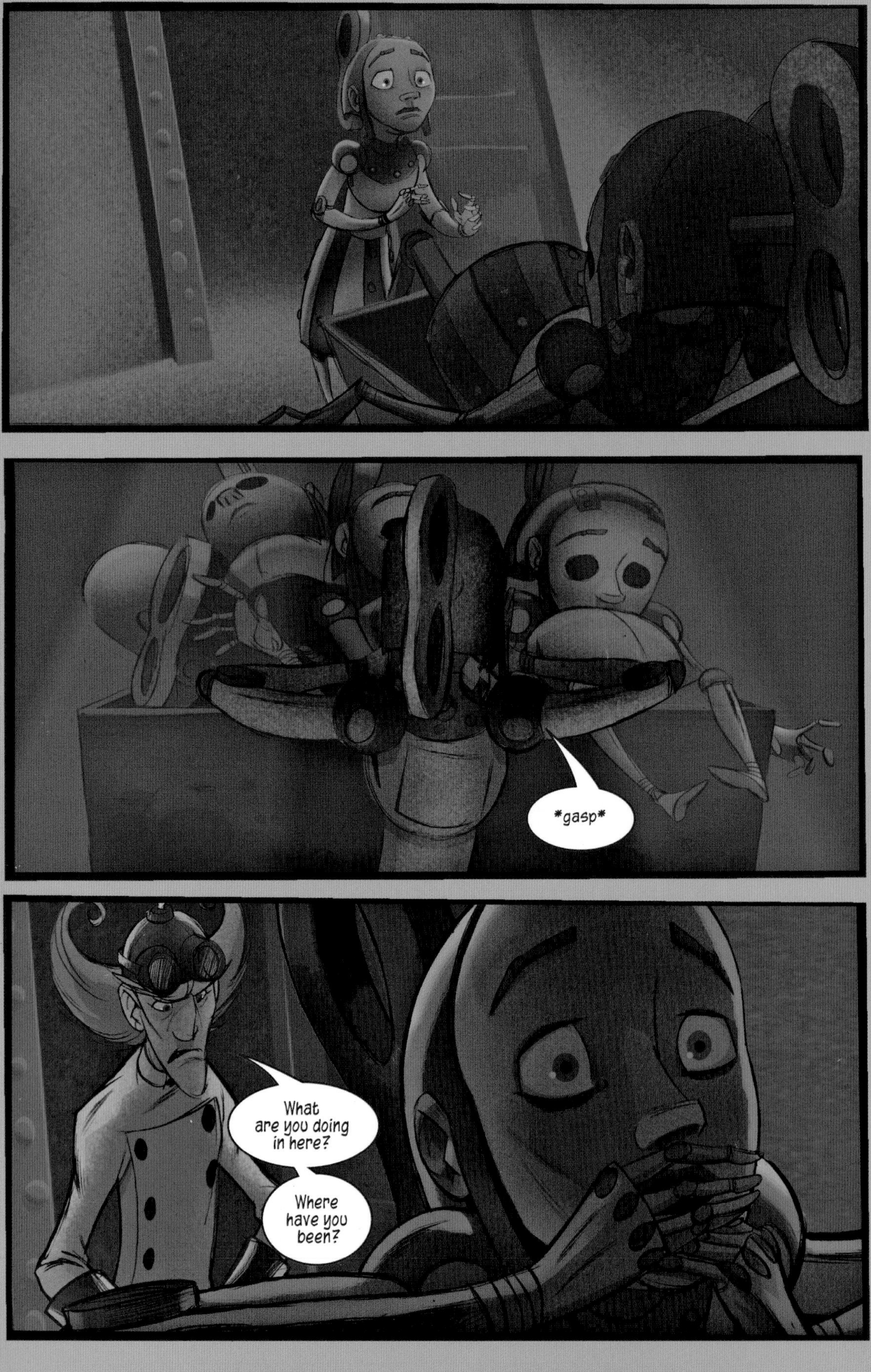
gasp
What are you doing in here?
Where have you been?

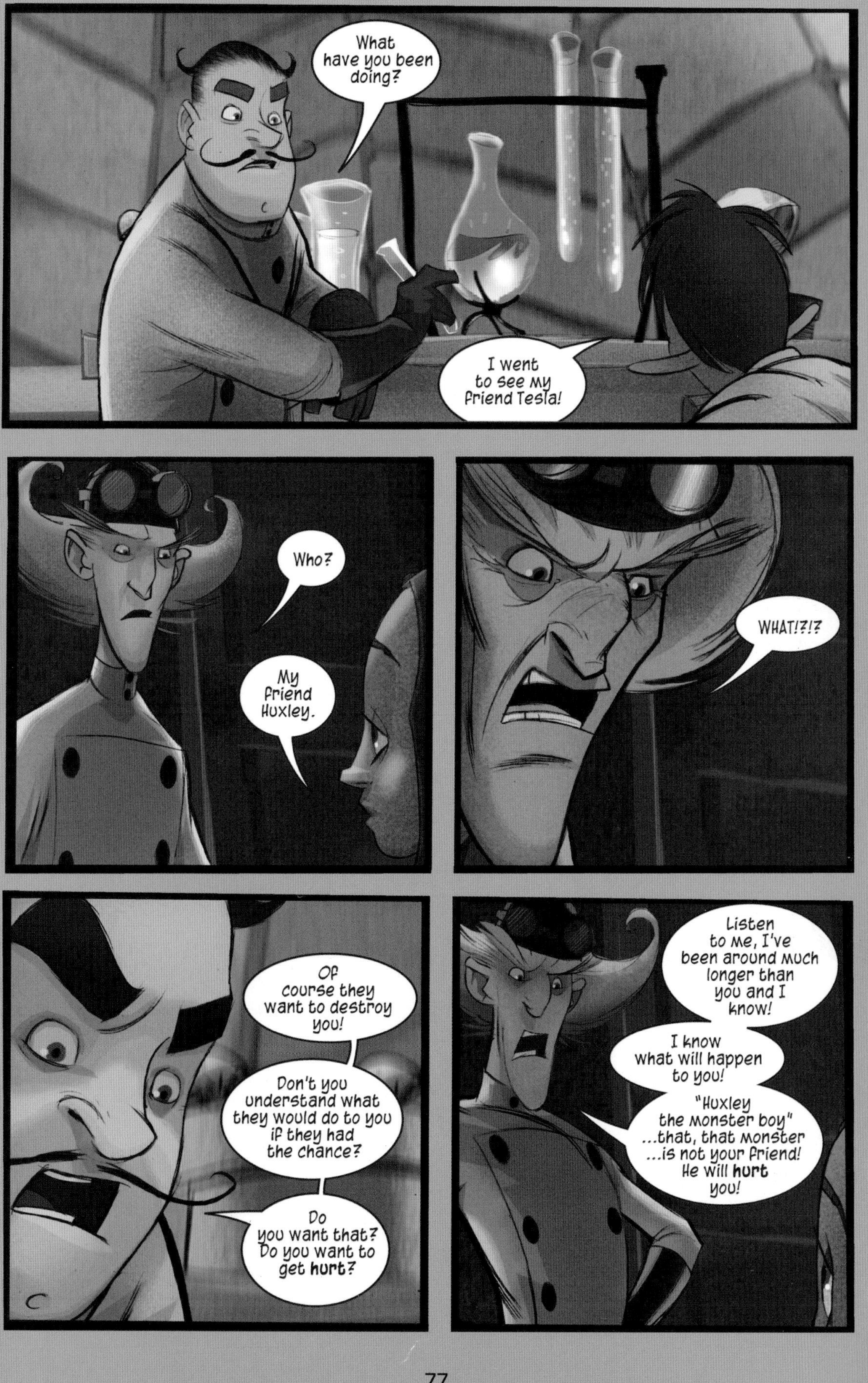
What have you been doing?
I went to see my friend Tesla!
Who?
My friend Huxley.
WHAT!?!?
Of course they want to destroy you!
Don't you understand what they would do to you if they had the chance?
Do you want that? Do you want to get **hurt**?
Listen to me, I've been around much longer than you and I know!
I know what will happen to you!
"Huxley the monster boy" ...that, that monster ...is not your friend! He will **hurt** you!

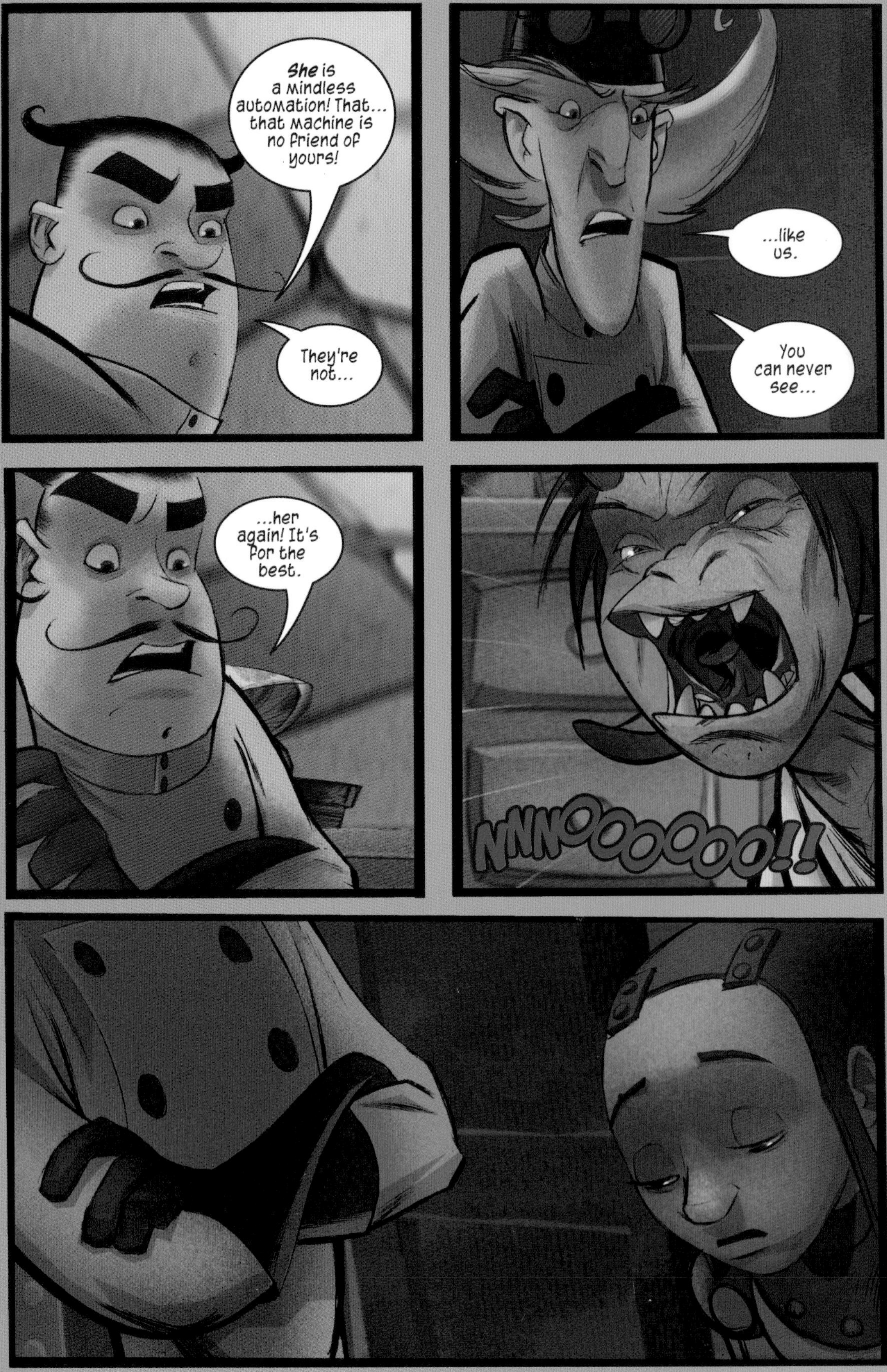
She is a mindless automation! That... that machine is no friend of yours!
They're not...
...like us.
You can never see...
...her again! It's for the best.
NNNOOOOOOO!!

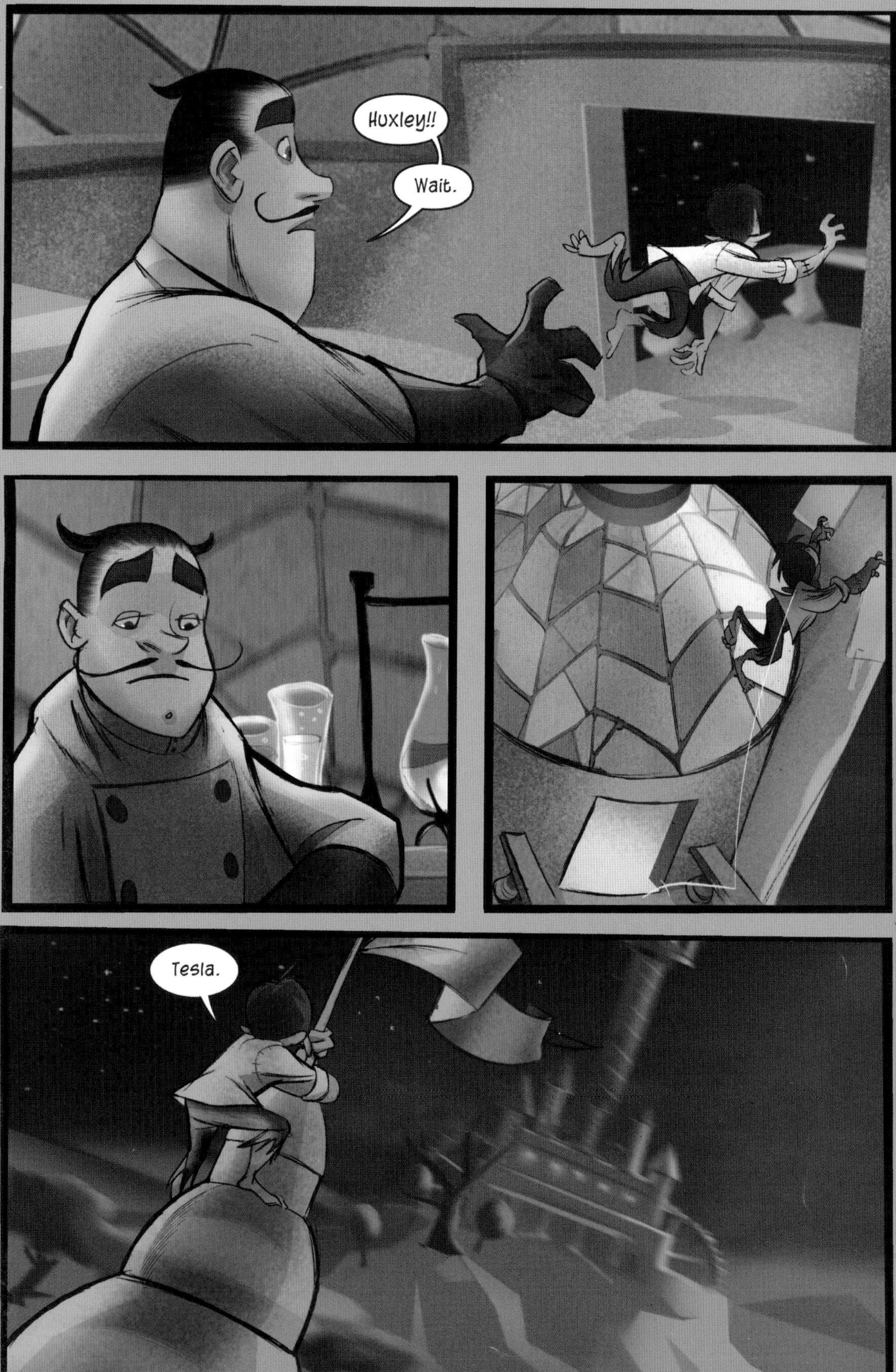
Huxley!!
Wait.
Tesla.

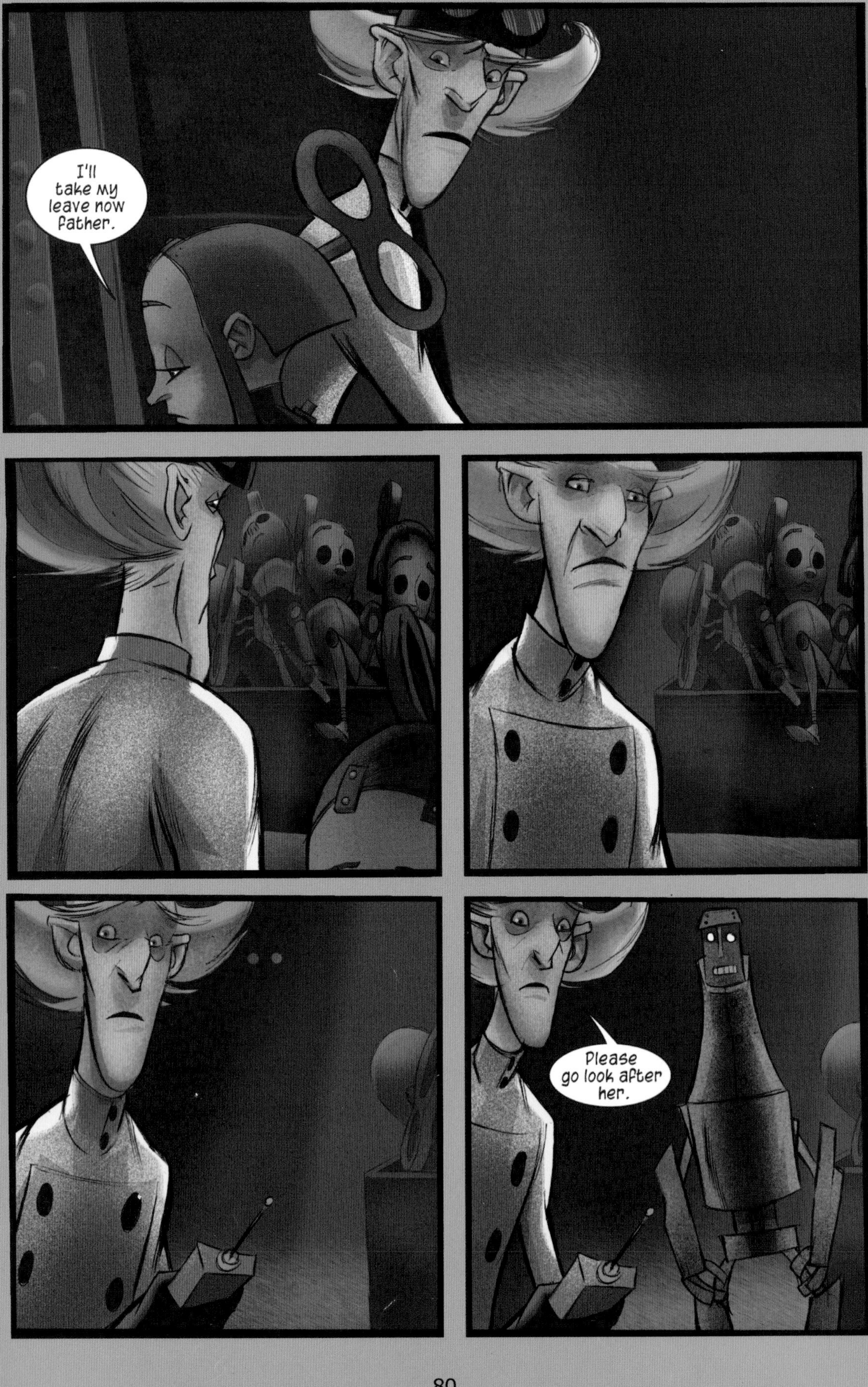
I'll take my leave now father.
Please go look after her.

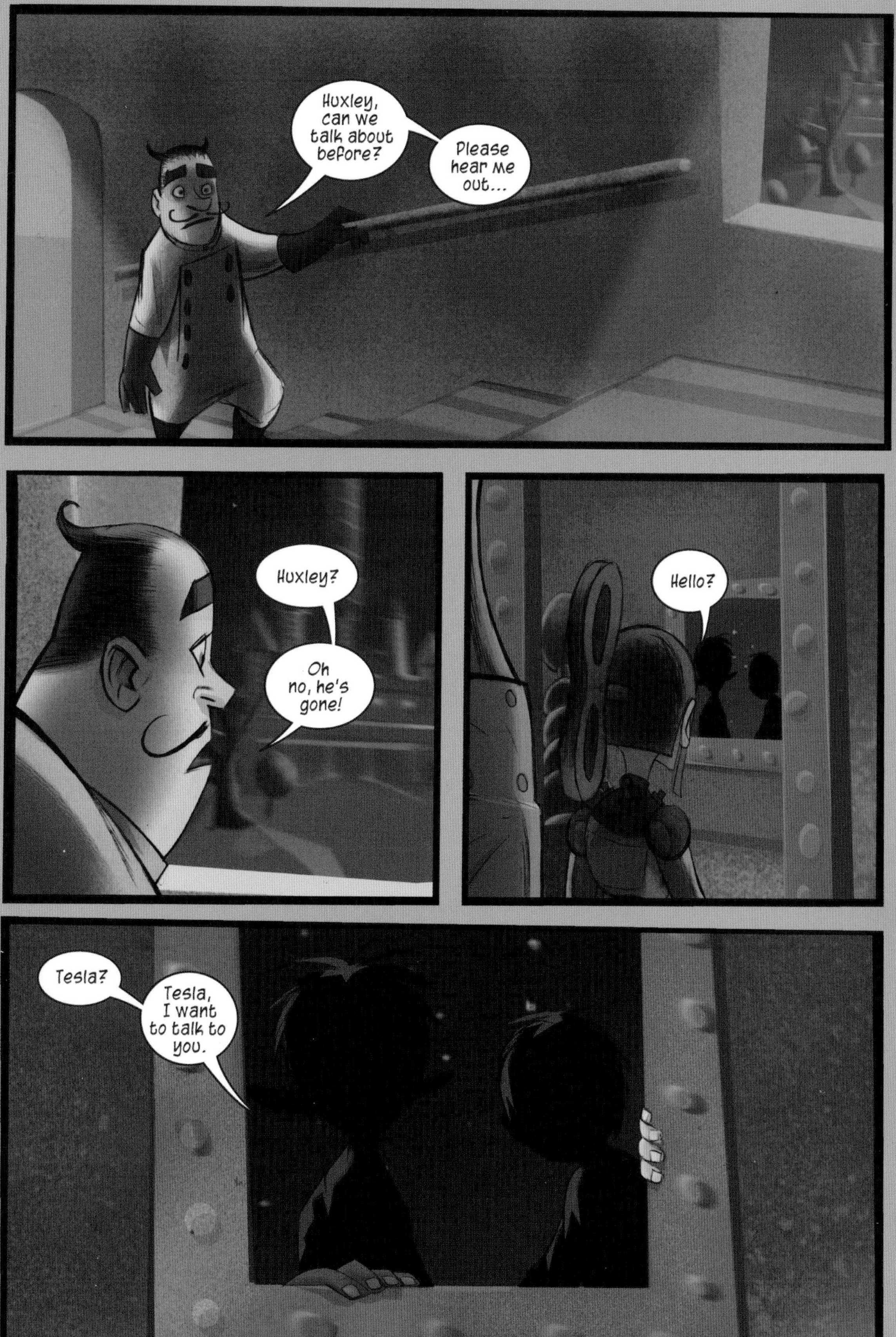
Huxley, can we talk about before?
Please hear me out...
Huxley?
Oh no, he's gone!
Hello?
Tesla?
Tesla, I want to talk to you.

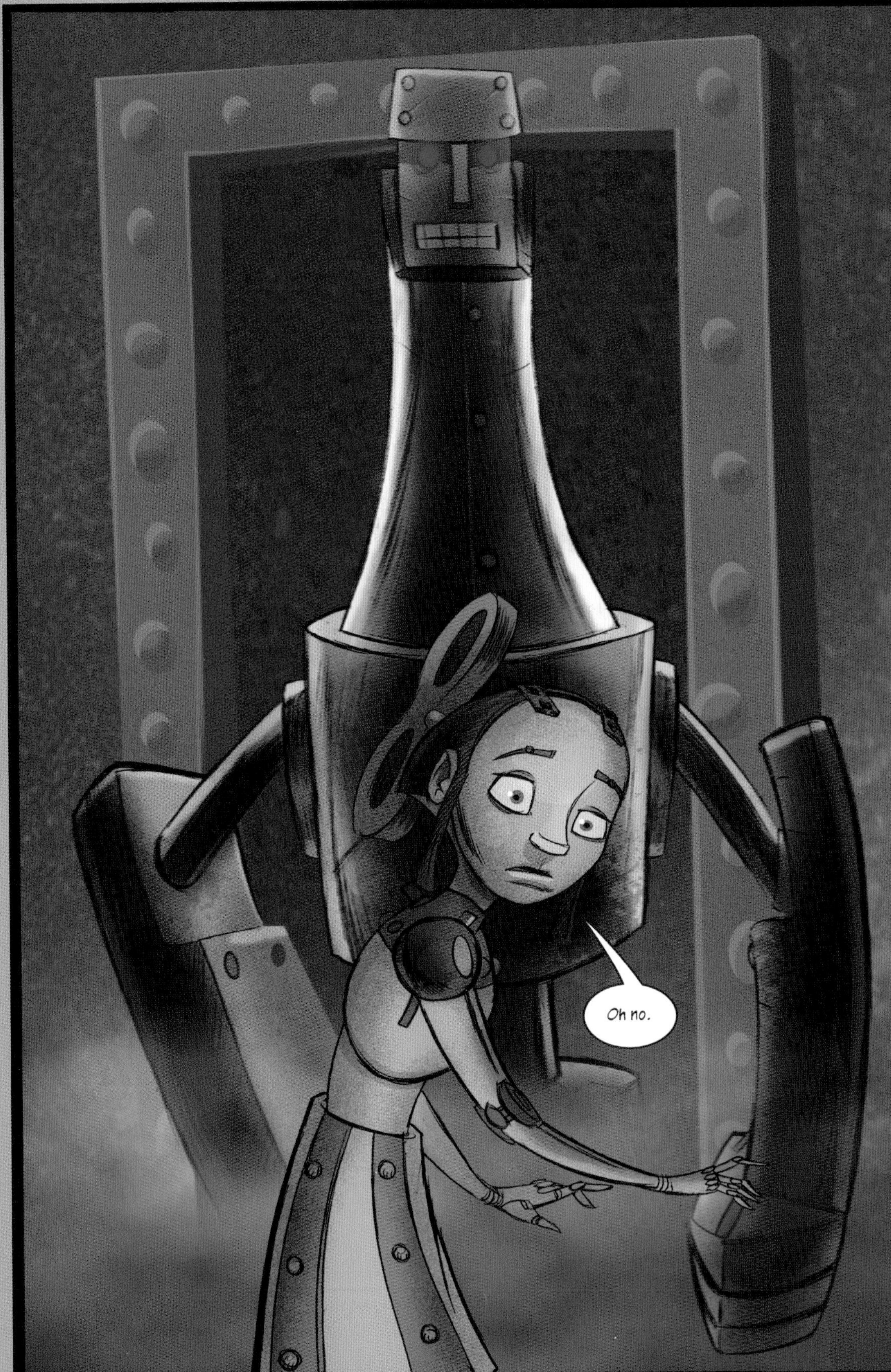
Oh no.

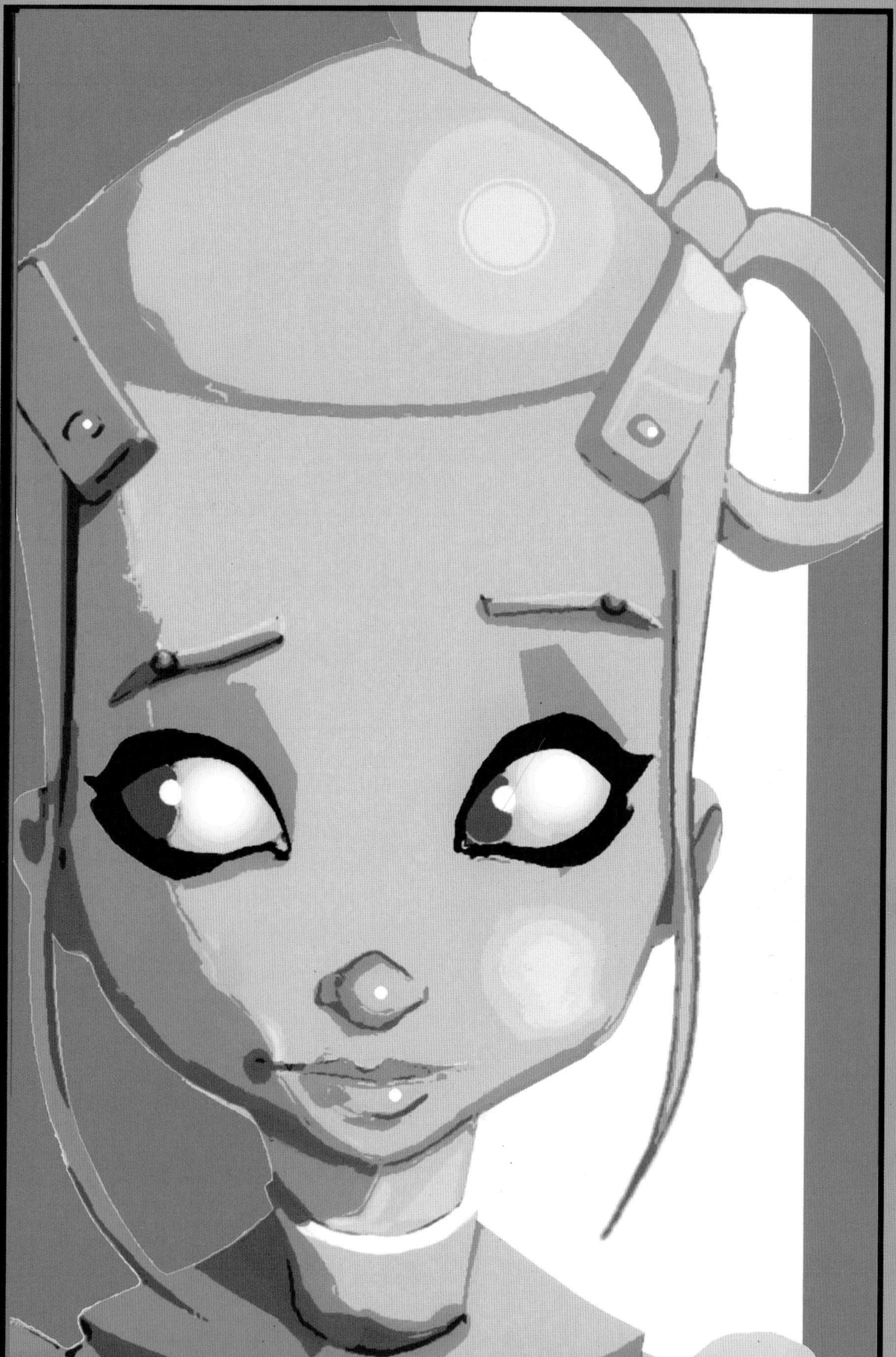

Chapter 4

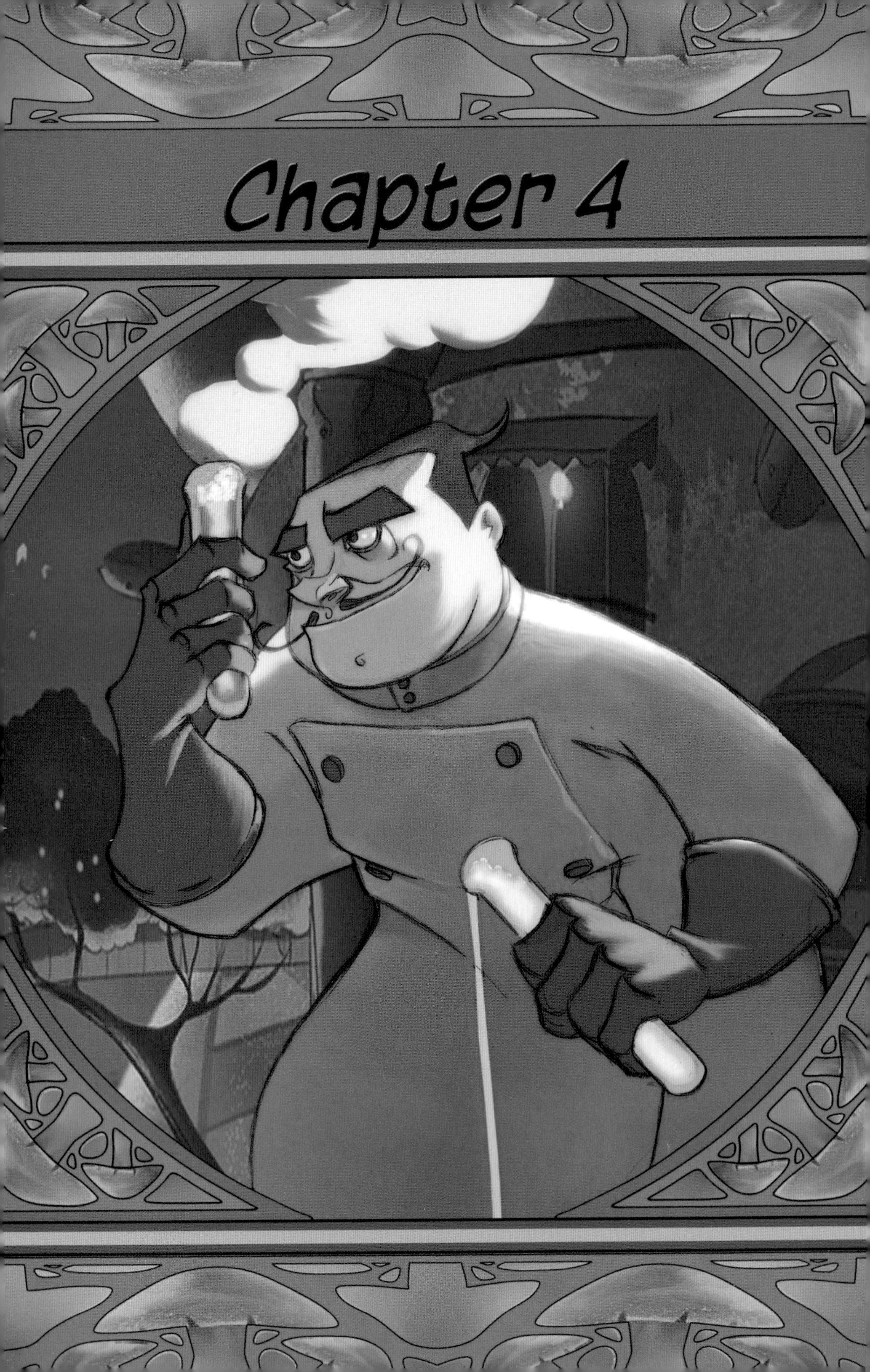

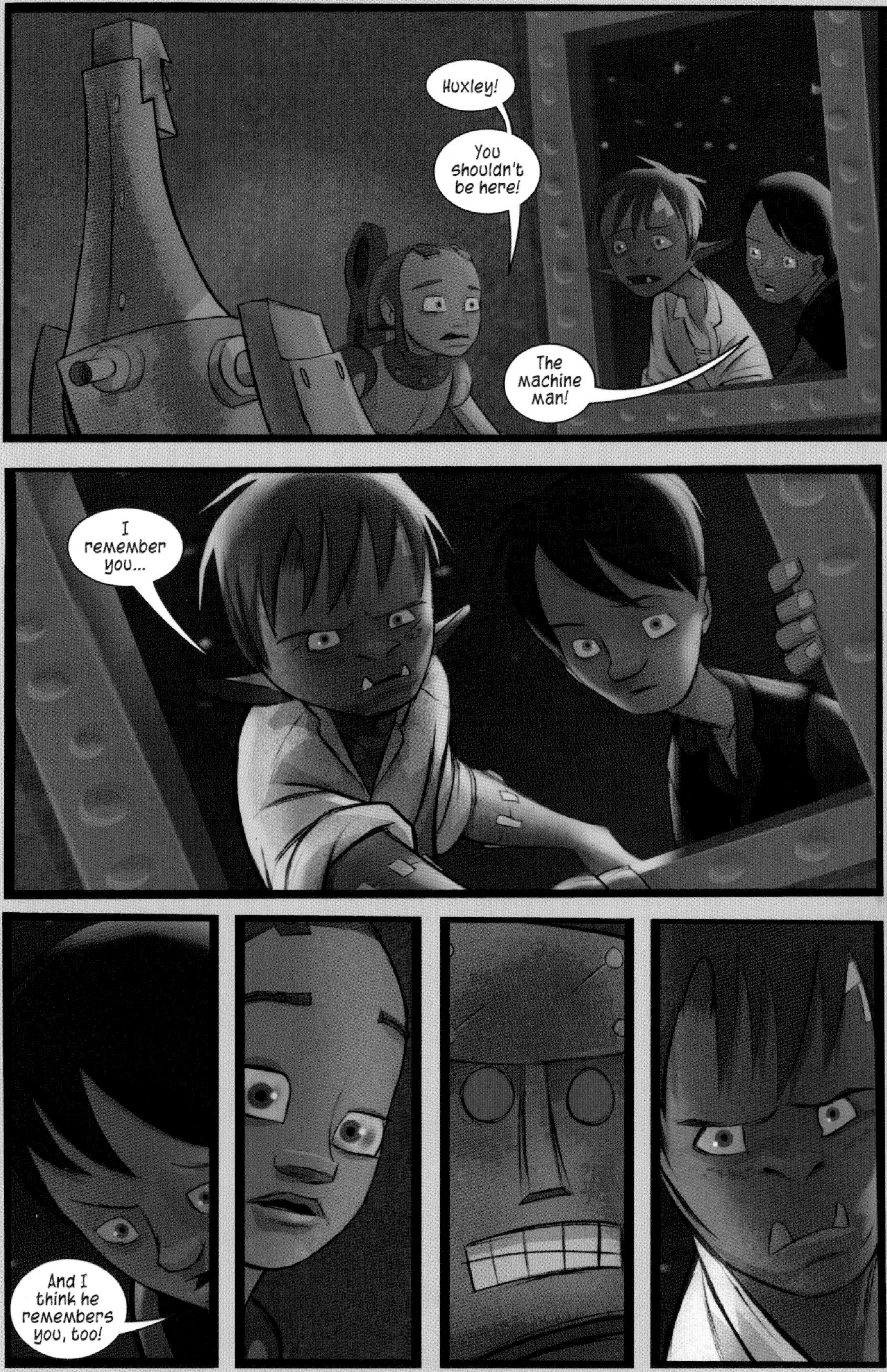
Huxley!
You shouldn't be here!
The Machine Man!
I remember you...
And I think he remembers you, too!

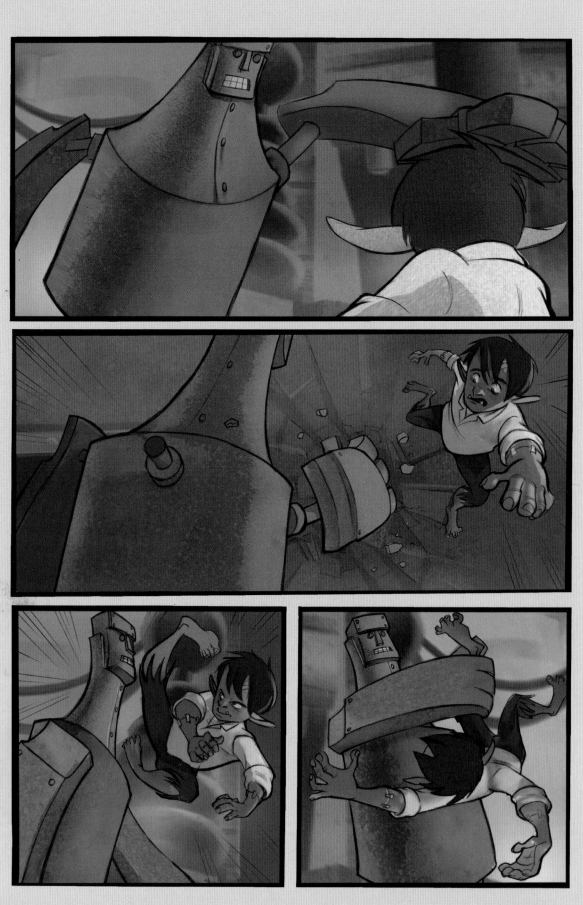

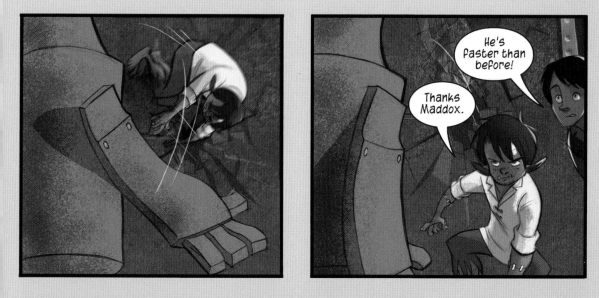

He's faster than before!

Thanks Maddox.

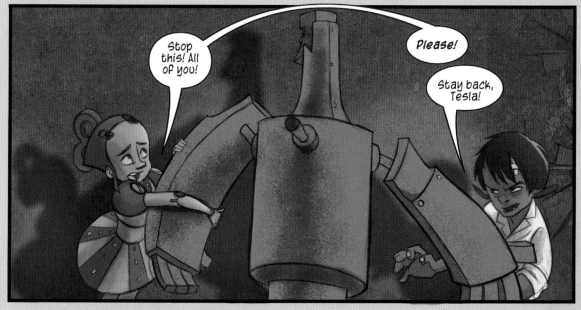

Stop this! All of you!

Please!

Stay back, Tesla!

OH!

Leave her alone!!!

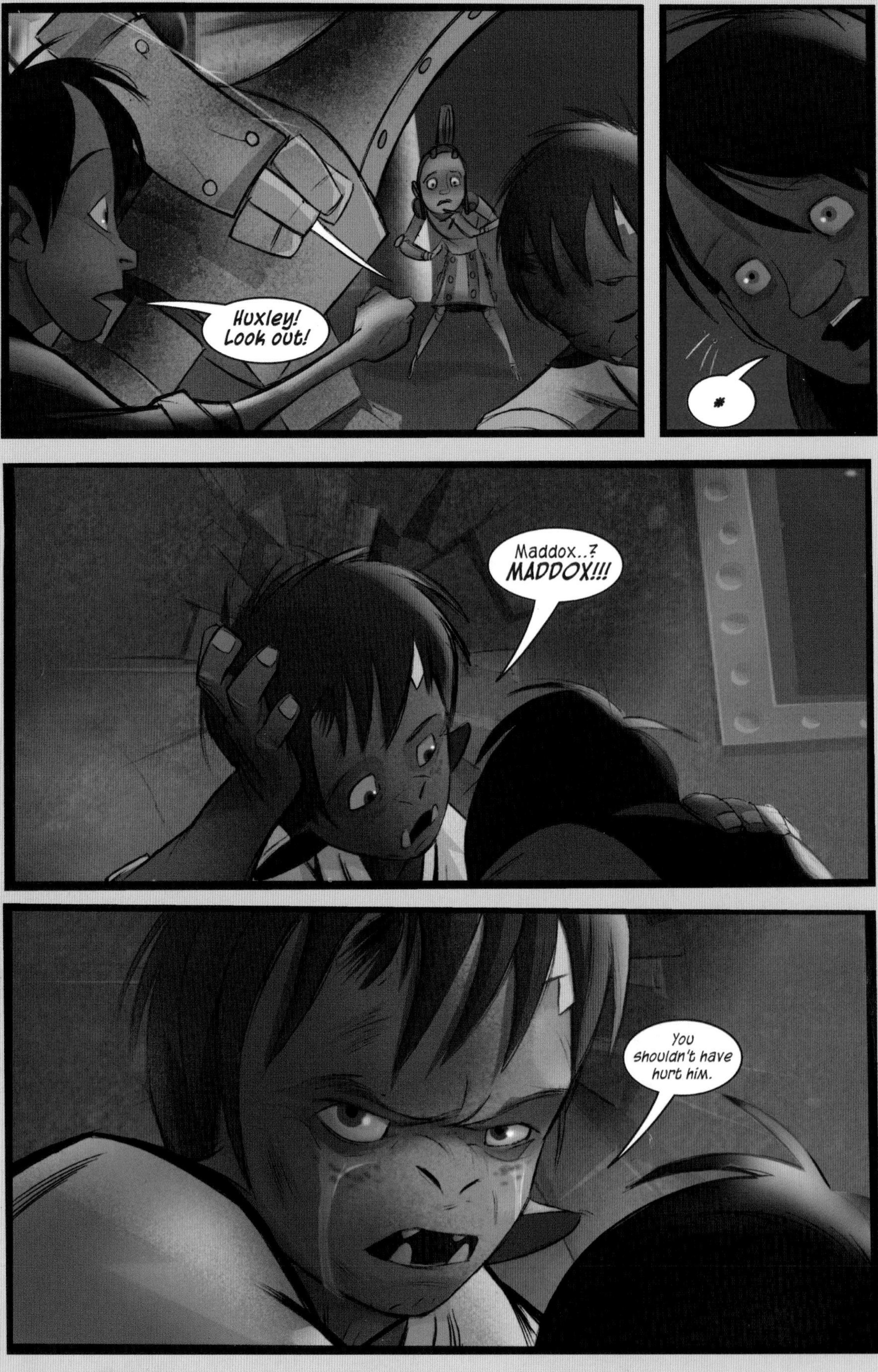
Huxley!
Look out!
*
Maddox..?
MADDOX!!!
You shouldn't have hurt him.

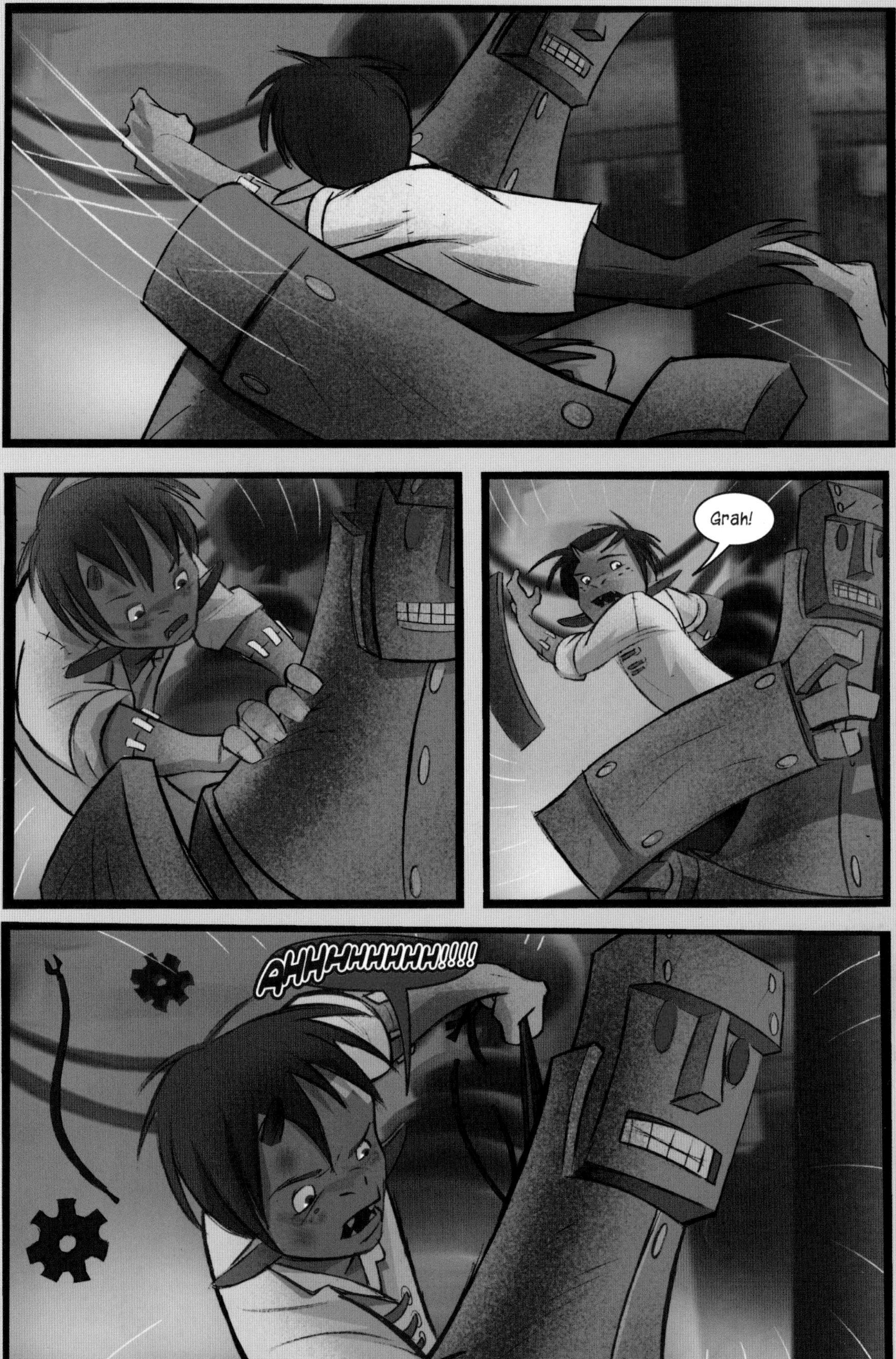
Grah!
AHHHHHHHH!!!!

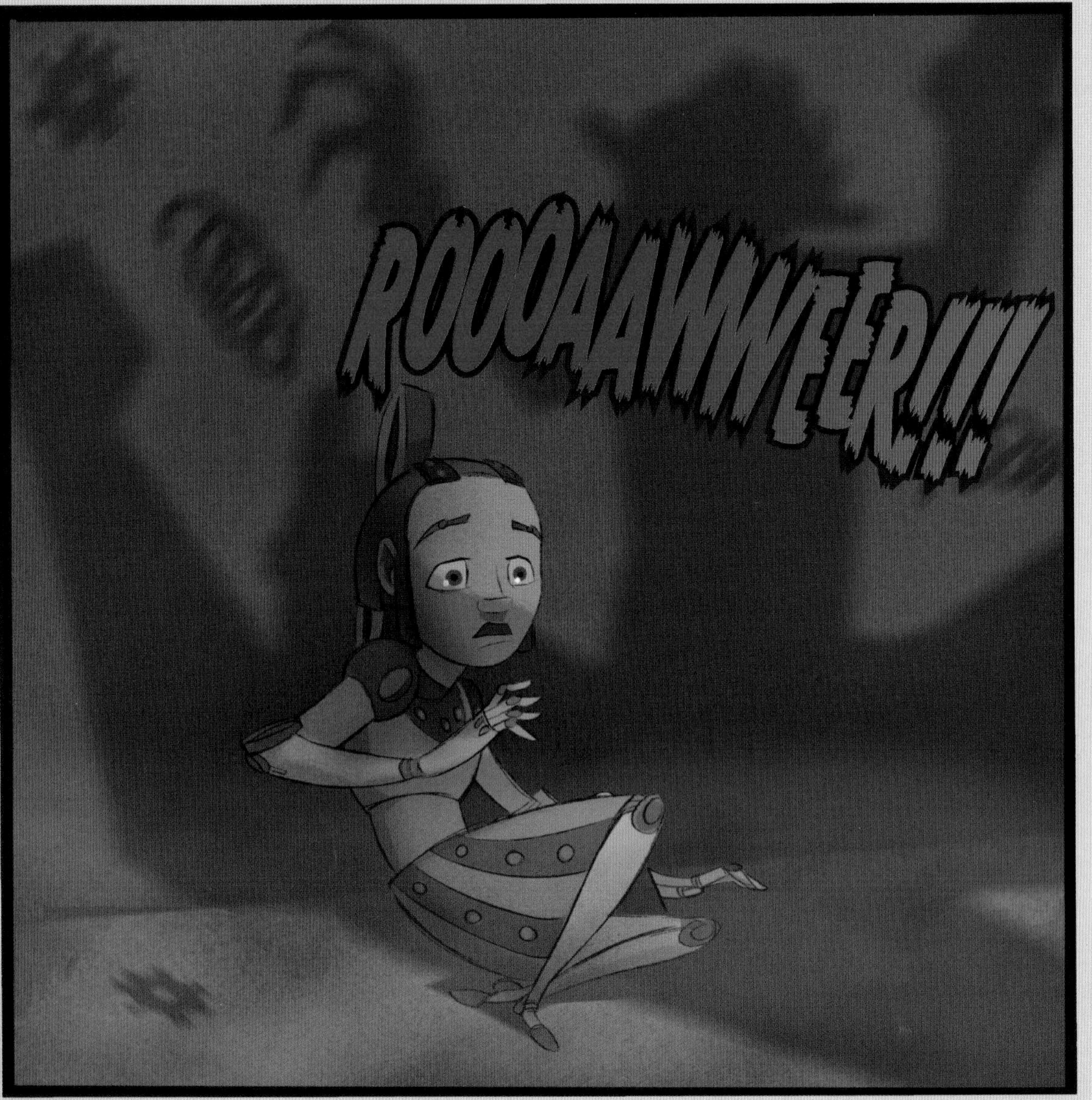
ROOOAAWWEER!!!

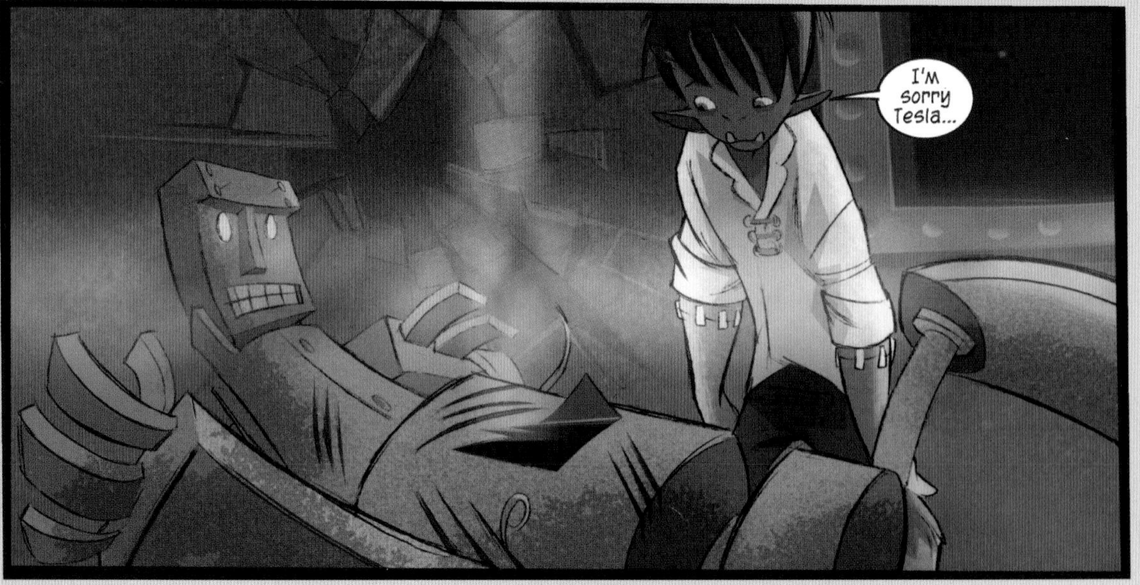
I'M sorry Tesla...

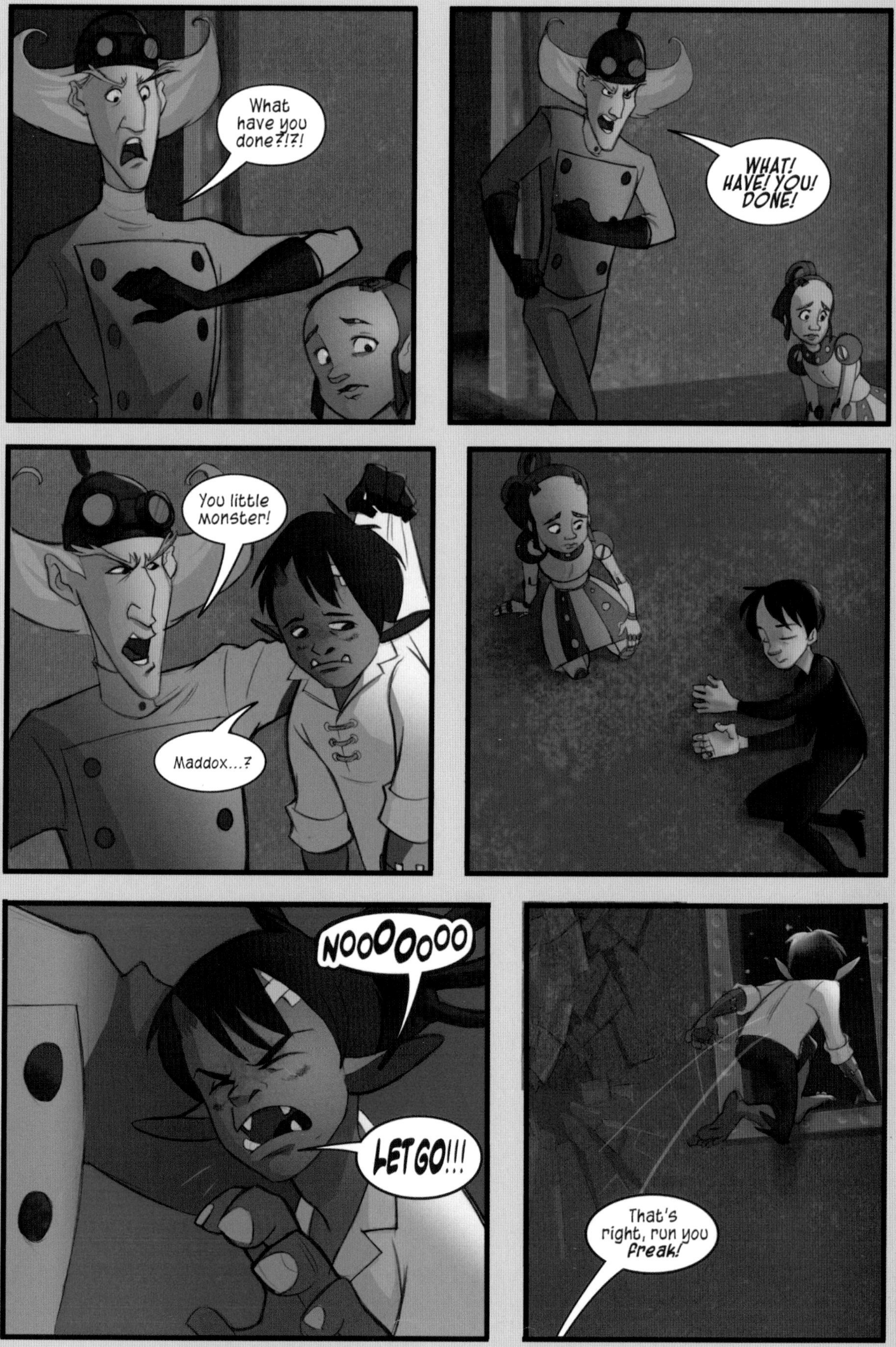
What have you done?!?!
WHAT! HAVE! YOU! DONE!
You little monster!
Maddox...?
NOOOOOOO
LET GO!!!
That's right, run you freak!

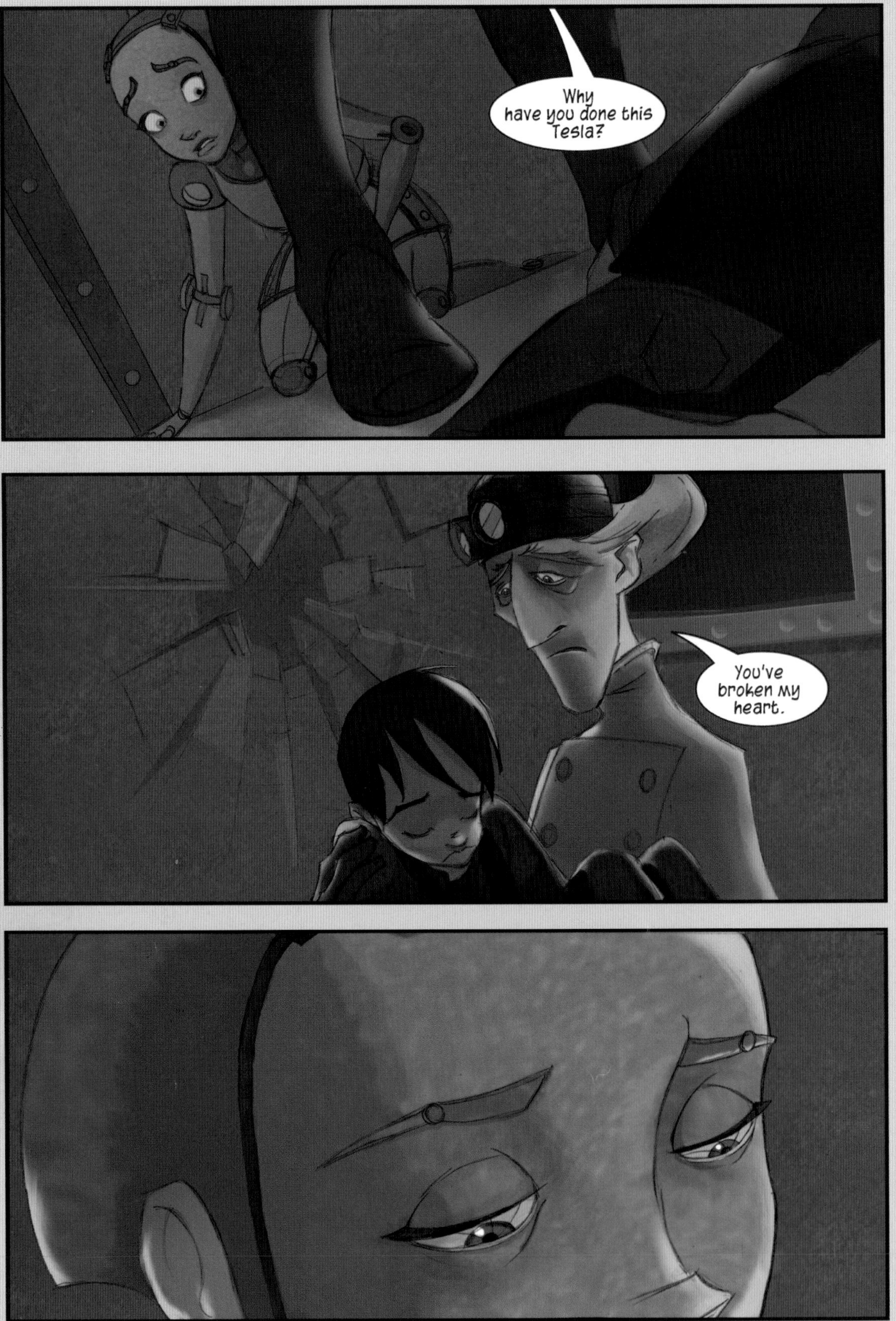
Why have you done this Tesla?
You've broken my heart.

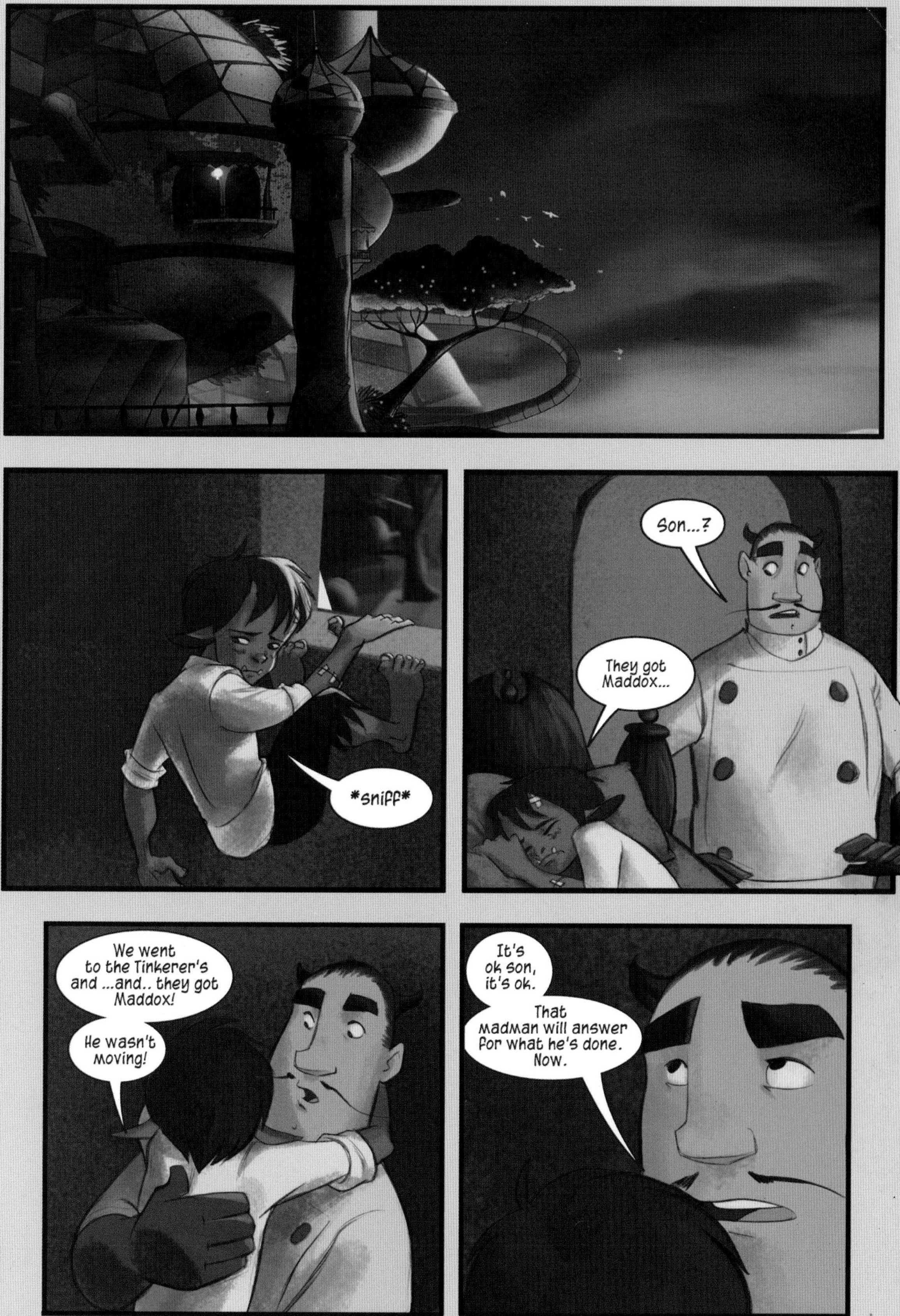
sniff
Son...?
They got Maddox...
We went to the Tinkerer's and ...and.. they got Maddox!
He wasn't moving!
It's ok son, it's ok.
That madman will answer for what he's done. Now.

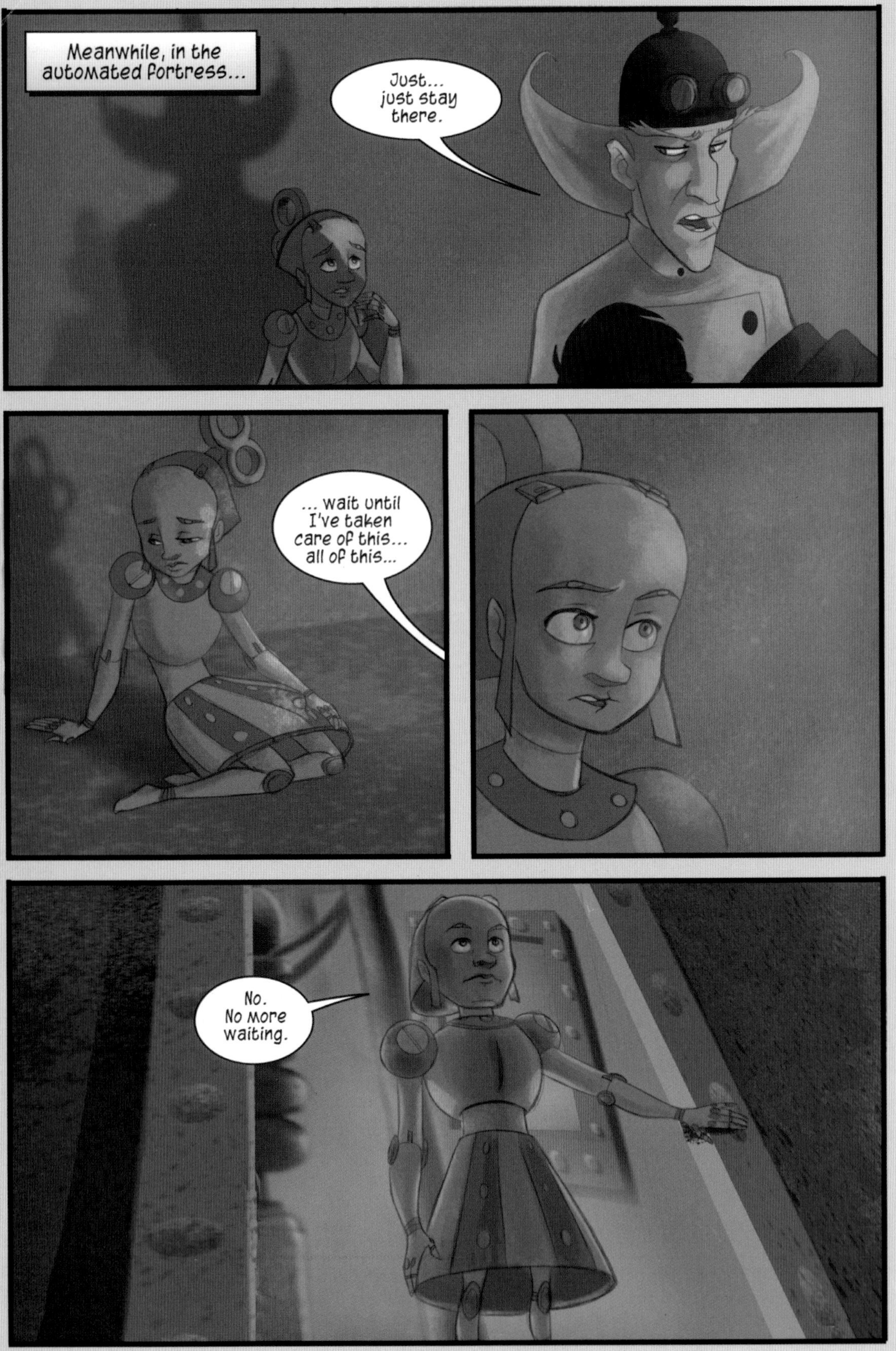
Meanwhile, in the automated fortress...
Just... just stay there.
... wait until I've taken care of this... all of this...
No. No more waiting.

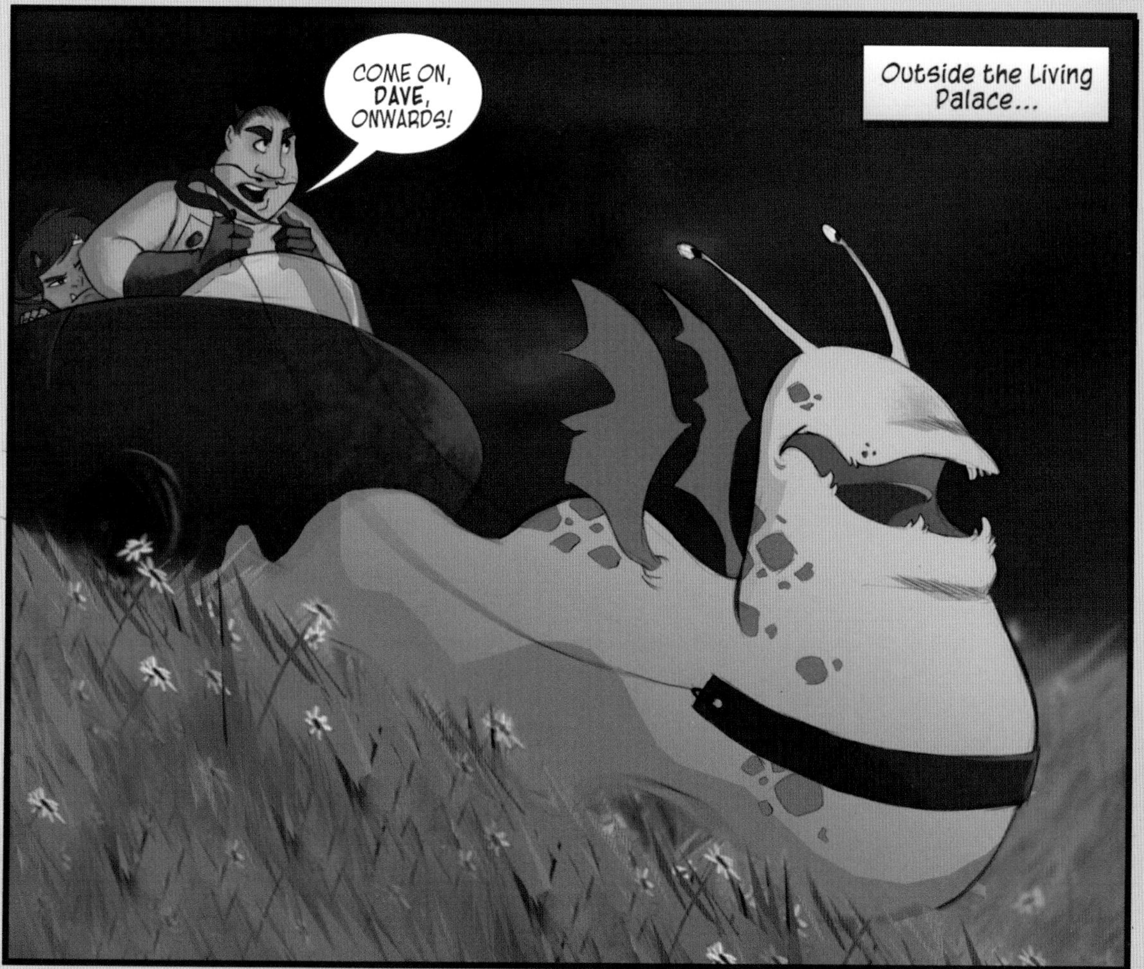
Outside the Living Palace...
COME ON, DAVE, ONWARDS!

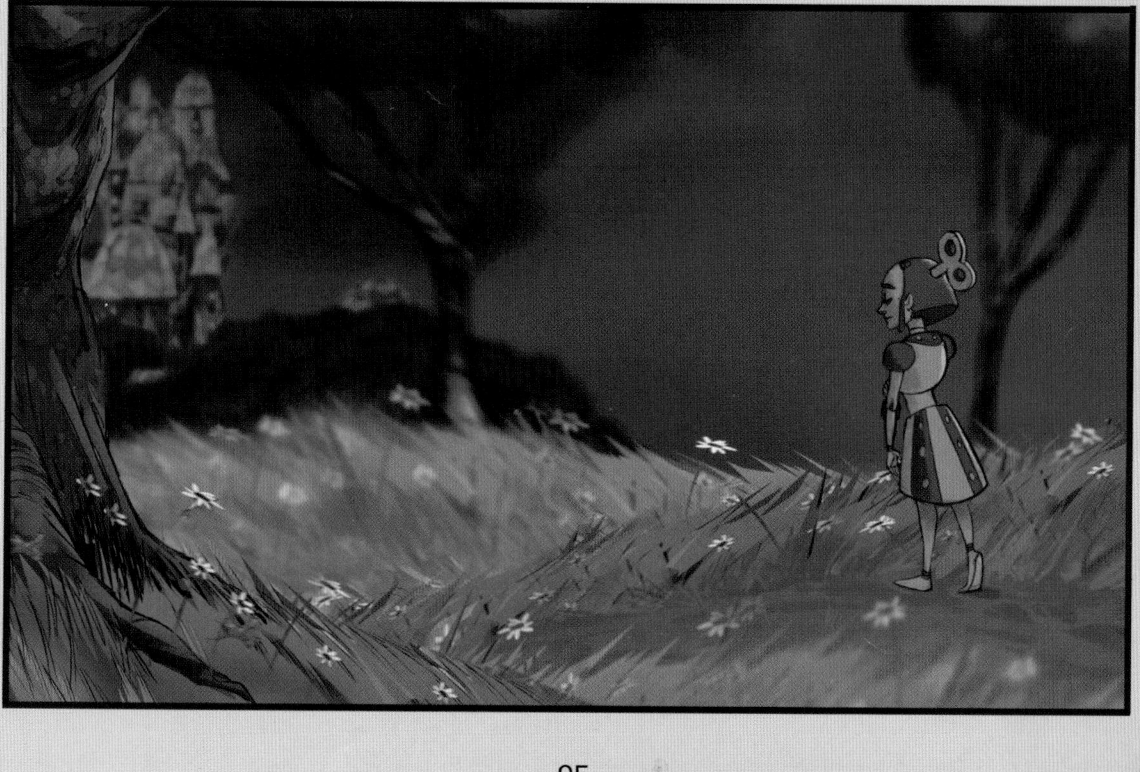

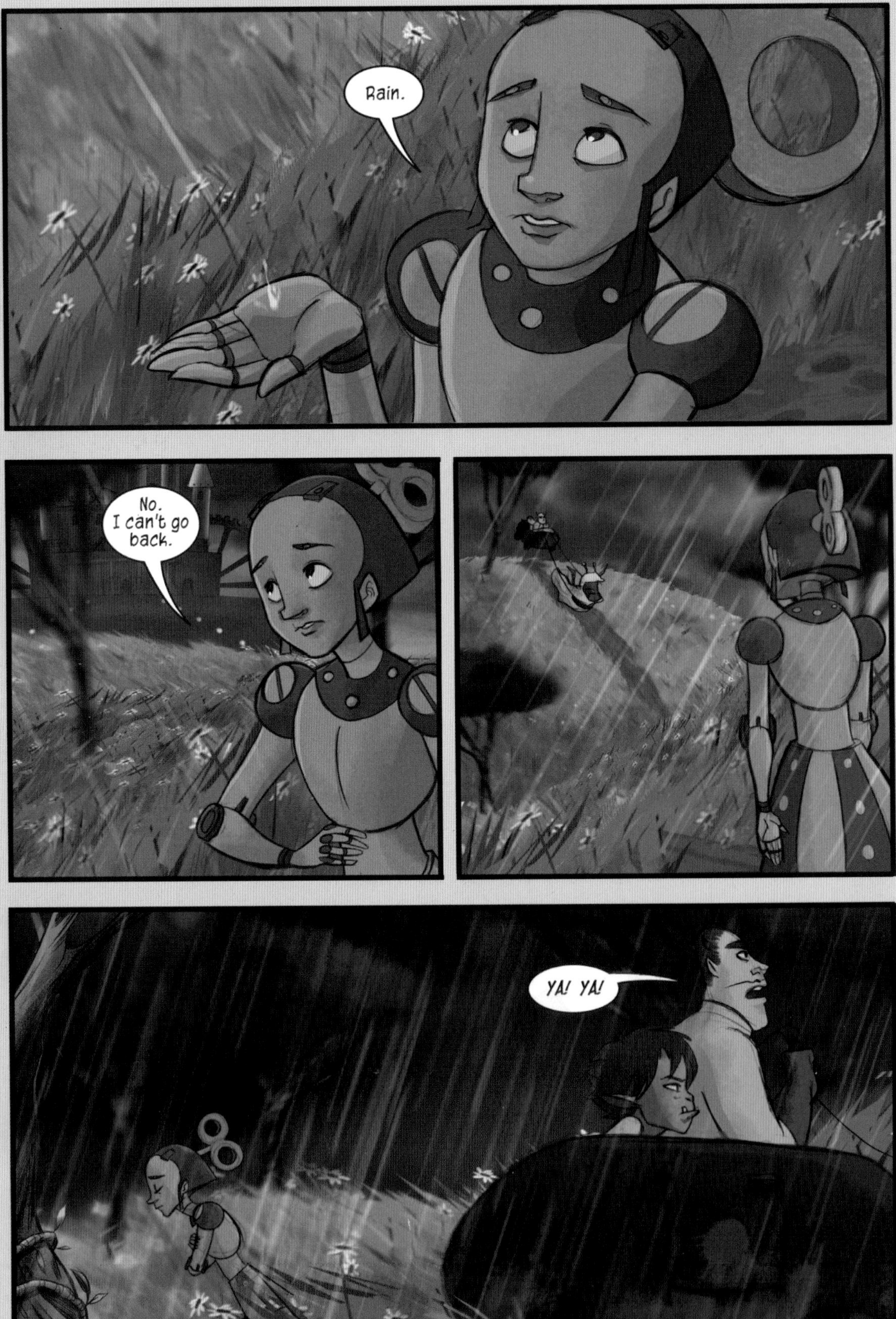
Rain.
No. I can't go back.
YA! YA!

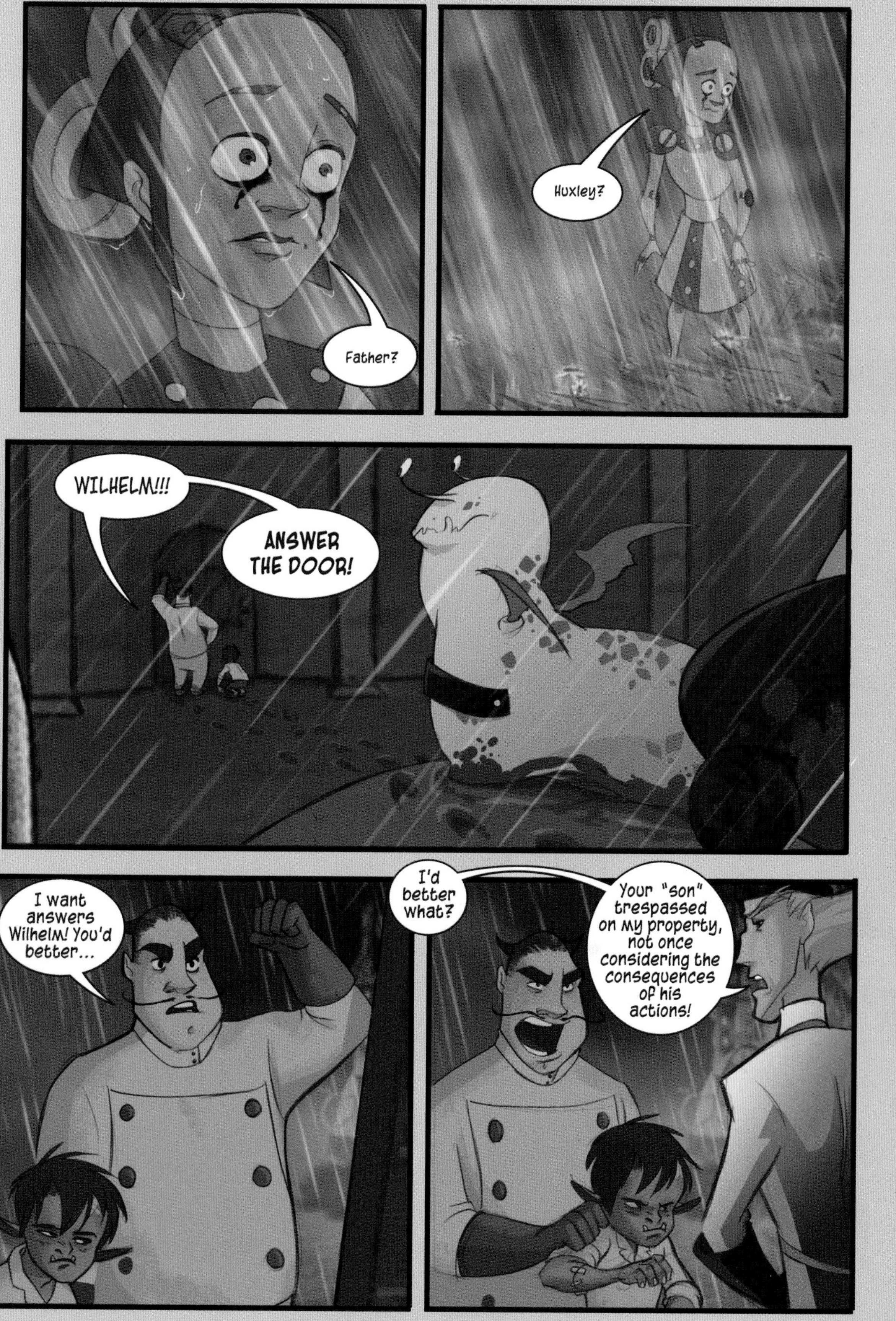

Father?
Huxley?
WILHELM!!!
ANSWER THE DOOR!
I want answers Wilhelm! You'd better...
I'd better what?
Your "son" trespassed on my property, not once considering the consequences of his actions!

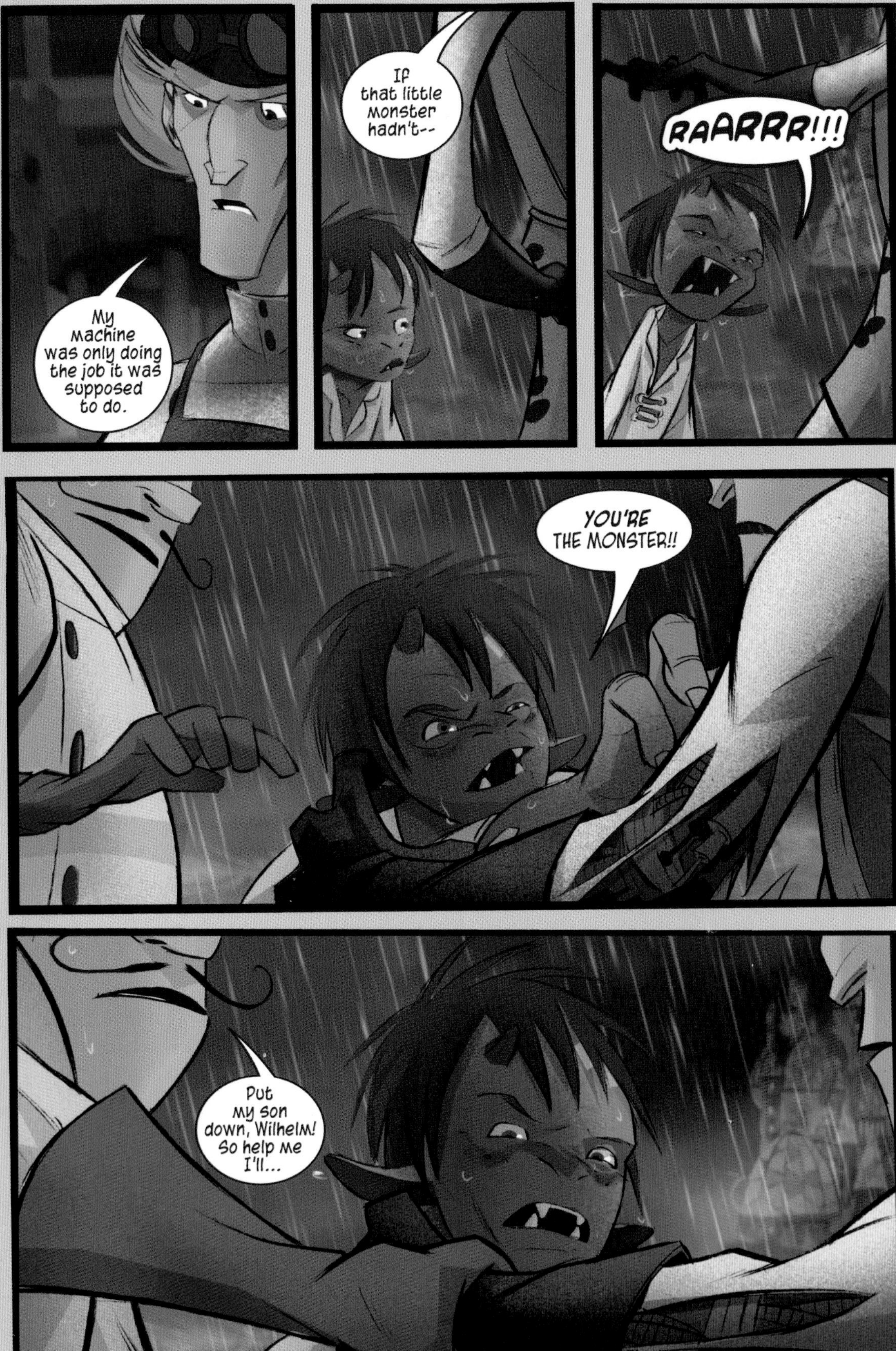
My machine was only doing the job it was supposed to do.
If that little monster hadn't--
RAARRR!!!
YOU'RE THE MONSTER!!
Put my son down, Wilhelm! So help me I'll...

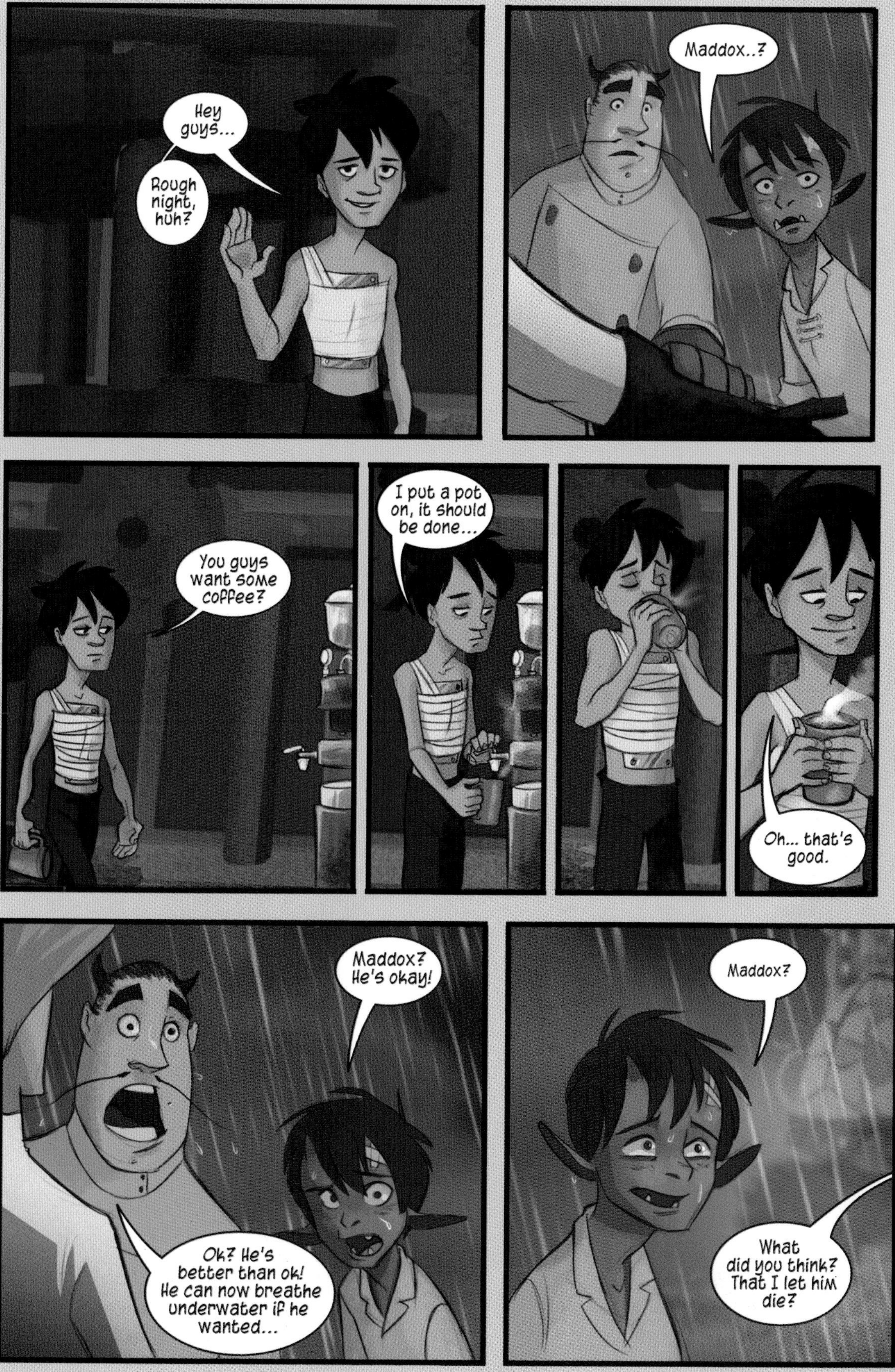
Hey guys...
Rough night, huh?
Maddox..?
You guys want some coffee?
I put a pot on, it should be done...
Oh... that's good.
Maddox? He's okay!
Ok? He's better than ok! He can now breathe underwater if he wanted...
Maddox?
What did you think? That I let him die?

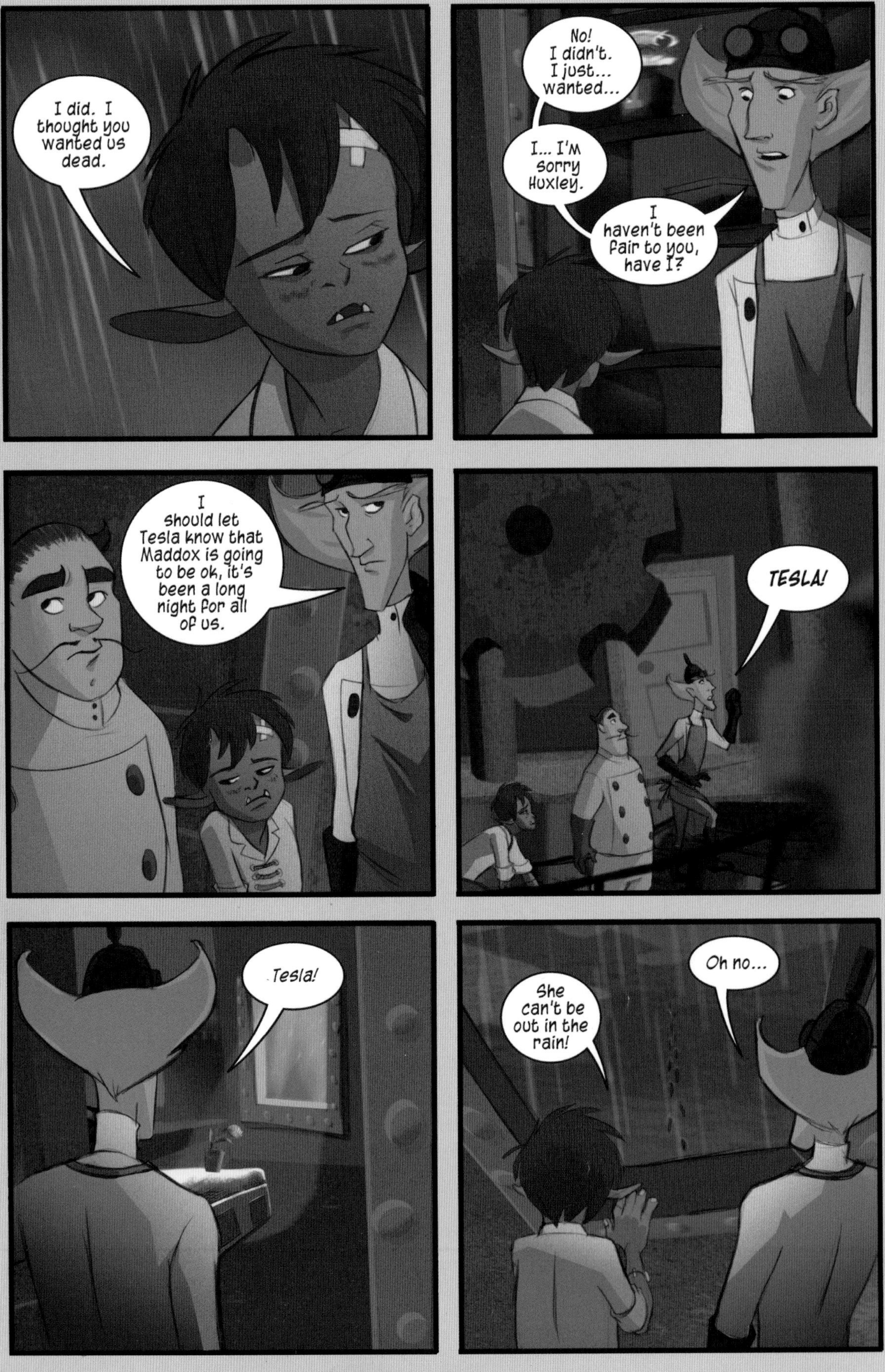
I did. I thought you wanted us dead.
No! I didn't. I just... wanted...
I... I'm sorry Huxley.
I haven't been fair to you, have I?
I should let Tesla know that Maddox is going to be ok, it's been a long night for all of us.
TESLA!
Tesla!
Oh no...
She can't be out in the rain!

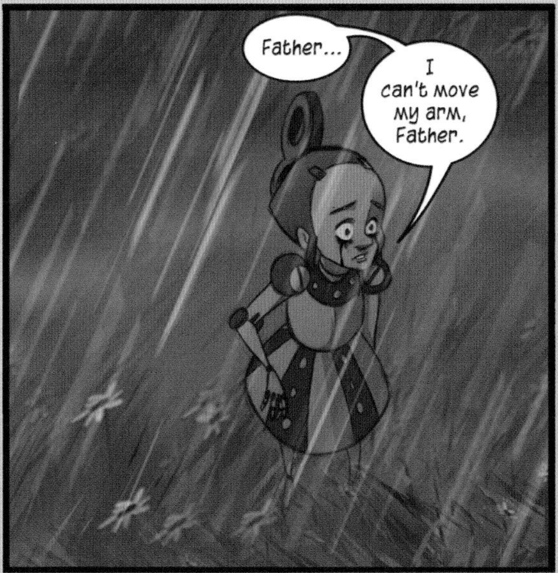
Father...
I can't move my arm, Father.

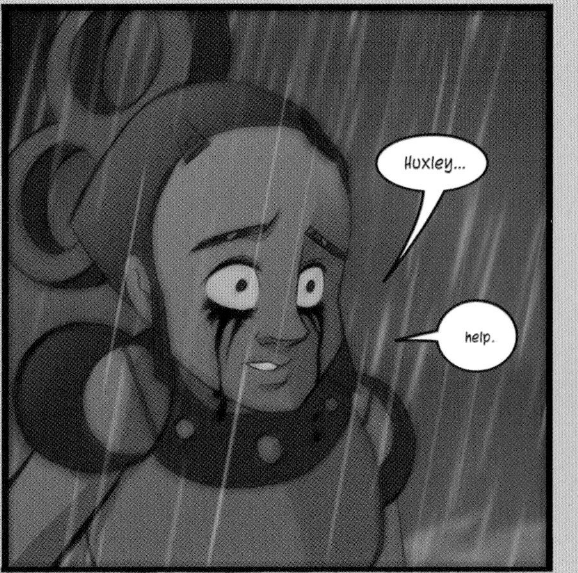
Huxley...
help.

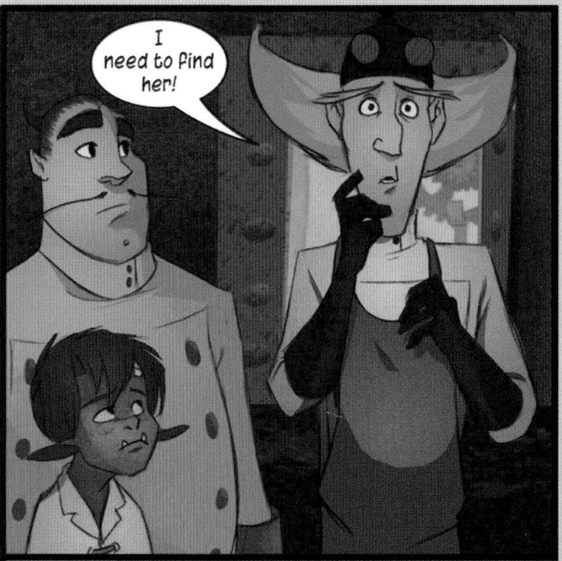
I need to find her!

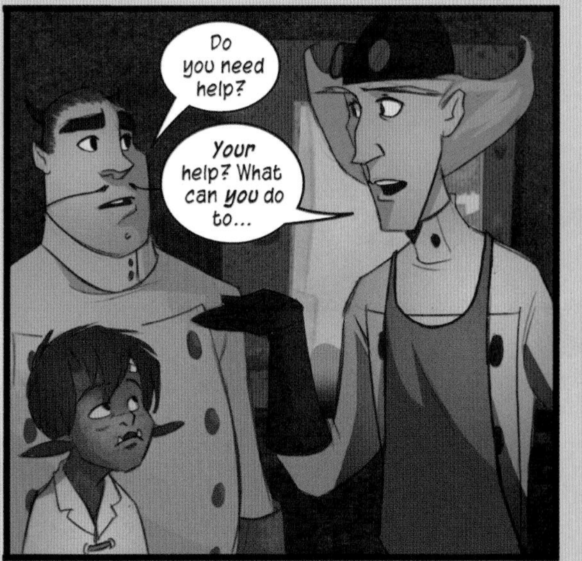
Do you need help?
Your help? What can you do to...

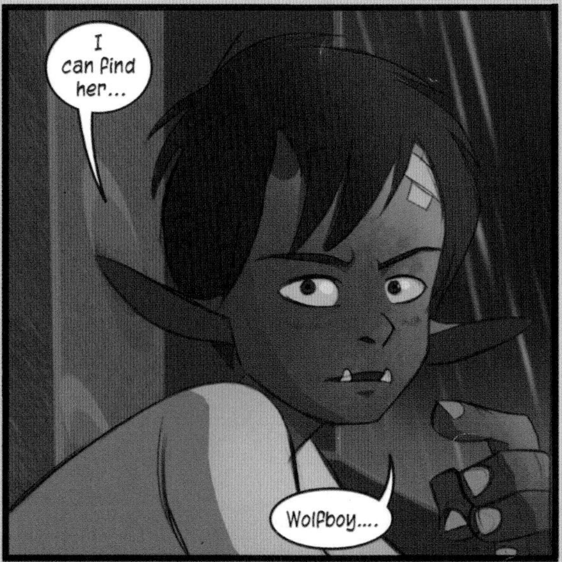
I can find her...
Wolfboy....

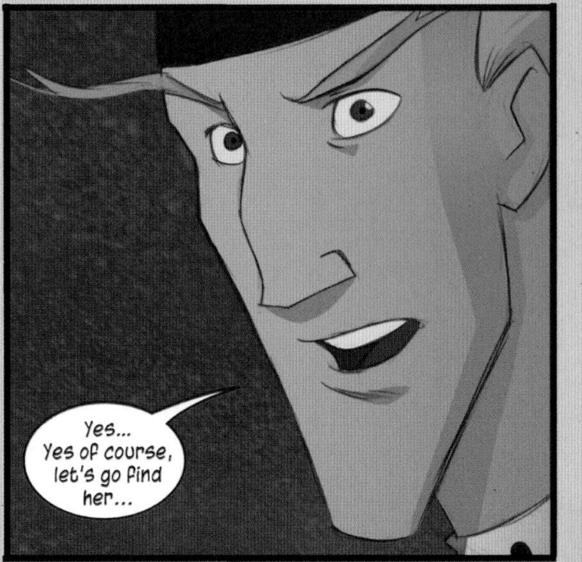
Yes... Yes of course, let's go find her...

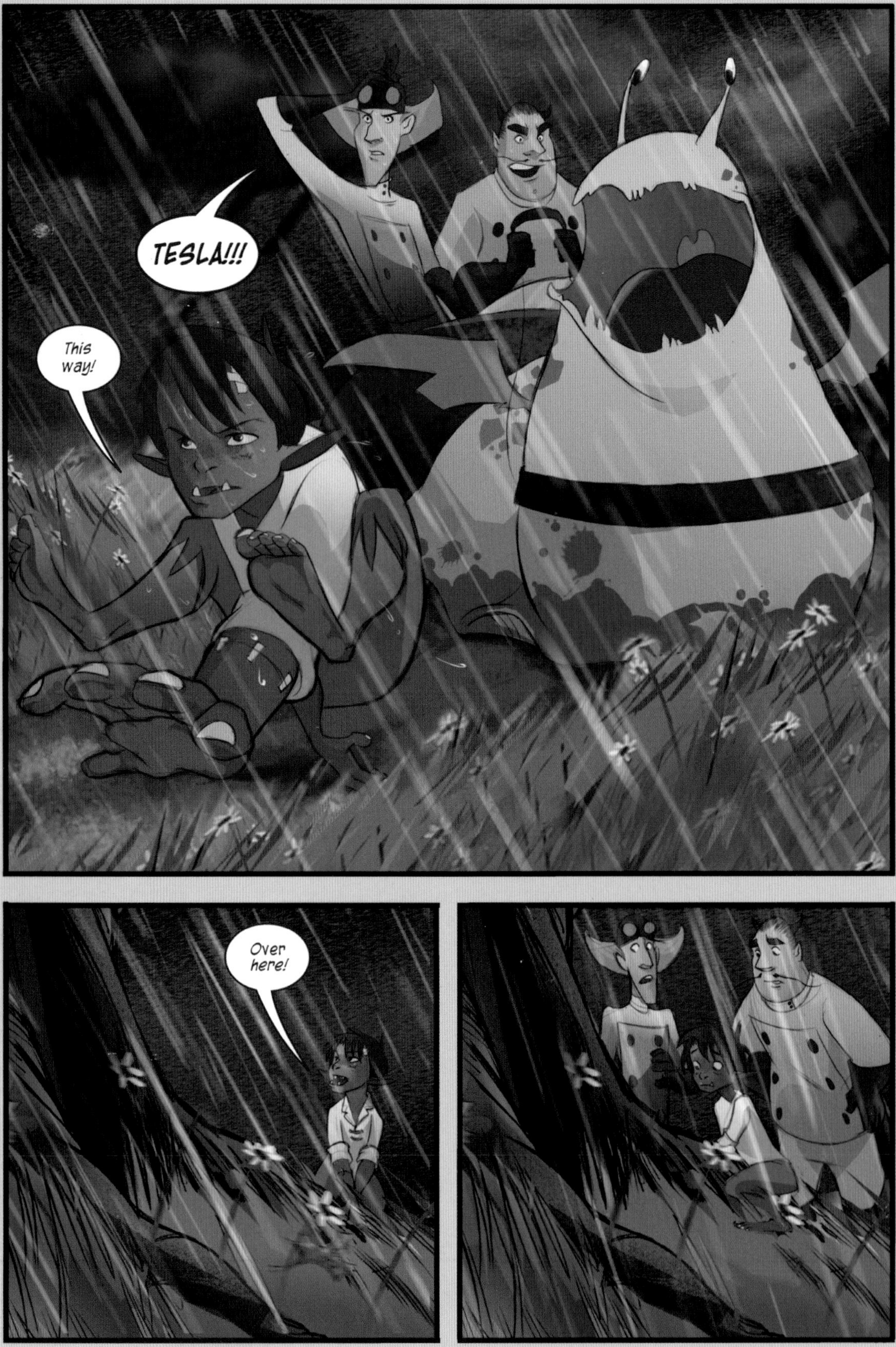
TESLA!!!
This way!
Over here!

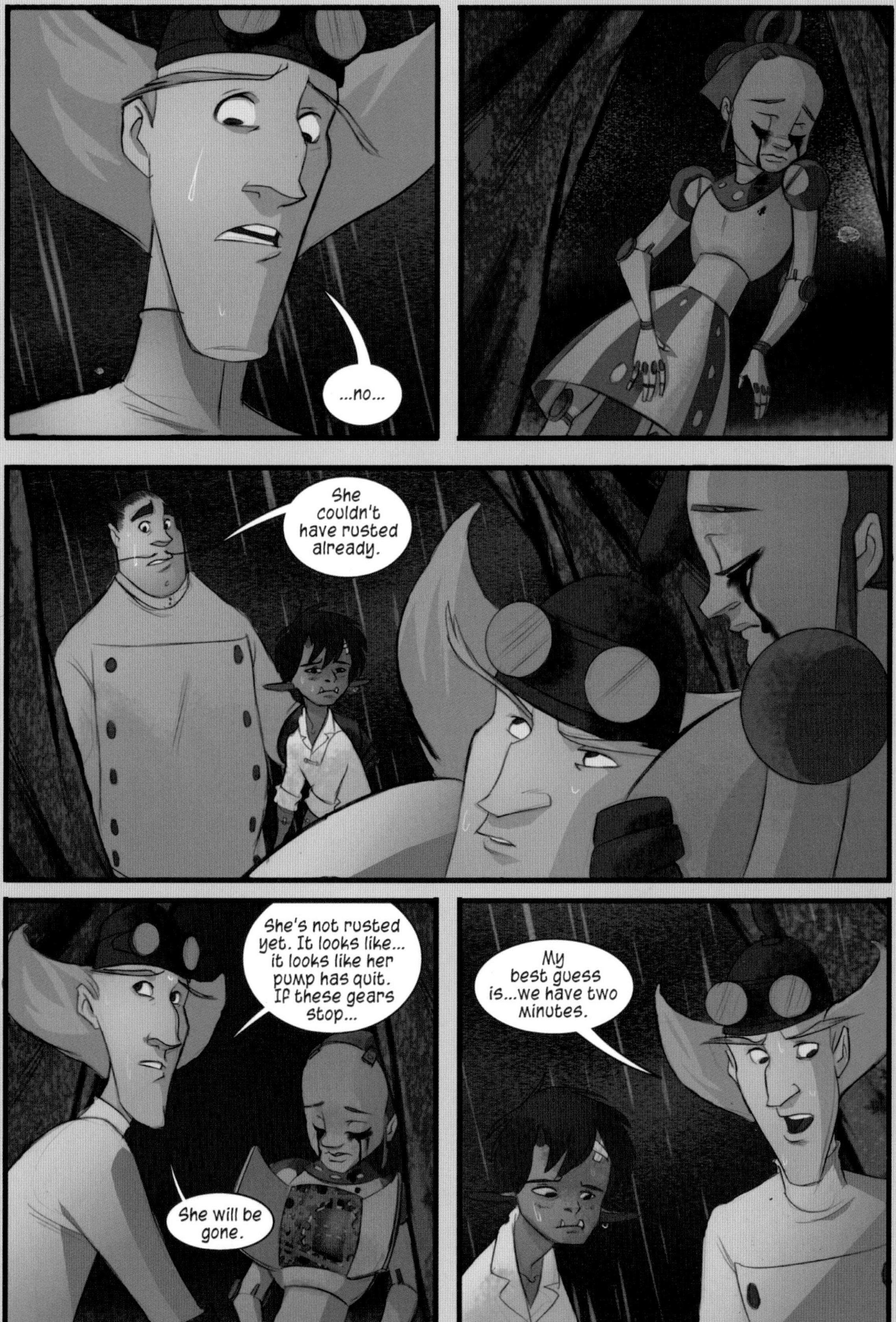
...no...
She couldn't have rusted already.
She's not rusted yet. It looks like... it looks like her pump has quit. If these gears stop...
She will be gone.
My best guess is...we have two minutes.

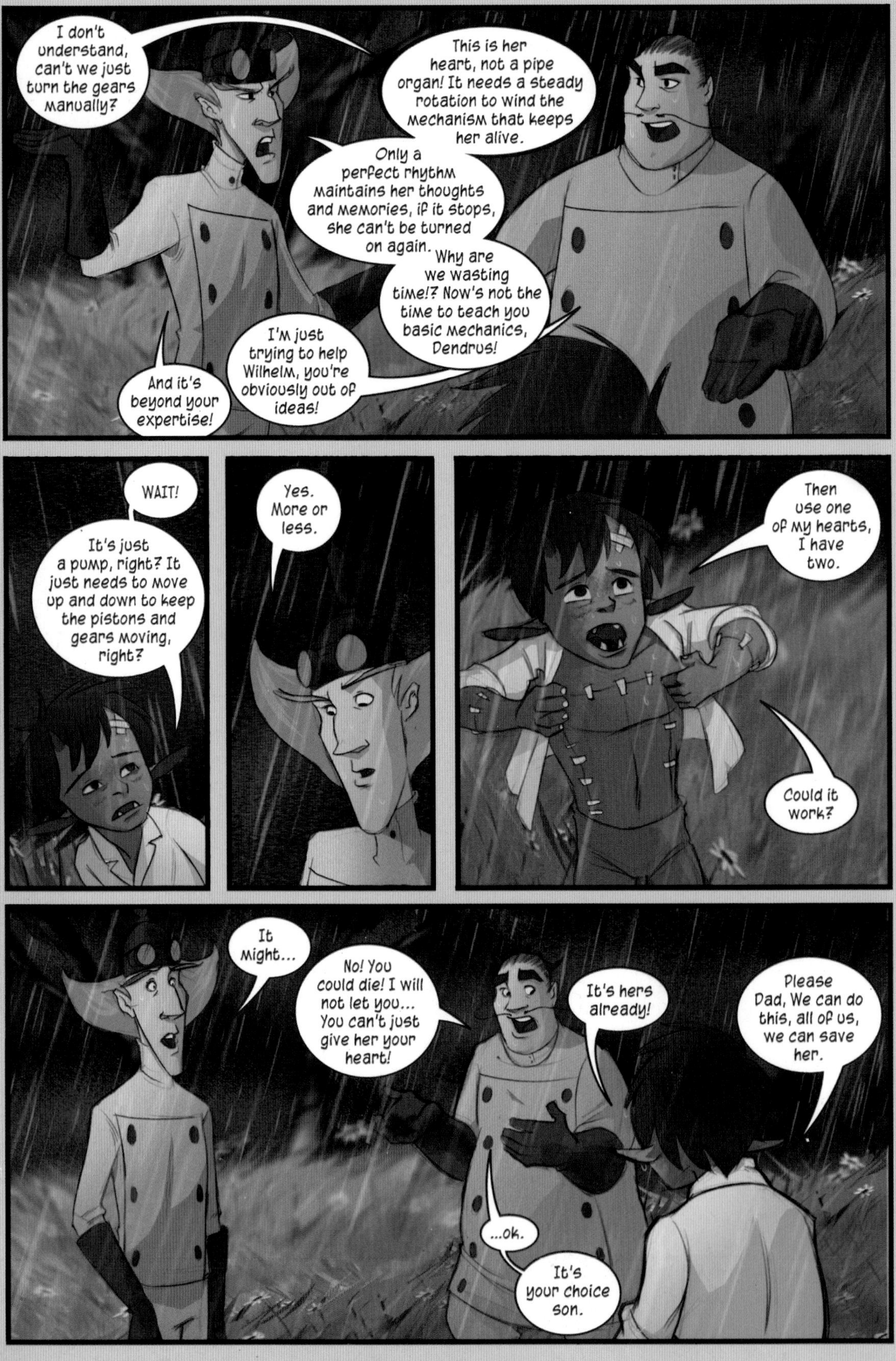
I don't understand, can't we just turn the gears manually?
This is her heart, not a pipe organ! It needs a steady rotation to wind the mechanism that keeps her alive.
Only a perfect rhythm maintains her thoughts and memories, if it stops, she can't be turned on again.
Why are we wasting time!? Now's not the time to teach you basic mechanics, Dendrus!
I'm just trying to help Wilhelm, you're obviously out of ideas!
And it's beyond your expertise!
WAIT!
It's just a pump, right? It just needs to move up and down to keep the pistons and gears moving, right?
Yes. More or less.
Then use one of my hearts, I have two.
Could it work?
It might...
No! You could die! I will not let you... You can't just give her your heart!
It's hers already!
Please Dad, We can do this, all of us, we can save her.
...ok.
It's your choice son.

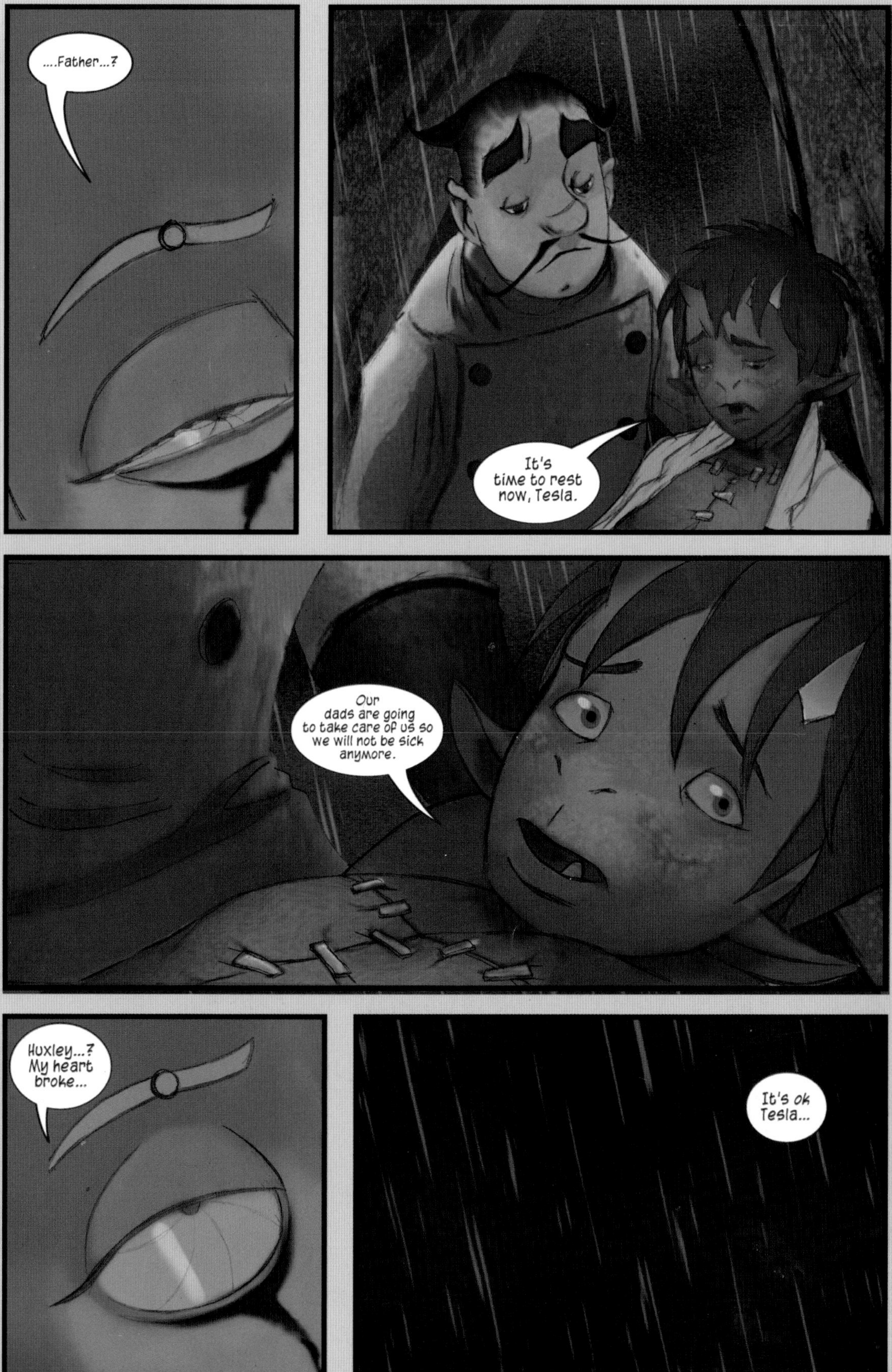
....Father...?
It's time to rest now, Tesla.
Our dads are going to take care of us so we will not be sick anymore.
Huxley...? My heart broke...
It's ok Tesla...

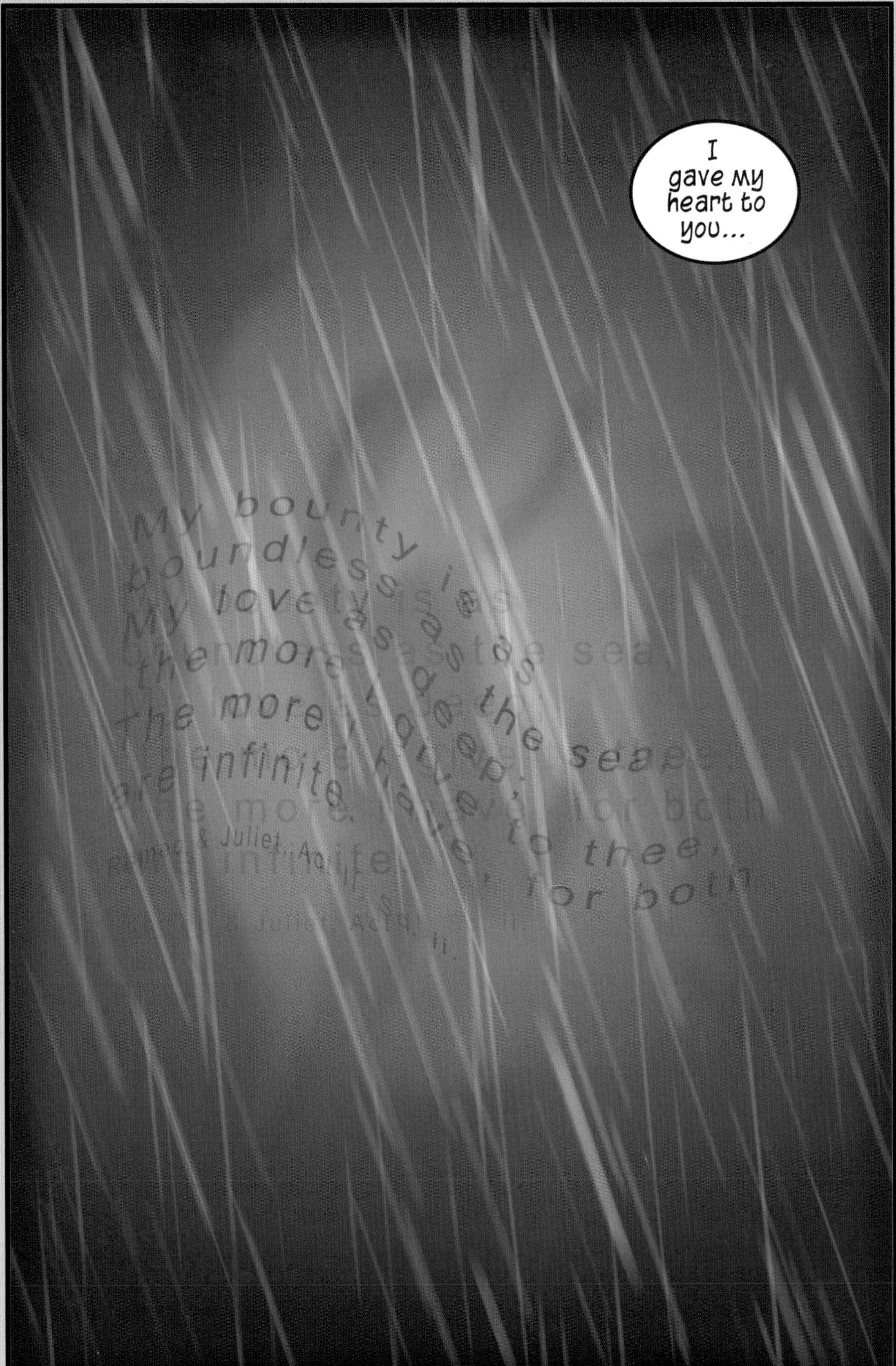
I gave my heart to you...

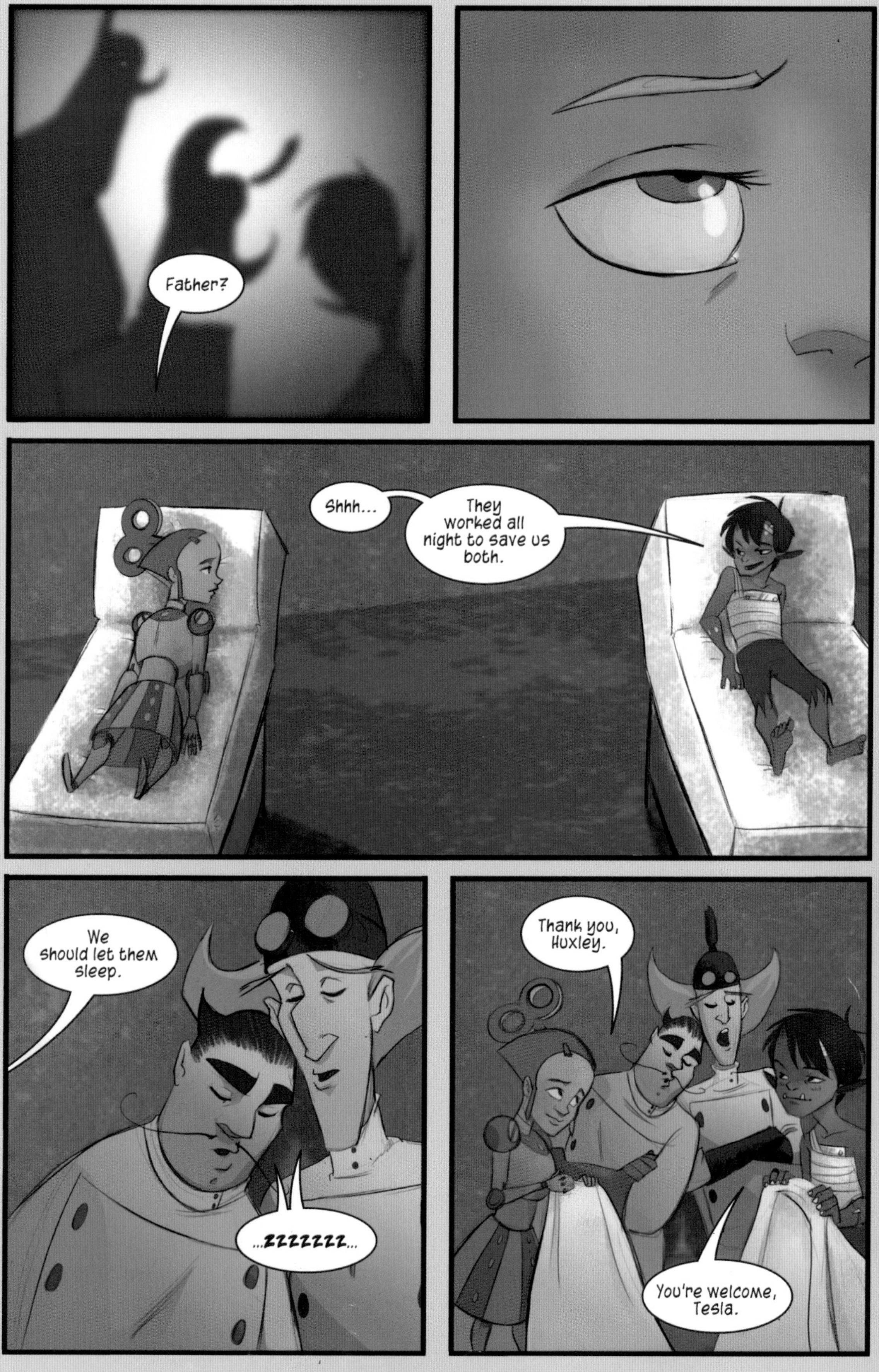
Father?
Shhh...
They worked all night to save us both.
We should let them sleep.
...ZZZZZZZ...
Thank you, Huxley.
You're welcome, Tesla.

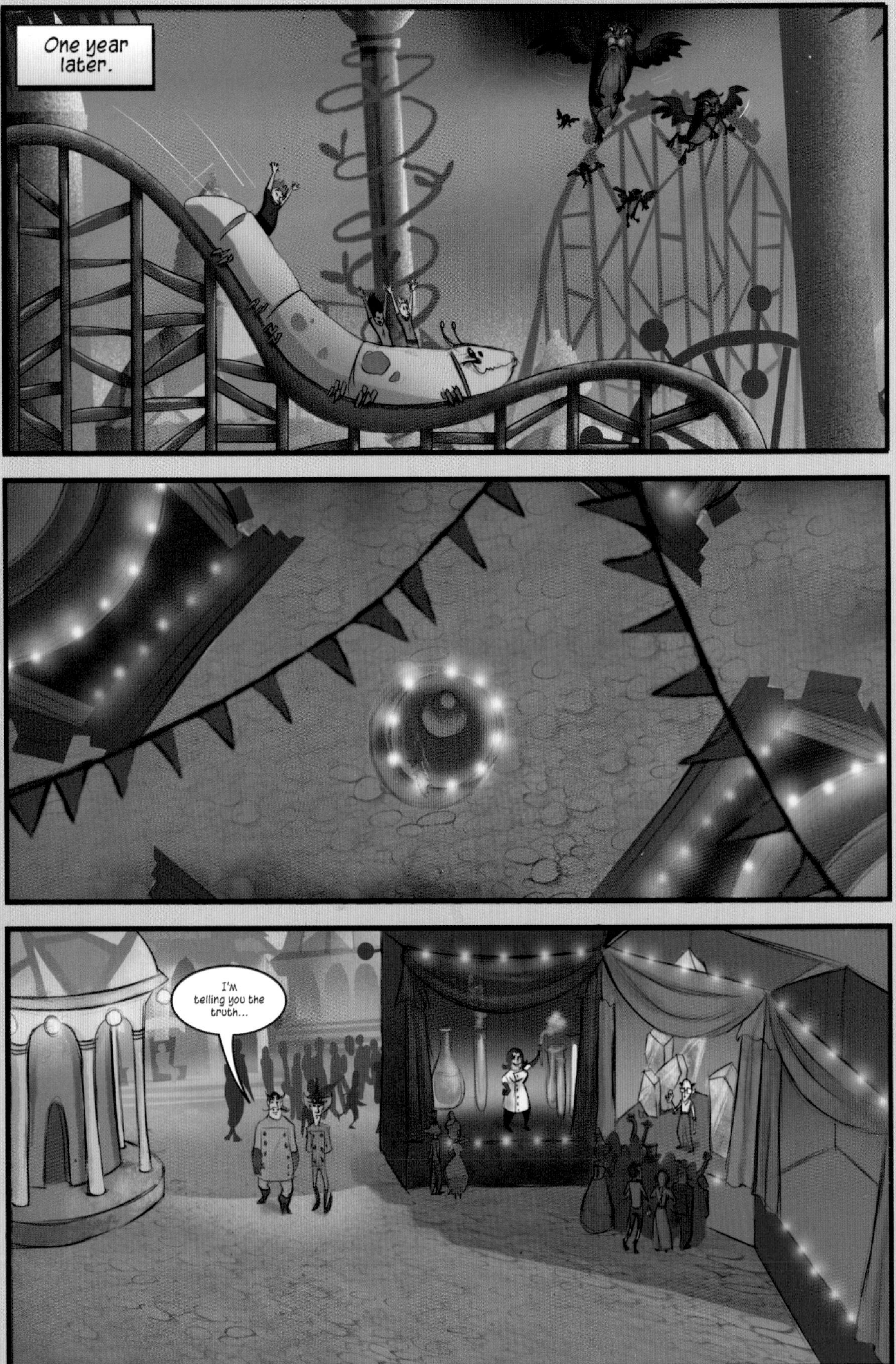
One year later.
I'm telling you the truth...

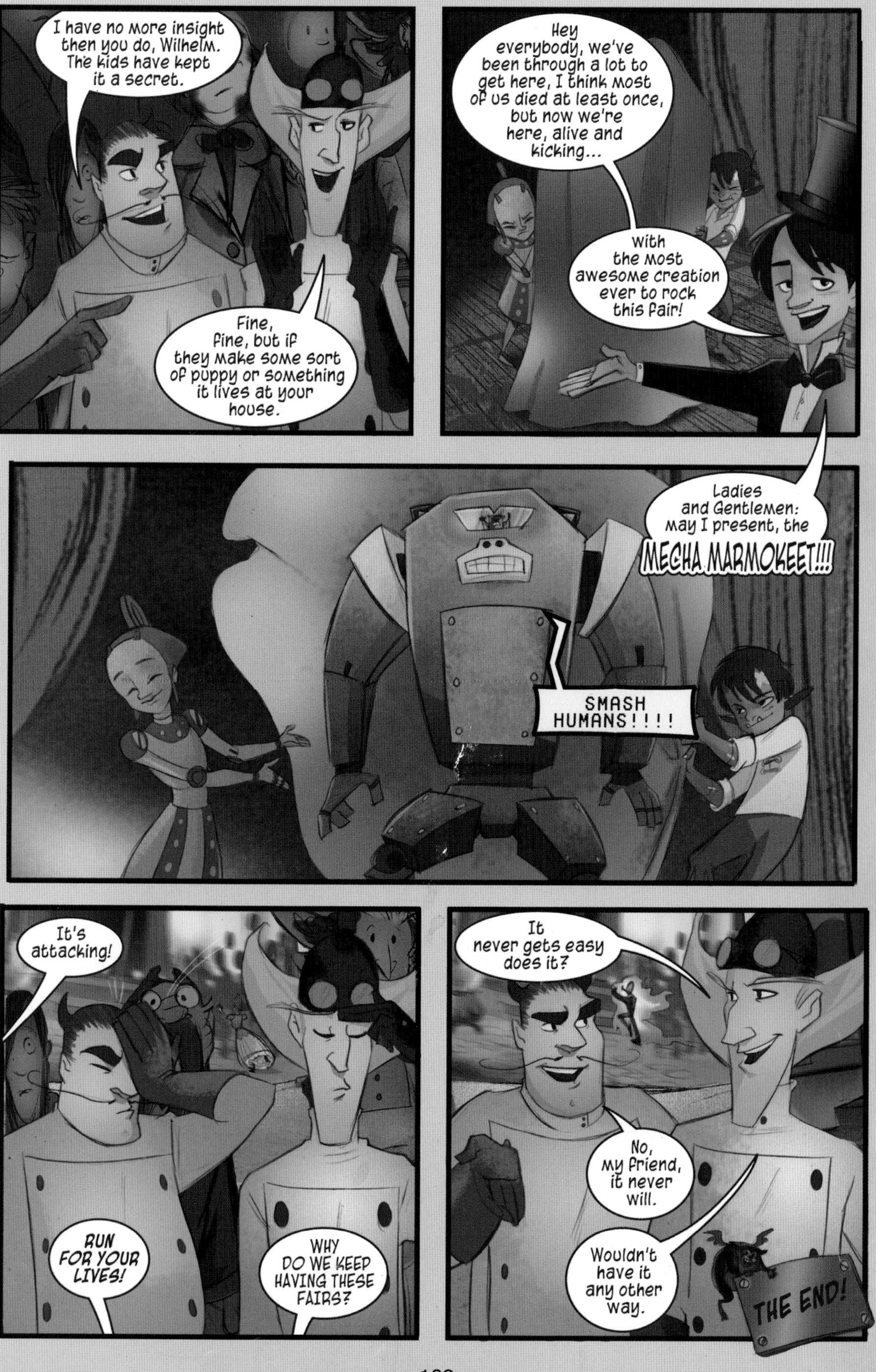
I have no more insight then you do, Wilhelm. The kids have kept it a secret.
Fine, fine, but if they make some sort of puppy or something it lives at your house.
Hey everybody, we've been through a lot to get here, I think most of us died at least once, but now we're here, alive and kicking...
With the most awesome creation ever to rock this fair!
Ladies and Gentlemen: may I present, the
MECHA MARMOKEET!!!
SMASH HUMANS!!!!
It's attacking!
RUN FOR YOUR LIVES!
WHY DO WE KEEP HAVING THESE FAIRS?
It never gets easy does it?
No, my friend, it never will.
Wouldn't have it any other way.
THE END!

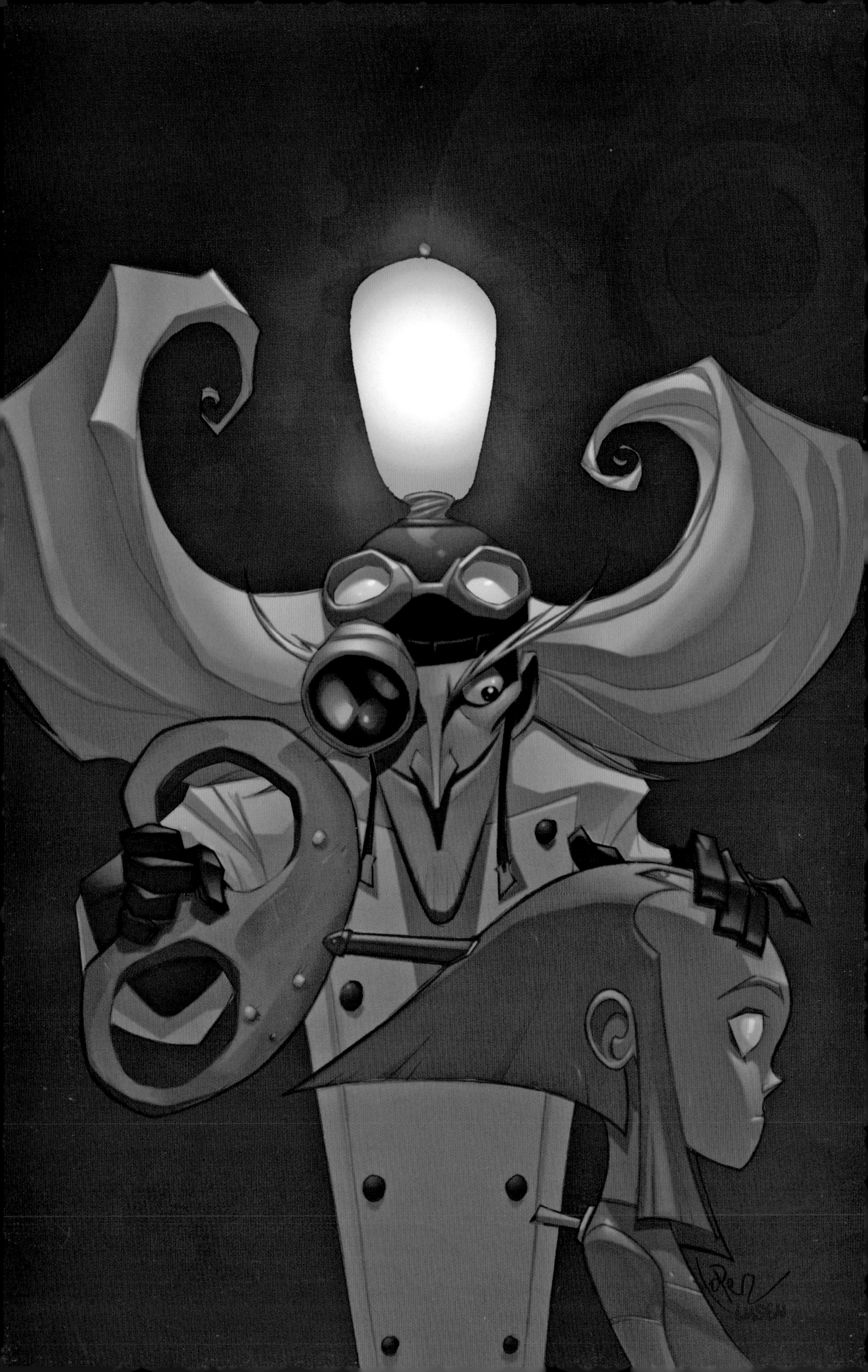

Gallery

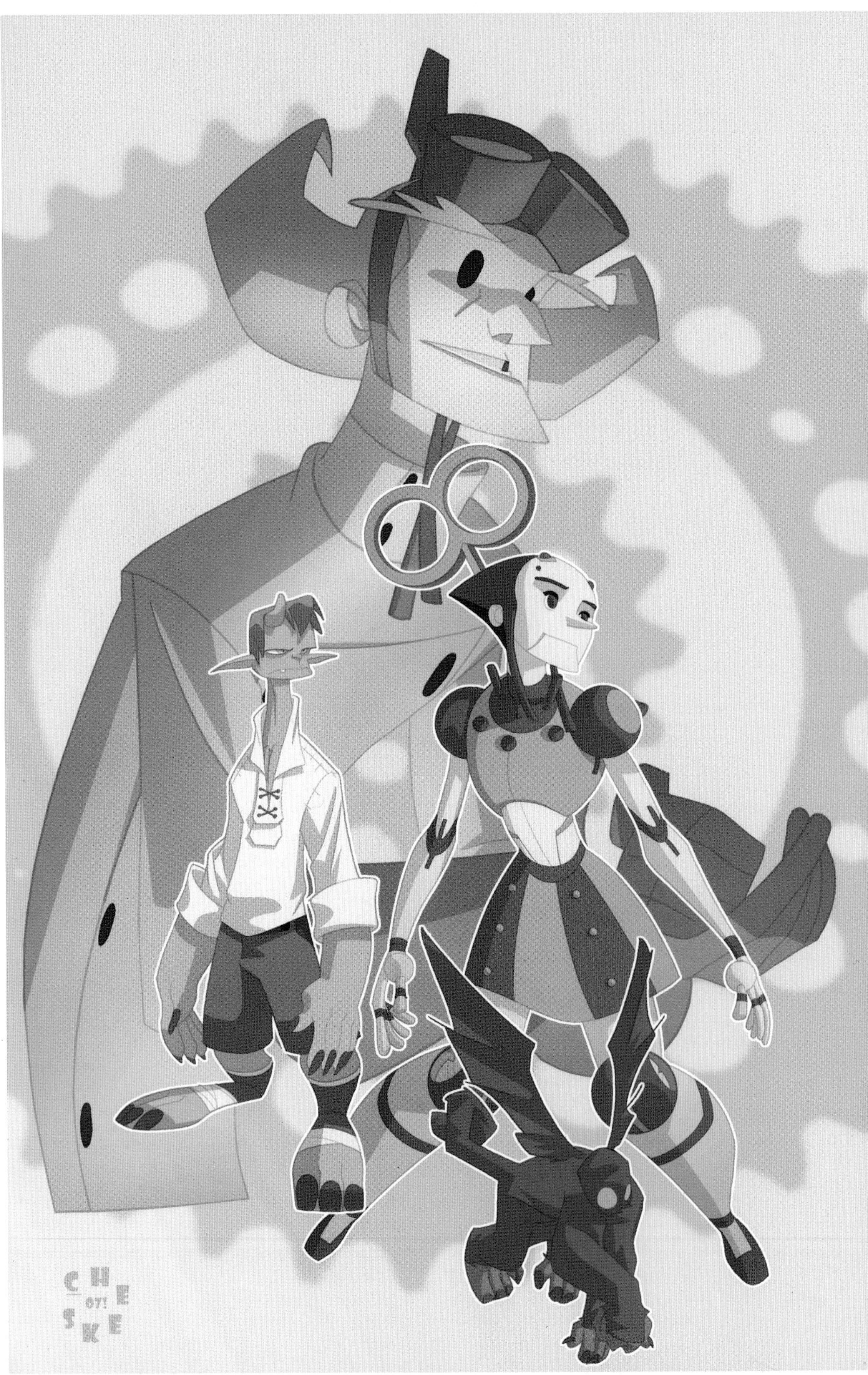
CHE
07!
SKE

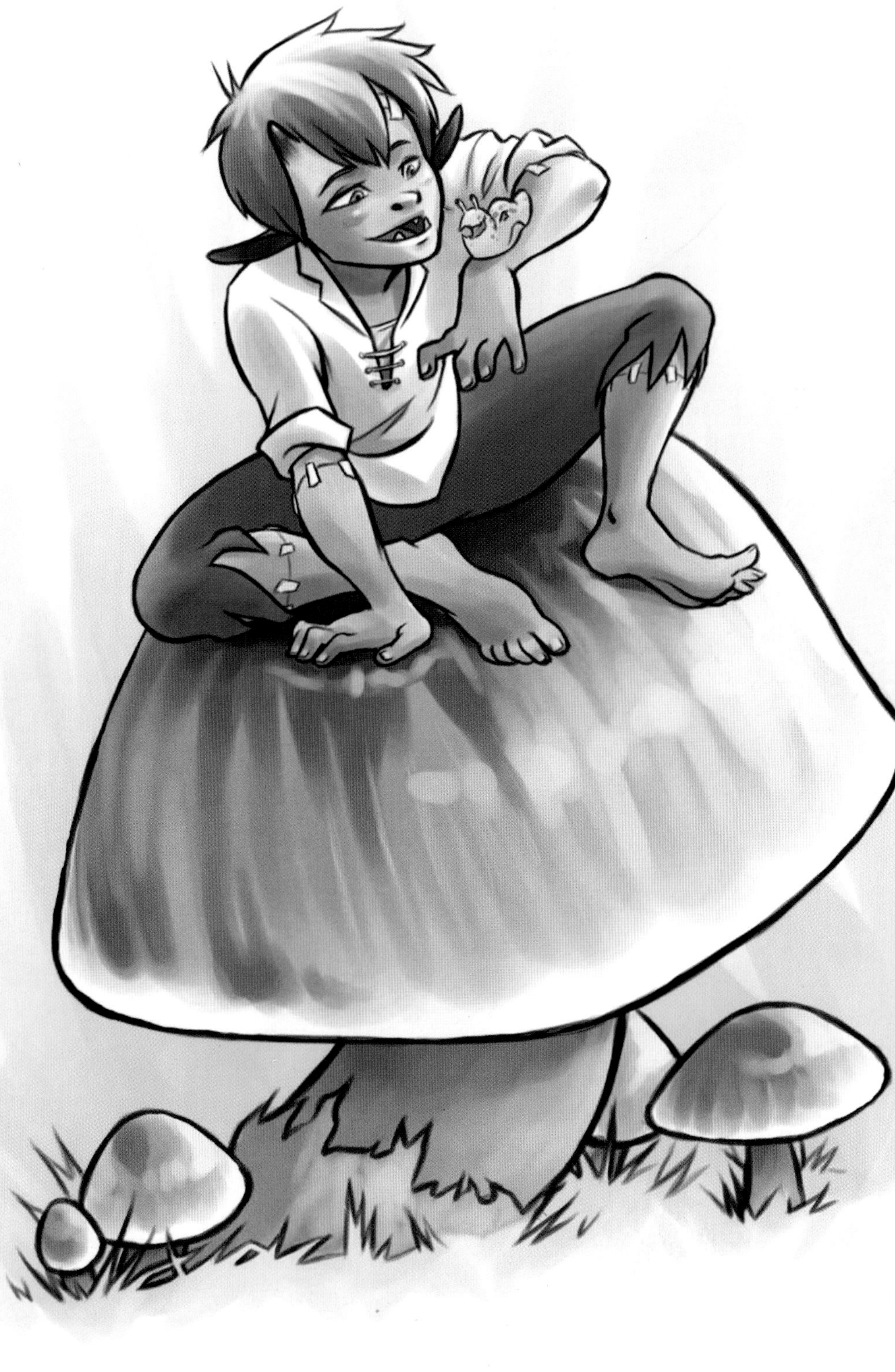

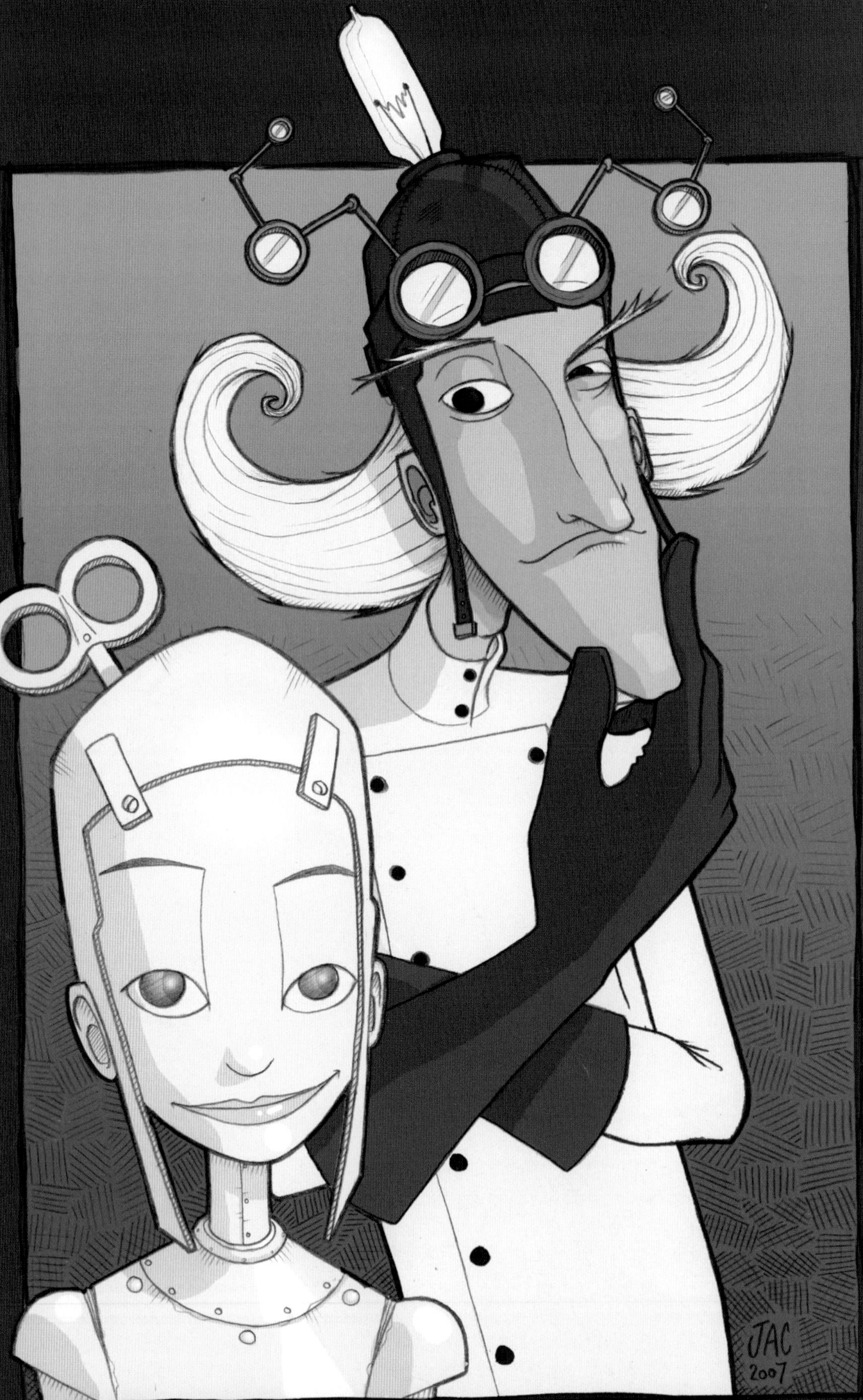
JAC
2007

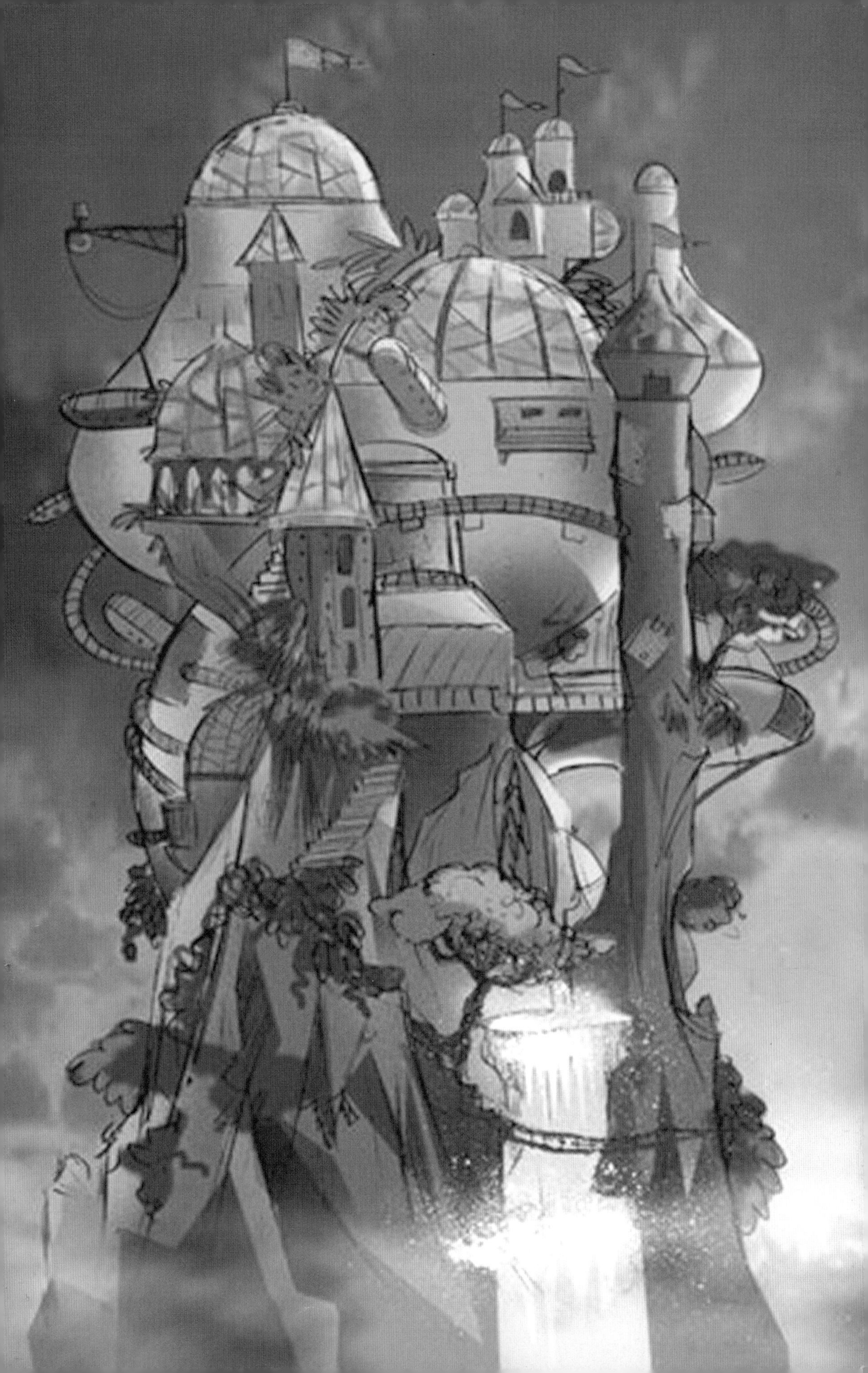

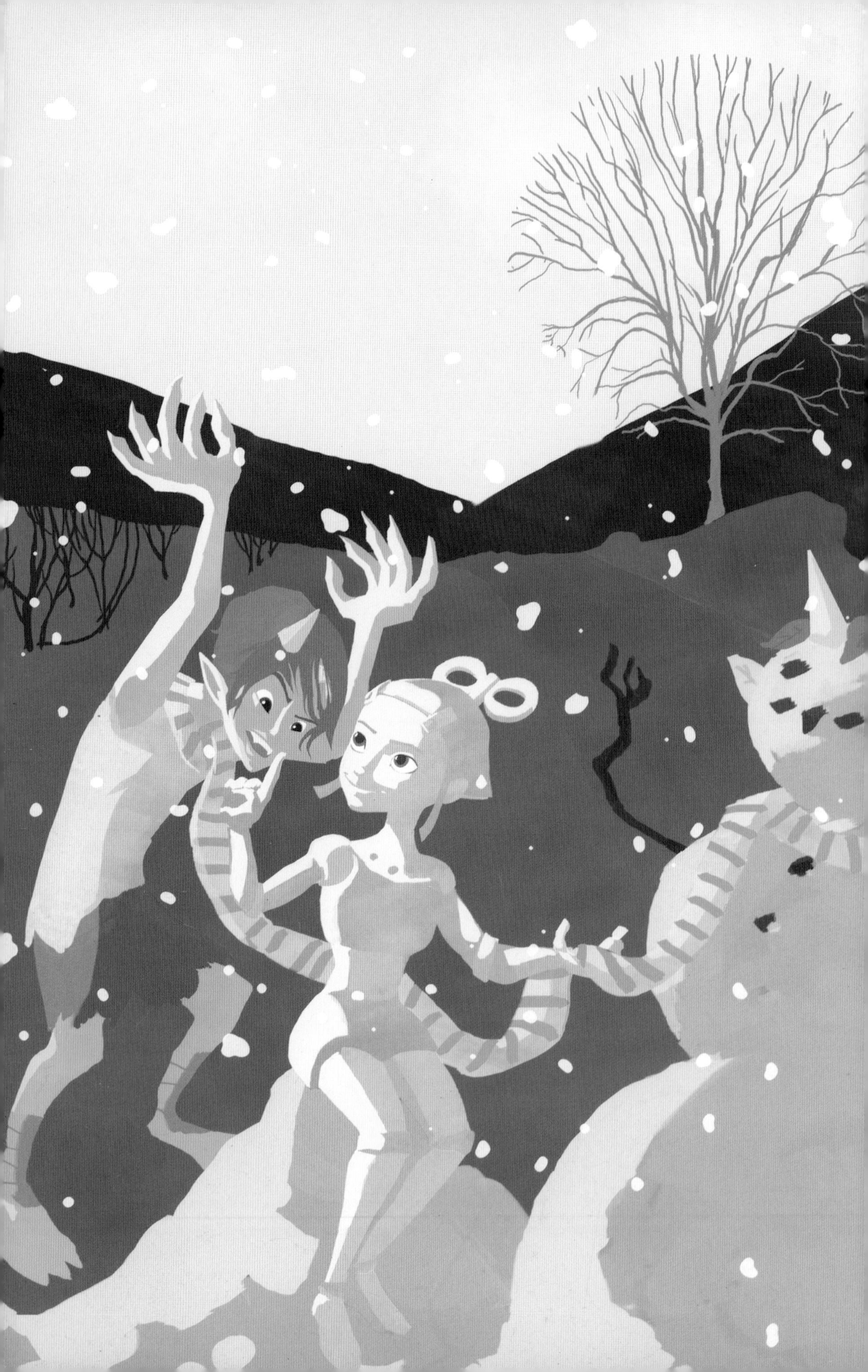

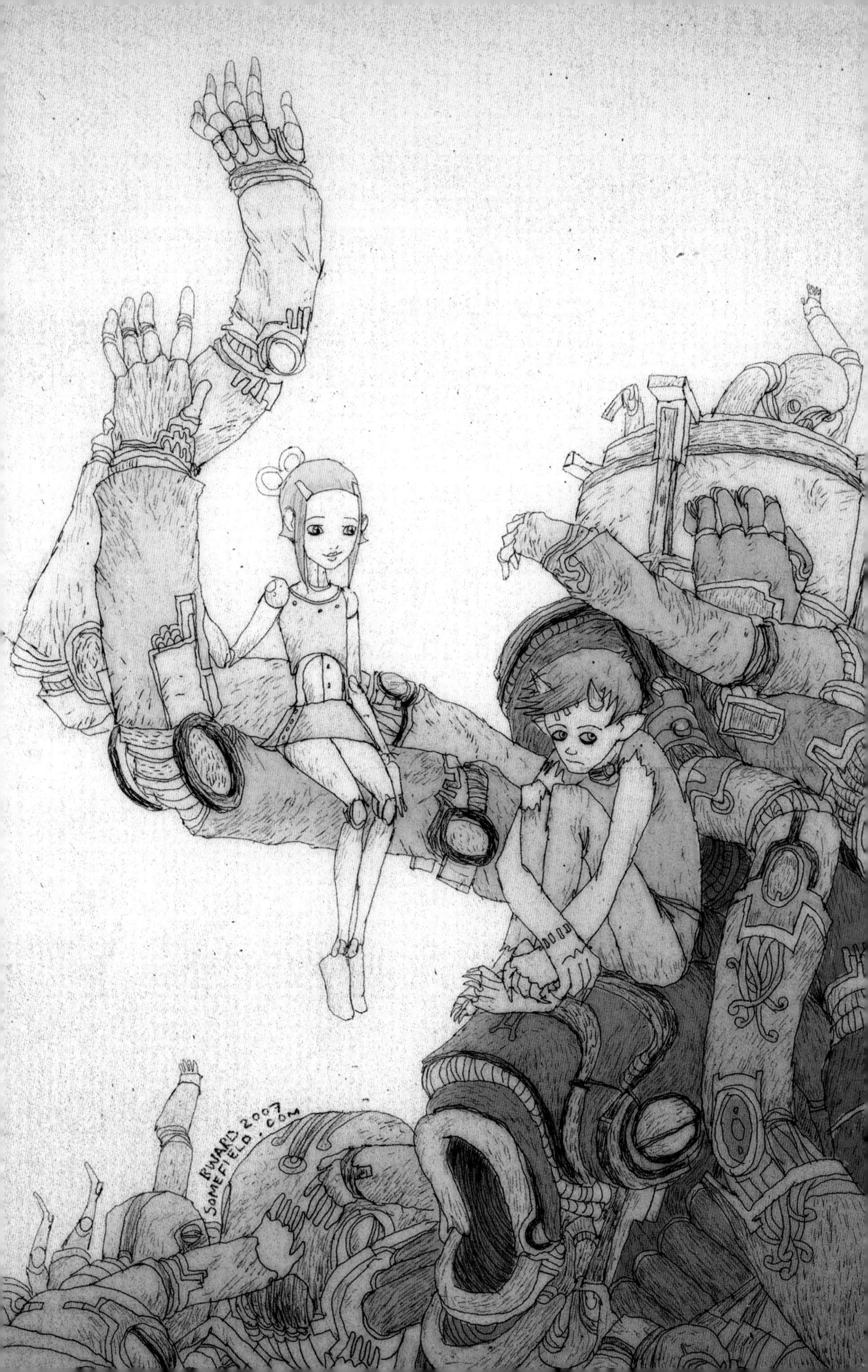
BWARD 2007
SOMEFIELD.COM

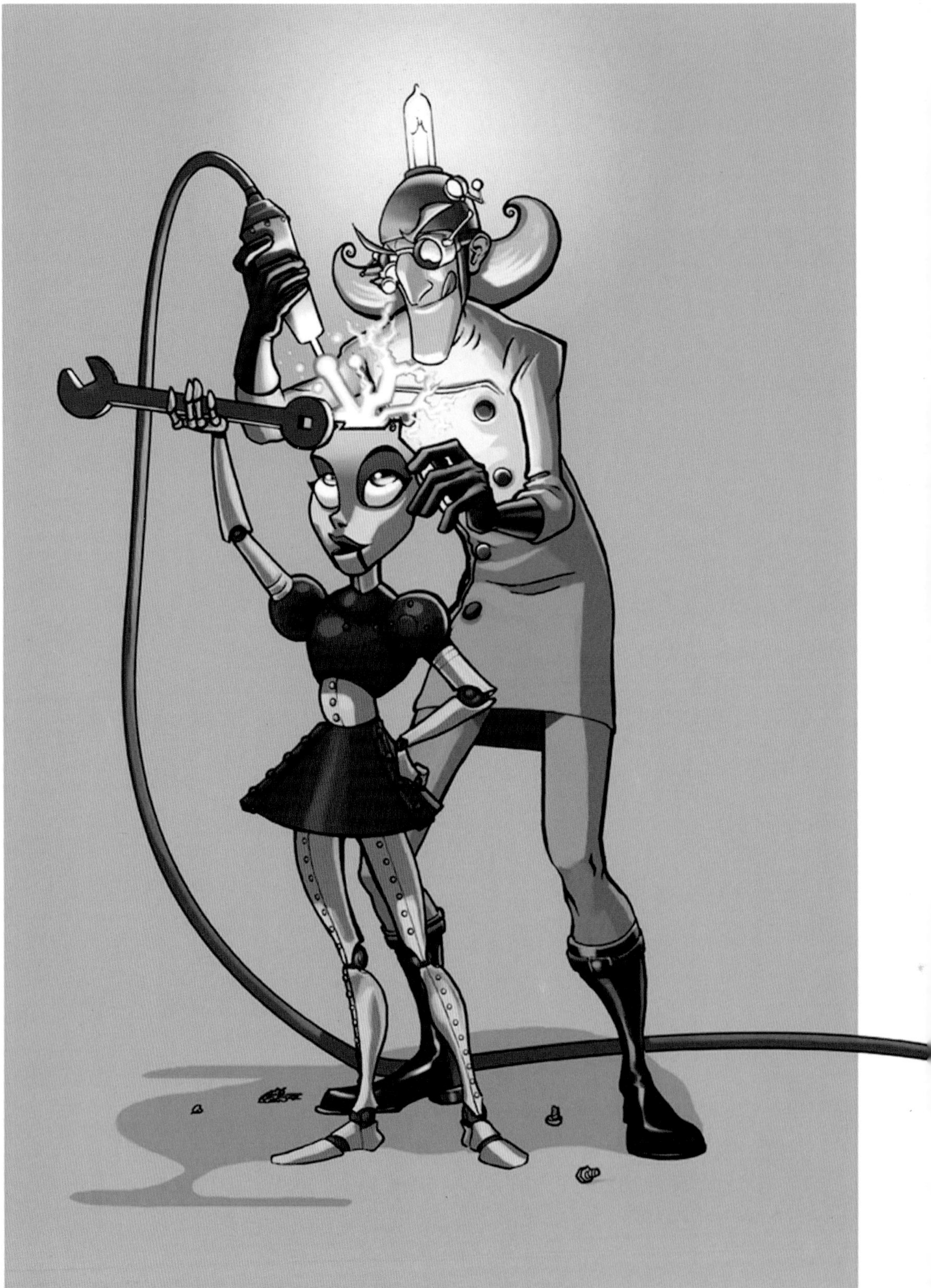

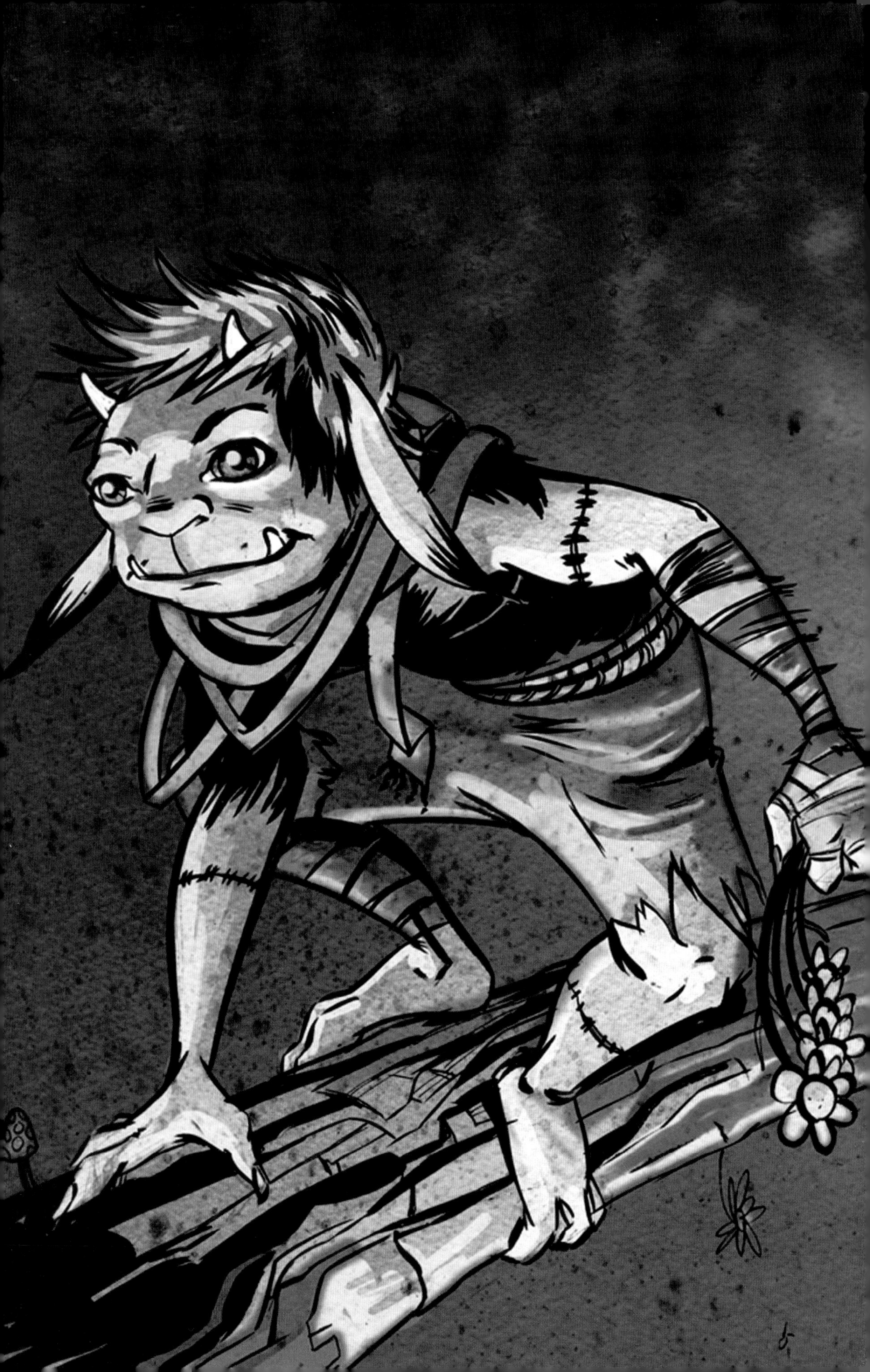

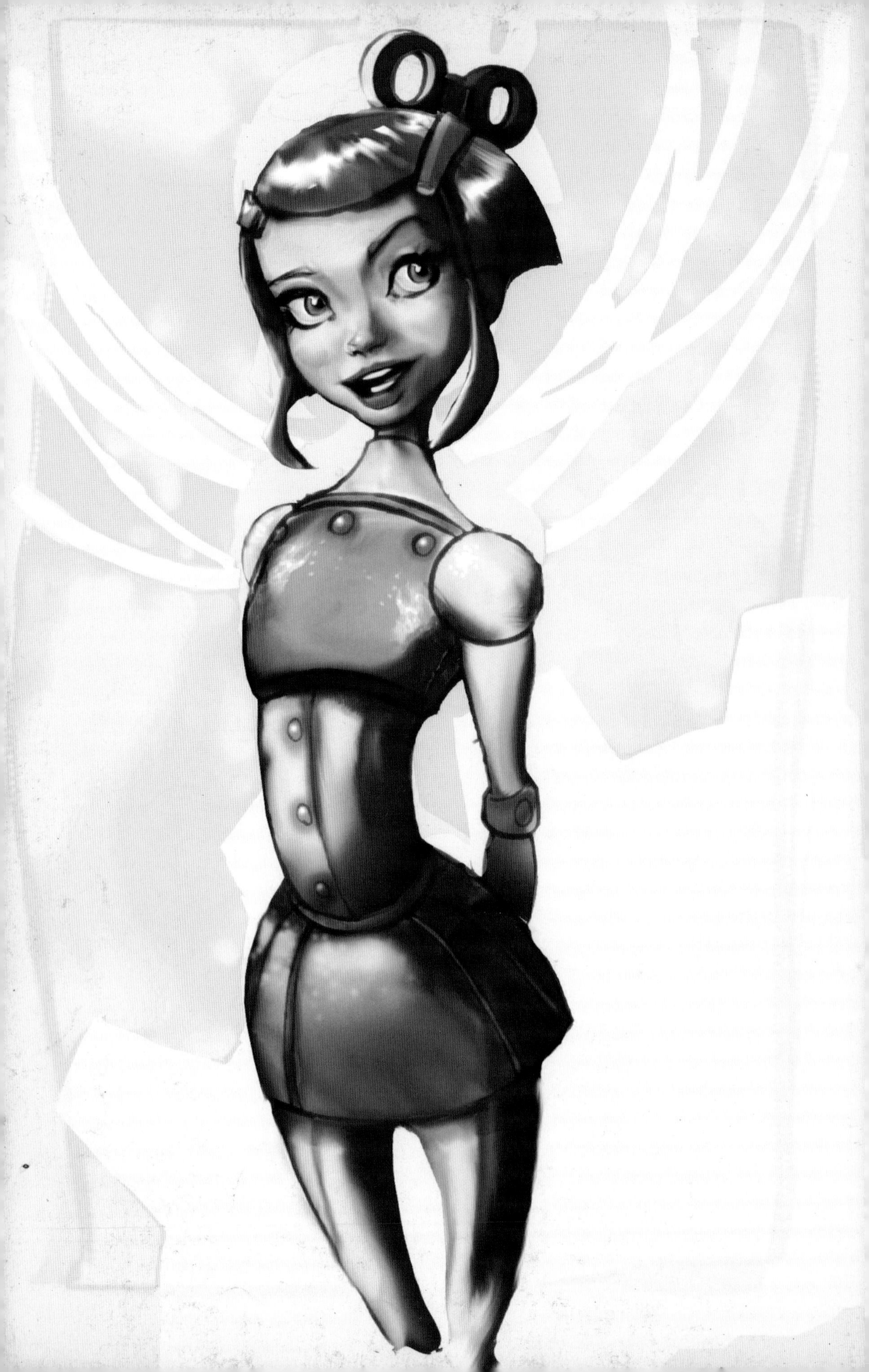

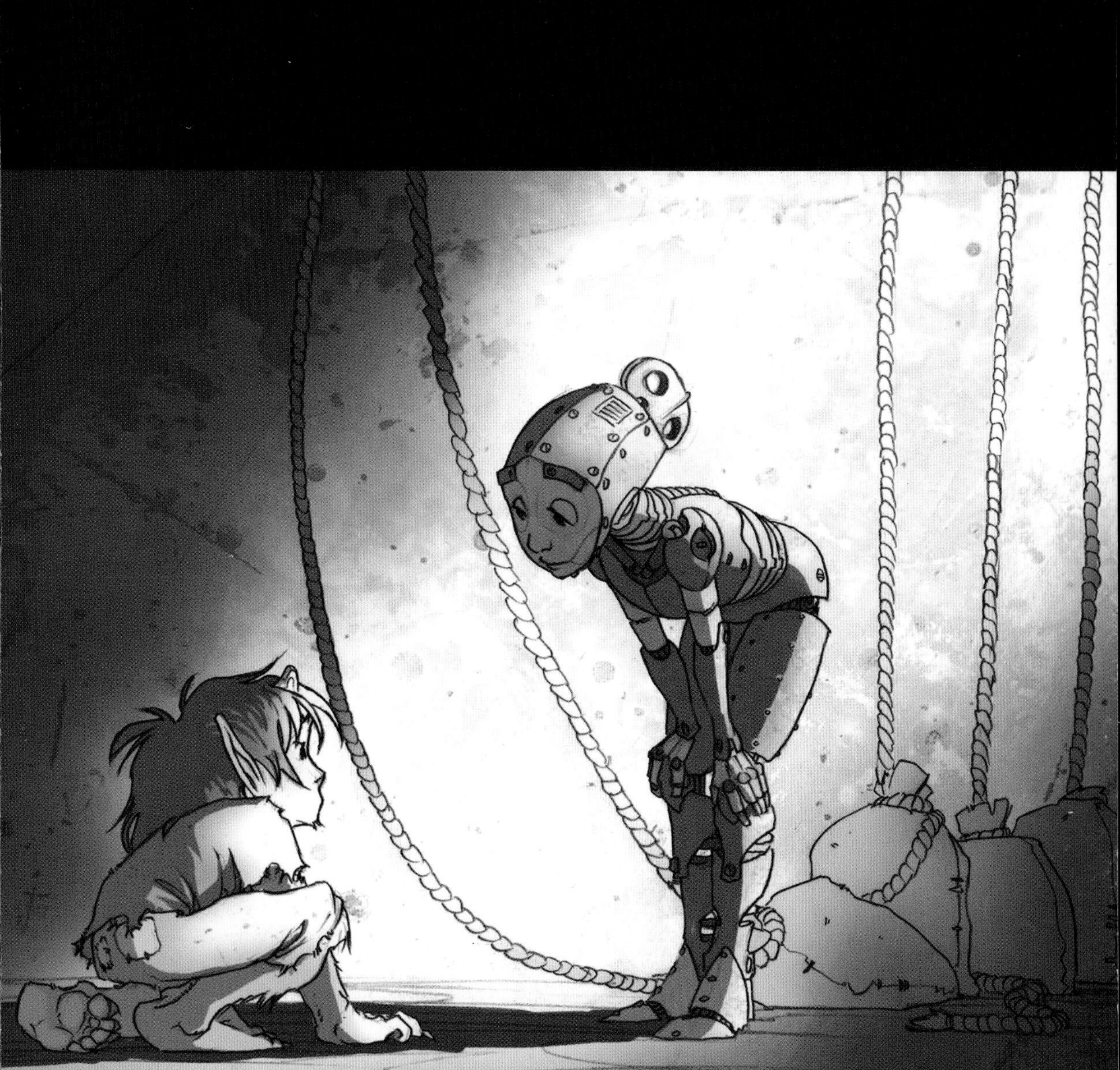

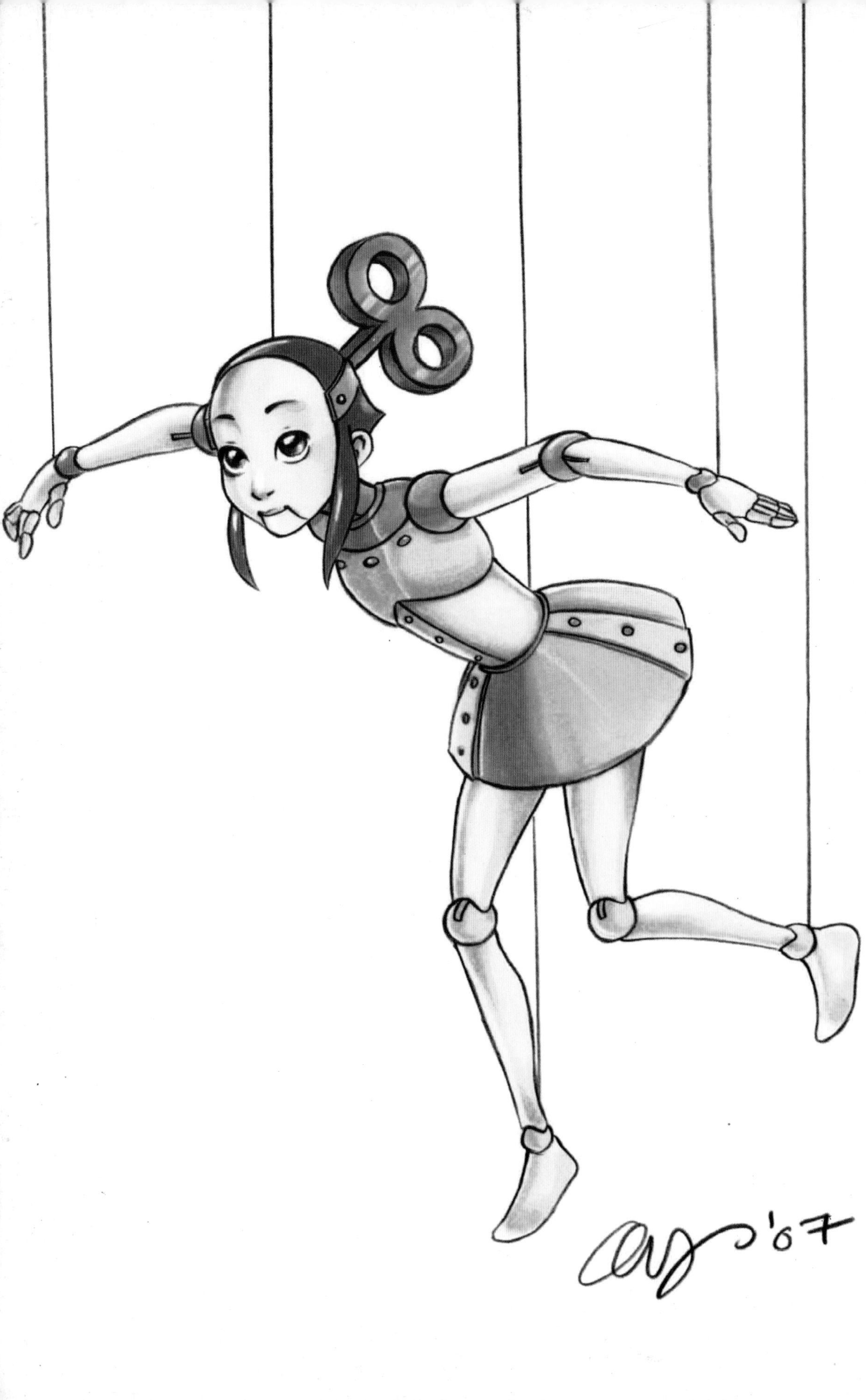

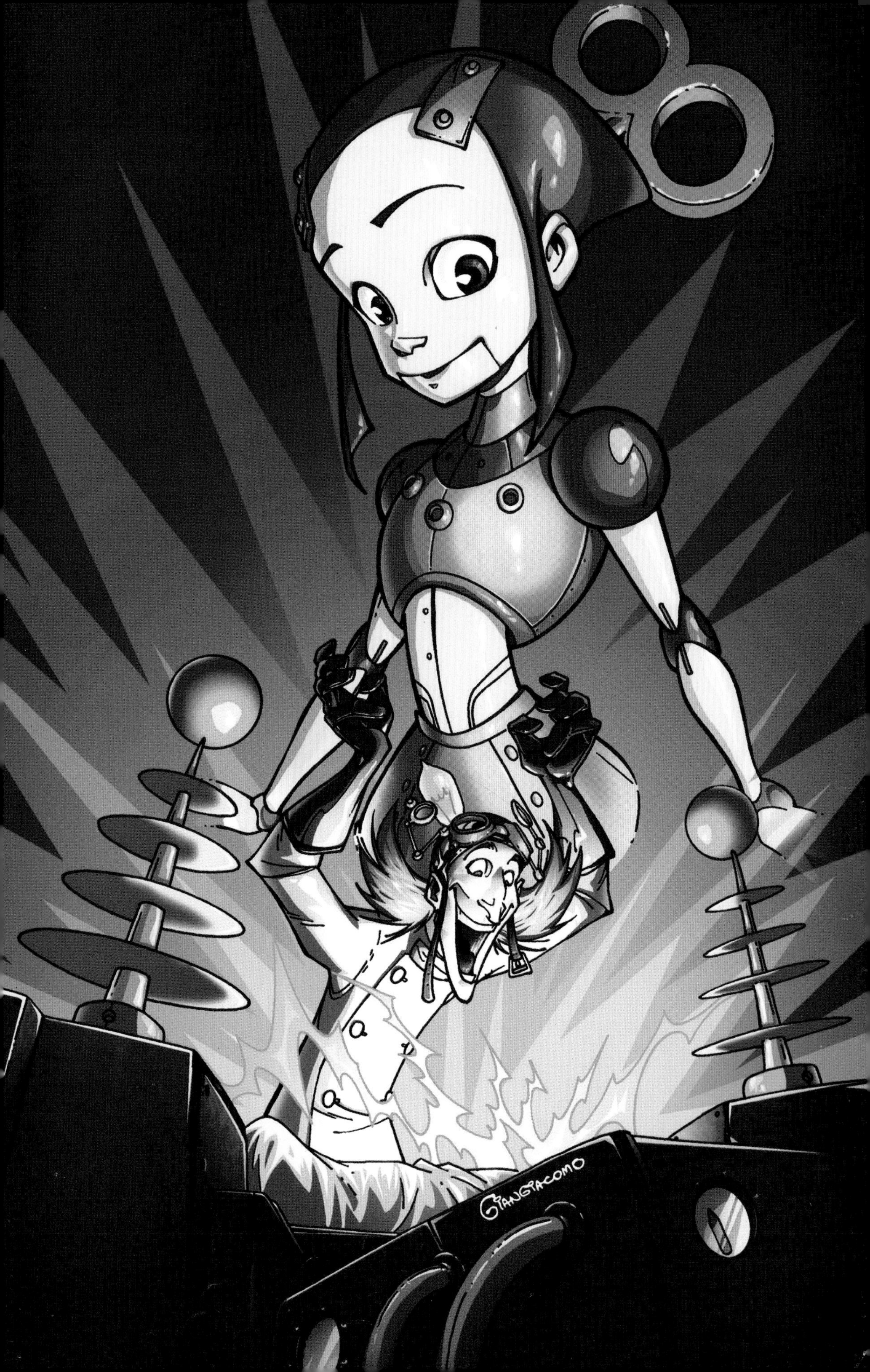
GIANGIACOMO

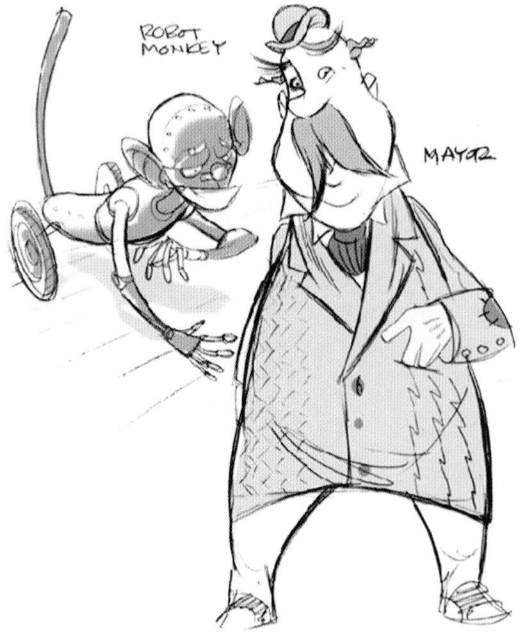
ROBOT MONKEY
MAYOR

story concept

Sean O'Reilly

Kevin created the Tinkerer long before the story of the Clockwork Girl, and the Tinkerer was the inspiration for the entire tale. Working with Kevin's vision, I brought in Shakespearean and scientific elements, and soon the characters and story took on a life of their own.

— Sean O'Reilly

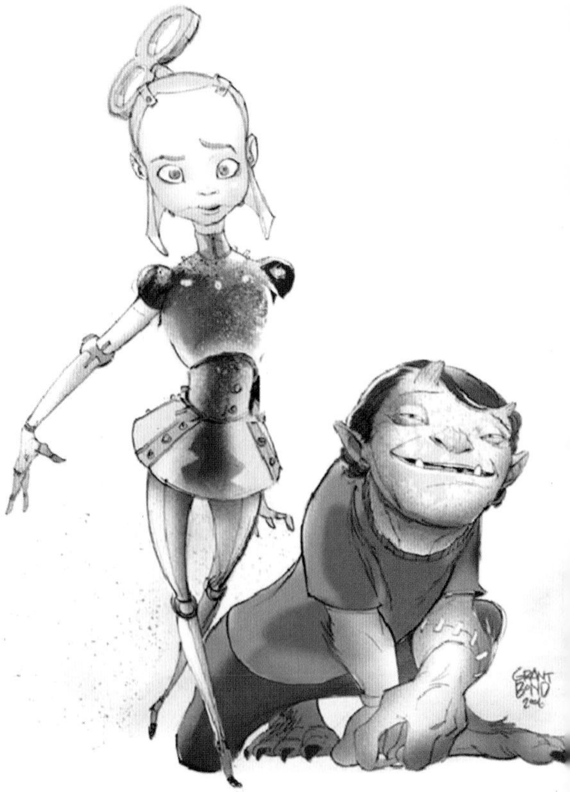

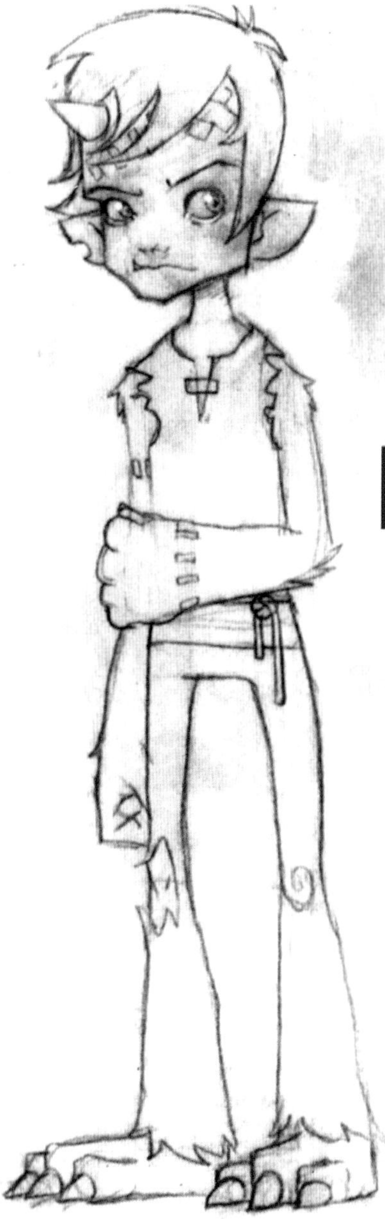

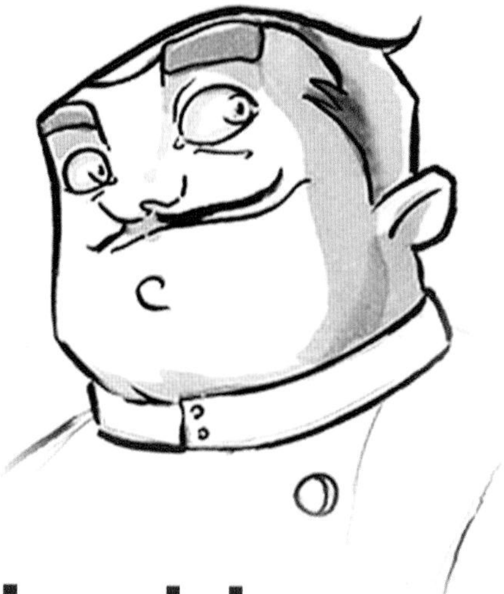

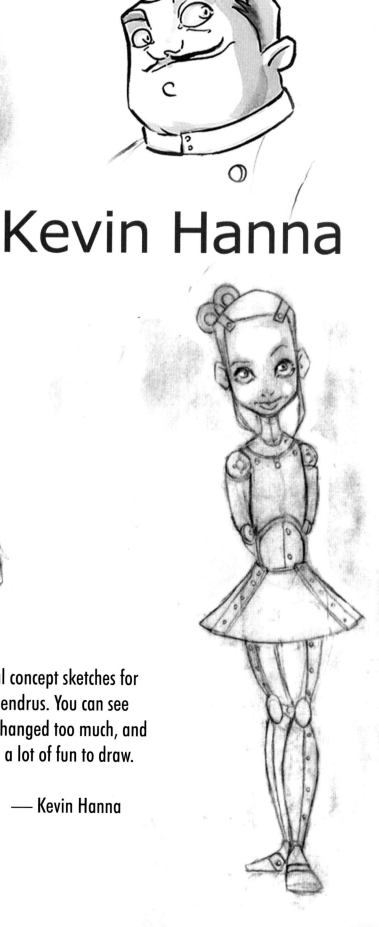

Kevin Hanna

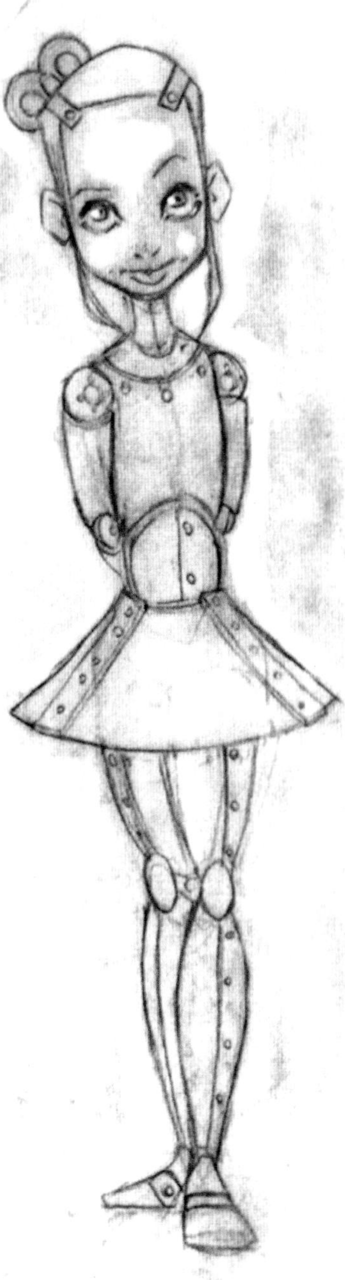

Here are my original concept sketches for Huxley, Tesla, and Dendrus. You can see they really haven't changed too much, and they've always been a lot of fun to draw.

— Kevin Hanna

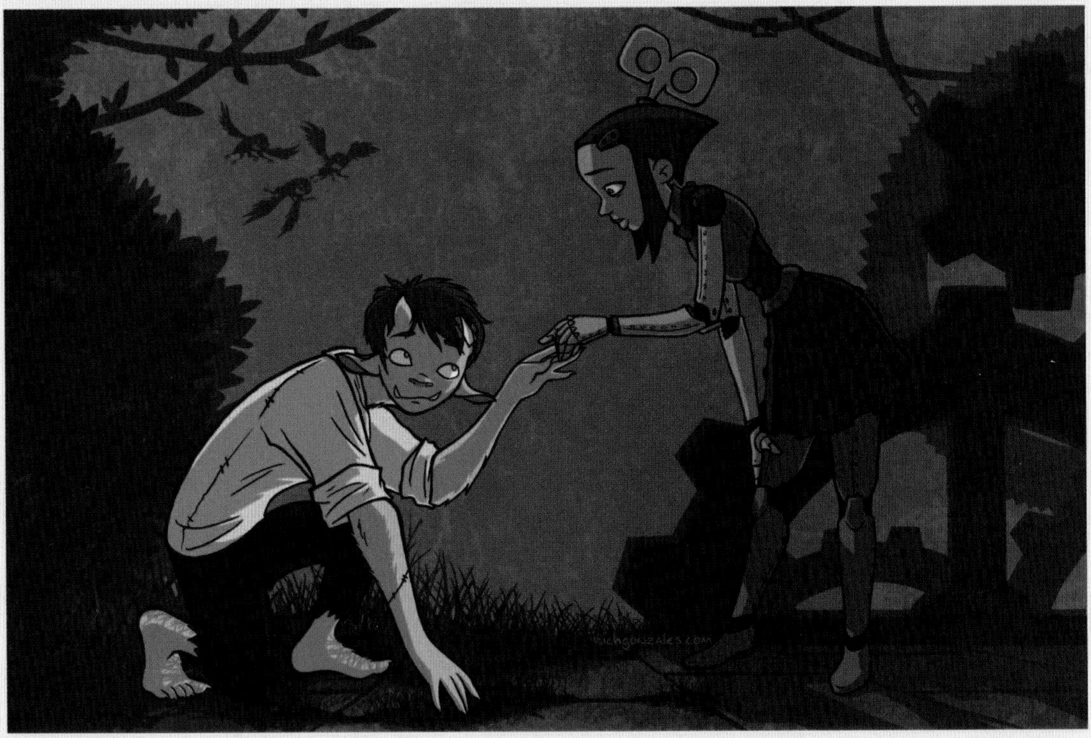
richgonzales.com

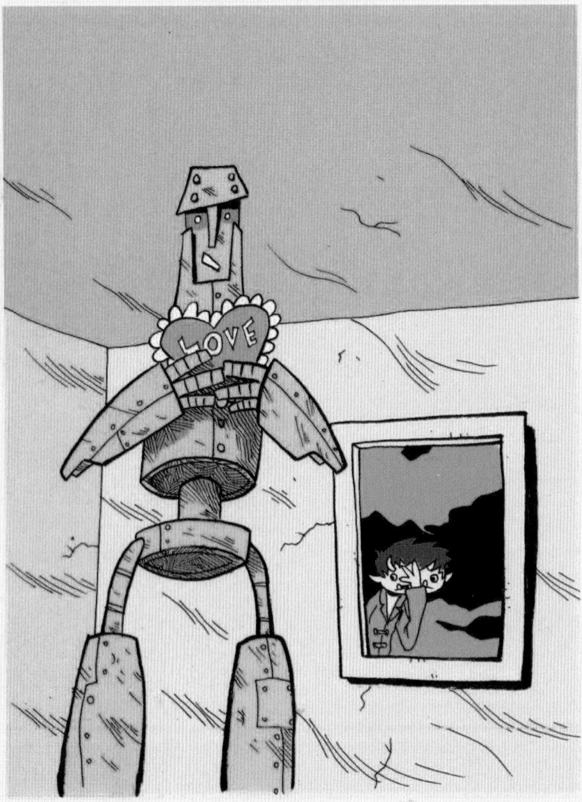
LOVE

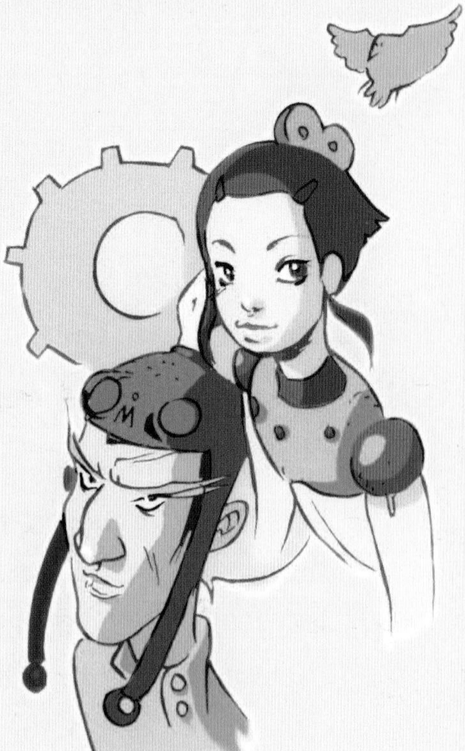
FOR
KEVIN

About the Authors

Sean O'Reilly

Sean O'Reilly is the founder and C.E.O. of Arcana Studio, an award-winning publisher of comic books and graphic novels. He is the author of a number of graphic novels, including *The Gwaii*, *Mighty Mighty Monsters*, *Pixies*, *Kade*, and *The Hope Virus*. He has also written and produced two films for Lionsgate Entertainment (*Circle of Pain* and *Beatdown*), and is continuing to build other branded story-worlds that work as transmedia projects.

Kevin Hanna

Kevin Hanna is the founder of Frogchildren Studios, a Seattle-based multimedia entertainment company. He has worked as an art director for Disney, Microsoft, Sony, and Google, but is especially dedicated to his work creating murals on the sides of large buildings. *The Clockwork Girl* is his first graphic novel.

Acknowledgments

Sean O'Reilly

With degrees in biology and technology, and my true love by my side, is why *The Clockwork Girl* is a story that is close to my heart. I could not have created it without the incredible support I have from my family—my wife, Michelle; my parents, Pat and Sue; and my incredible children, Summer, Kiefer, Phoenix, and Harmony—whose encouragement allows me to pursue my dreams. A special thank-you also goes out to Kevin Hanna, my partner and friend, who has been an amazing partner and is a true visionary; and to Josh Redmond who finished the short film and saw us through the entire journey of creating our feature film.

Kevin Hanna

This book would not exist without the help of my children, Kendra, Kenton, and Aubrey, whose imagination inspired me to start it; my wife, Claire, whose pragmatism drove me to finish it; and Sean, my friend and collaborator, without whom I would never have fulfilled my childhood dream of making comics.

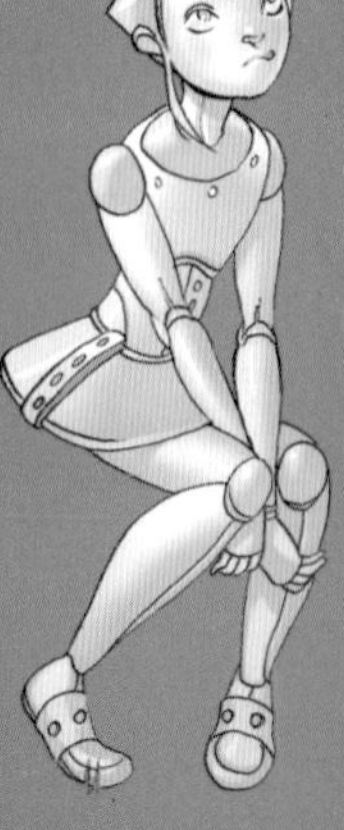

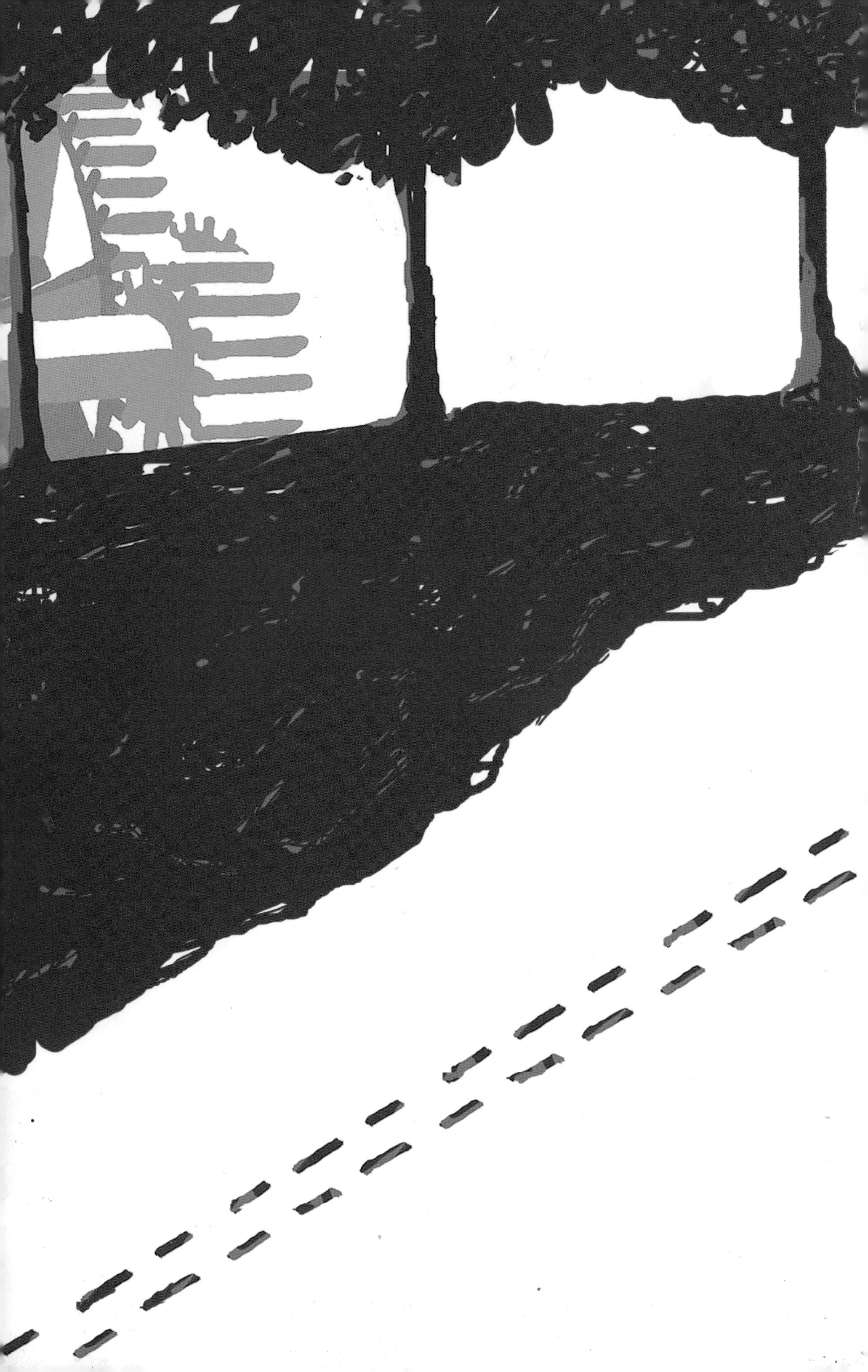